Christmas 1987

Kayaks Down the Nile

To Rod & Claire —
Two wonderfully talented
kindred spirits, whose contributions
I deeply admire!
With warm friendship
and great appreciation.

John Goddard

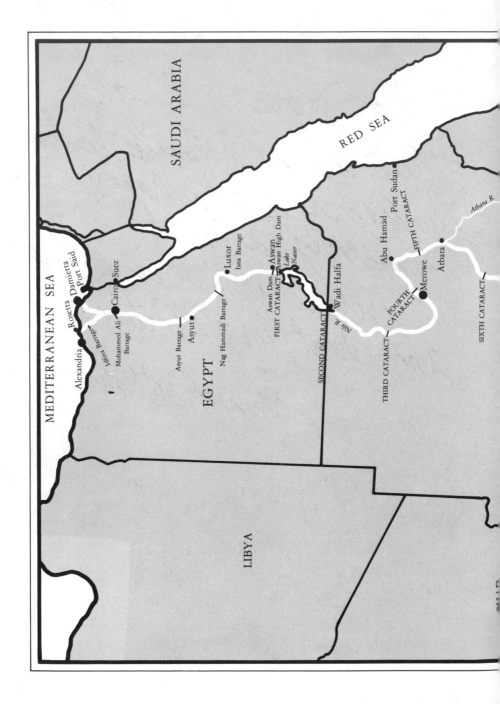

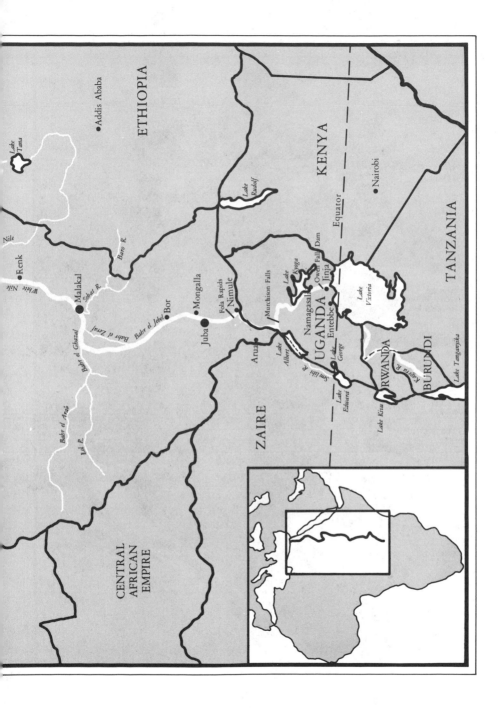

From top: John Goddard, André Davy, and Jean La Porte.

John Goddard

Brigham Young University Press

Library of Congress Cataloging in Publication Data

Goddard, John M   1924–
  Kayaks down the Nile.

  Includes index.
  1. Nile Valley–Description and travel. 2. Goddard,
John M., 1924–   I. Title.
DT115.G62   916.2'04'4   78-14203
ISBN 0-8425-1575-5
ISBN 0-8425-1365-5 pbk.

*To my fellow
adventurers on the Nile,
Jean LaPorte and
André Davy,
two of the bravest
individuals I have
ever known.*

Contents

Acknowledgments

Most of my African friends will never read this account of the Nile Expedition or know of its outcome. It is unlikely that I shall associate with them again; yet their memory will never fade, and their acts of hospitality will never be forgotten.

I feel deep gratitude toward the many officials and citizens of France, French Somaliland, Kenya, Uganda, Rwanda, Burundi, Sudan, and Egypt, who extended their warmest friendship and contributed so liberally to the success of what I will always consider the most outstanding experience of my life.

Throughout the expedition my parents, Jack and Lettie Goddard, were a constant source of inspiration. Their faith, support, and encouragement never wavered.

For those wondering why three men with sound minds and healthy bodies would want to risk their comfort and security—even their lives—in exploring the largely untamed Nile River, I offer the reasons why the river intrigued me.

The 4,145-mile Nile is the longest river on earth, and one of the greatest of all natural wonders. For 6,000 years it has been the world's most important watercourse, with a vital role in the development of the human race. And the Nile Basin's million square miles contain the world in miniature: a fantastic variety of races, animals, terrain, agriculture, and weather.

The water of the Nile is the source of life for an immense population of humans representing dozens of races, from the fair-skinned to the dark, from the pygmy to the giant, from the pagan to the Moslem and Christian. The largest city in Africa, Cairo, is near the river's mouth; Lake Victoria, the world's second largest freshwater lake, is located at its head. To the natural scientist, the Nile offers the greatest variety of birds in the northern hemisphere; to the social scientist, the shores of the Nile are lined with the world's most magnificent wonderland of archaeology. Following the Nile brings you past the three-mile-high Mountains of the Moon—the Ruwenzori Range in Uganda, with exotic Alpine vegetation giving way to thick equatorial rain forest—and leads you to the scorching, rainless deserts of Sudan and Egypt. Between the two extremes is the largest swamp in the world.

Since the dawn of civilization the Nile has been—and will continue to be—the dominant feature of Africa. It has had its greatest impact and has fulfilled its richest destiny in Egypt, where its water and fertile silt have spawned a ribbon of oasis in an otherwise barren land. If there hadn't been a Nile, there never would have been an Egypt—and without Egypt the entire course of human history would have been altered.

This great river has fascinated and challenged men since the earliest stages of human history. Through the ages numerous expeditions have attempted to trace its interminable channel through Africa to solve one of the oldest and most debated mysteries of geography—the secret of its sources. Yet, prior to our successful project, there was no historical record of any organized group or individual having successfully traveled the Nile from sea to source or the reverse—one of the factors that made our attempt a transcendent challenge. The ancient Egyptians must have felt extreme frustration at their inability to locate the genesis of the stream that created and nourished their entire nation, although they were familiar with the river from its outlet on the Mediterranean Sea southward to the confluence of the White and Blue Niles at Khartoum.

In 457 B.C. Herodotus journeyed upstream as far as the First Cataract at Aswan—600 miles from the sea. Eratosthenes, the Greek scientist of Alexandria, published a map in the third century B.C. that traced the river southward to present-day Khartoum. Ptolemy, the Greek astronomer and geographer of the second century A.D., summed up the total knowledge of the Nile to his day; and then for seventeen hundred years, virtually nothing new was added, though there is evidence that in the first century some Romans penetrated perhaps as far as the Sudd, the great papyrus swamps of the southern Sudan.

It was not until 1827 that Adolph Linant, a Belgian, ascended the White Nile 132 miles south of Khartoum, the first known European to achieve this feat since the first century A.D. After his expedition, Mohammed Ali, Viceroy of Egypt, sponsored three Egyptian expeditions up the White Nile in 1839, 1841, and 1842. The first group reached a village near Bor; the second and third made it farther south to Juba (Gondokono).

But the mystery of the Nile's southern sources was finally solved by John Hanning Speke, who in 1858 discovered and named Lake Victoria and in 1862 established that the lake was the Nile's main source when he discovered the river pouring forth from the lake's overflow at its northern edge. In 1864 Sir Samuel Baker discovered Lake Albert, the second source. Yet the river had never been explored in its entirety—the explorers had each visited only certain stretches of the Nile. And that became our unwavering dream and our goal—to conduct the first exploration of the great river from its sources in central Africa to its mouth at the Mediterranean Sea.

"A trip down the Nile in those cockleshells?" blurted the British customs officer as we presented our equipment for inspection. "You must be crackers!"

Possibly we were! I had to laugh at his tactless but honest reaction—for as we arrived at Mombasa, the chief port of Kenya, our kayaks looked pathetically inadequate for traveling down the longest river in the world. We found that his reaction was echoed by every official, every authority, and every expert (self-styled or genuine) we had met from Paris to central Africa.

"A foolhardy attempt at the impossible!" we were told.

"A journey dangerous beyond words."

"A triple suicide by kayak!"

Not that anyone tried to hinder us—officials were all helpful and hospitable, willing to cooperate with what they saw as utter recklessness, but feeling duty-bound to warn us about all the obstacles facing us: dangerous wildlife, trackless swamps, roaring cataracts, disease, hunger, sandstorms, hostile peoples, and relentless heat. And, of course, they were right. Our own research had forewarned us about these obstacles. Also, many friends and relatives had found it difficult to understand why we would leave the security of civilization and sacrifice our comfortable and familiar surroundings to embark on such a project. We had tried to convey to them our need to experience the unknown, our eagerness to encounter rare sights and peoples and adventure, and to enjoy the enchantments of pure wilderness. I had always had a problem making these people understand the immense inner rewards and self-fulfillment I had gained from such sources. But if they could only stand as my French companions, Jean and André, and I did, 6,700 feet high on an isolated windswept mountaintop in Burundi and look down from its grass-covered highlands to see the alluring vastness of Africa, perhaps they, too, would feel the siren call that beckoned us down the longest river on earth.

In those grassy highlands, ten tiny springs gurgle out of the rocky hillside, the southernmost headwaters of Lake Victoria's main feeder, the Kagera River. A ten-foot stone pyramid faced with whitewashed concrete held a bronze plaque that bore the Latin words *Caput Nili*—"the head of the Nile." The German explorer Burkart Waldecker had built the monument in 1938 to honor all those who, from ancient time, had sought the source of the river of the Pharoahs.

Though we were not the first there, we were the first to stand at Kasumo Springs, almost four degrees below the equator, determined to travel with the eternal stream ever downward until the clear waters of the springs swept into the Mediterranean. It had taken many months of intensive research and preparation, with frequent setbacks and disappointments and thousands of miles of travel, but at last, on 2 November 1950, we stood at the threshold of our expedition.

Originally we had planned to begin where the waters of Lake Victoria empty into the Nile, since the lake is generally accepted as the most distant source of the Nile. But since the headsprings of the Kagera are the ultimate source of the Nile, hydrologically, we decided our commitment to travel the Nile should begin here. We knew it would add time and trouble to our journey; we didn't know, however, that it would lead to near fatal disaster.

How long was the journey ahead? *Alpha* was the group of ten springs; *Omega* would be the small Egyptian town of Rashid on the Nile delta, bordering the Mediterranean Sea. Between lay a distance equivalent to one-sixth of the earth's circumference. The journey would be as long as a trip from Los Angeles to Lima, Peru; from New York to Naples, Italy. And we would travel that distance, not in an airplane or a ship, but in small Eskimo-type boats operated solely by our own muscle power. We were about to do what no one had ever done before, what no one had even attempted. And we were determined to succeed.

1

The Start— and Nearly the Finish

November 2: *The biggest red-letter day for us to date. The source of the Nile to the village of Rutana, Burundi.*

We were deeply moved but jubilant at reaching the headsprings this morning. From here on we will be continually working our way northward toward the Mediterranean. I fished out a tin cup from my pack, filled it with water from one of the oozes, and offered it to Jean and André as a toast to our success. And then I sipped my first taste of Nile water—the first of several hundred gallons—and found it deliciously pure and cool.

After we had filmed the pyramid, springs, and surrounding hills, we piled into the pickup truck driven by our Belgian friend Jacques Lamy, a young district officer who had driven us to the Nile source from his headquarters at Rutana, a village only eighty-five miles from Ujiji on Lake Tanganyika, where in 1871 the historic meeting of Stanley and Livingstone took place.

Bouncing down a dirt road little better than a cowpath, we kept in sight of the shallow brook gradually growing as the water from the tiny freshets converged. Ahead of us a wide watershed added more water, and the brook turned into a river, assuming a succession of lyrical African names—Mukasenyi, Kigera, Luvironza, Ruvuvu, and finally Kagera River, Lake Victoria's largest tributary, which supplies the lake with more water than any other source except direct rainfall.

Three miles downstream from the springs, we jumped out of the truck, tramped across green fields, and shot pictures of a small waterfall—the first falls of the Nile. Then we returned to Rutana, where we enjoyed a meal cooked by

Jacques's wife. He told us of a man-eating lion in his district that had killed fifteen Hutus before a government hunter had tracked it down and shot it.

When it came time for us to leave, the Lamys seemed genuinely regretful. They rarely had white visitors, and seemed to regard our visit as a major event. They offered to mail two cablegrams for us—one to the President of France and the other to the French Explorers Society—announcing our arrival at the source and the beginning of our Nile journey.

"I almost envy you," Jacques said wistfully as we left him. "You're embarking on a type of adventure that happens once in a generation. If you succeed, you will make history."

November 9: *Kakitumba, Uganda, near the border of Rwanda. (We have lived one month in equatorial Africa.)*

At Kakitumba, the customs station in Uganda, we picked up our kayaks and the bulk of our gear, which had been stored while we sought out the Kasumo Springs. Monsieur Klaus, the customs inspector, a middle-aged Belgian, greeted us in fluent though heavily accented English. He insisted we stay with him for the night in his neat little brick bungalow, a touch of Europe in the wild, game-filled African bush. No one in his right mind roams this country after sundown; nocturnal predators aren't picky about what or whom they eat. Jean and André are asleep now in the one bed, and I am on a mattress on the brick floor.

November 10: *Kakitumba to the Kagera River*

Just before dawn we were wakened by shouts from the huts a stone's throw away. We scrambled into our clothes, ran outside, and found our host, clad only in shorts, trying to calm a group of Africans. "A leopard has snatched a sleeping baby from one of the huts and has carried it off into the jungle," Klaus explained. "They want me to get my rifle and track it down with them."

At first light, Klaus set off with several trackers, but soon lost the spoor in high grass and came home, forced to accept the incident as another jungle tragedy.

That wasn't to be the only hunting that day. I was "breadwinner" of our expedition. So far that had meant grocery shopping at local *dukas*—merchandise shops. But now it was time to begin hunting for food, and while Jean and André caught up on their correspondence, I unpacked our 12-gauge shotgun and cleaned, oiled, and loaded it.

I was looking for guinea hen or some other fowl along the banks of the Kakitumba when I was chilled by a series of agonized, humanlike shrieks—the

2

sound of a monkey in agony. The sound quickly turned into gasping, and I knew what was happening: a big snake, probably a python, had enveloped the hapless animal and was crushing it to death. I crashed along for a hundred yards, hoping to find the monkey, but I was brought up short at the river. The sounds were coming from the opposite bank. There was nothing I could do, and so the death-to-the weakest, food-to-the-strongest drama was played out to its fatal conclusion. I stood on the bank, frustrated and saddened, silently condemning the implacable brutality of jungle law that decrees for every living creature a host of predators seeking it as a victim.

I reached an open stretch of grassland and was stopped by the sight of a movement in the yellow grass less than forty feet away. A young female bushbuck, ears alert and eyes fearful, was staring at me. I raised my gun for an easy shot—a much better supply of meat than a few hens. Yet I couldn't pull the trigger. It wasn't buck fever that kept me from shooting. Rather, something passed between me and the antelope, a magic sense of communion, and for a

Jacques Lamy and African assistants.

moment I felt that this was not a man-animal encounter, but rather a meeting of fellow creatures of a common Creator.

The antelope stretched forward, nose quivering, eyes wide—not with fright, now, but with curiosity. The affinity was strong. But the ancient inborn distrust of the stranger proved stronger, and after a few seconds the spell was broken. The graceful animal bounded away.

The episodes with the leopard, the monkey, and now the antelope ended my interest in hunting that day. I had never hunted for sport; I had never understood how anyone could gain pleasure from a pastime that inflicted death and misery. Hunting, of course, has its place as a means of protecting life, procuring food, and harvesting game in overpopulated areas. However, as a means of bolstering the hunter's ego or proving his "macho," hunting is indefensible.

I had met a wealthy American "sportsman" only a month before in Nairobi. He and his two American partners had just returned from a hunt in Tanganyika (Tanzania)—a comfortable affair, since they had taken along a collapsible bathtub and a portable refrigerator with a built-in bar. In four weeks

André, Jean, and Goddard with disassembled kayaks at Kagera River campsite.

the men had shot everything from an elephant to a dik-dik (a pygmy antelope fourteen inches high at the shoulder); yet all that remained of the slaughter were two small tusks and a few of the choicest trophy heads. The rest of the game had been left for the hyenas.

The same hunter told me of an elephant that had gone on a rampage and trampled a village into the dust. After he had shot the elephant, he noticed that its right tusk was loose and dripping pus at the base. In cutting the flesh from the tusk, he found a two-foot-long, pus-filled abscess at the root, caused by an old bullet wound. The agony from the festering sore had driven the animal insane. In its frenzy, the rogue had attacked the village and massacred eight people before it died.

And now, returning from my own unsuccessful hunt, I thought what a rewarding novelty it would be if we were to go through Africa without killing one animal! Considering the circumstances of our trip, it would be unprecedented; and, of course, some people would think we were foolishly sentimental. Nevertheless, I decided not to use my gun during the expedition except in extreme necessity—to protect our lives or to get food when there might be no other source. I would bag trophies with my cameras, and instead of ending life, I would preserve it in action on film.

On the way back to the village, I met a troop of about forty baboons creeping through the tall grass, shepherded by a large grey male. He paused to size me up, looking like a venerable old philosopher as he squinted at me with one hand shading his intelligent-looking eyes. Apparently I passed inspection, and he leaped into the trees.

I found an ideal campsight overlooking the junction of the Kakitumba and Kagera rivers, a flat, open glade in a grove of spiky thorn trees, punctuated here and there by several large termite nests, conical mounds of grey earth taller than I and resembling stalagmites. In a hurry to rejoin my companions and set up camp before dark, I almost stumbled into the cavernous nest of an antbear, or aardvark, an animal best known because its name is usually the first to appear in dictionaries and encyclopedias. But the aardvark's real claim to fame is that it is, for its size, the fastest excavator in the animal kingdom.

Jean, André, and I were not exactly enthusiastic about the prospect of carrying all our gear on foot to the campsite beside the rivers. Klaus came to the rescue by generously offering, "Throw your bags in the back of my safari wagon, and we'll see if we can ride as far as the river."

But we had no sooner loaded up the wagon when a car came down the dirt road, trailing red dust. It was the slender, grey-haired District Commissioner, and he had only just heard about our proposal to descend the Kagera. He had hurriedly driven the sixty miles from his headquarters at M'barara in an attempt to warn us of the dangers ahead.

"I wish you chaps would reconsider this idea of boating down the Kagera," he said. "I've lived twelve years hereabouts, and no one I know, African or white, can tell you much of anything about the country, let alone the river. There are swarms of hippos everywhere, though—bloody awful beasts when they're stirred up. If they tip you in the drink, they'll either finish you off higgledy-piggledy, or the crocs will snatch you up before you can crawl out. The rapids are devilish, too, and—"

And I thought, "Here we go again." But I listened patiently as he finished cataloging the disasters awaiting us. Finally he asked to see our boats, and when he saw our disassembled kayaks lying in the bottom of the truck, he was appalled. "You can't mean you're going to try for Lake Victoria in these *toys!*"

André spoke only a little English, and Jean not at all, so it was my duty to answer. He was even more dismayed when I said, "Not only to Lake Victoria, but right on down the Nile to Egypt." And then we explained our expedition.

"I can't give you my official permission," he finally answered gravely. "If you and your partners insist on doing the Kagera, you do so entirely on your own responsibility. All I can say is I hope you make it." And then we returned to pleasant conversation for a few moments, and he drove off with a warm "Cheerio and good luck! Don't forget to send me a full report. I'll be anxious to know how you make out."

"Well, at least he didn't tell us we were crazy," I said to André.

It took us an hour to reach the campsite, the little truck jolting along behind André and me, as we led the way on foot over the rough terrain. We unloaded and waved goodbye to Klaus as he drove back. Dinner was an omelet cooked by André, and as we ate, bats swooped around our heads in the dim light of a delicate new moon.

As I write this by the combined light of the moon and a flashlight, Jean and André lie wide-eyed in their sleeping bags, kept awake by the nightsounds around us. From the surging river a few yards away, a hippo bellows, deep and thundering, against a background of barking and scolding from the troop of baboons bedding down in the banyan tree at the water's edge. The weird whooping of a hornbill or the maniacal wail of a prowling hyena occasionally rings out to obscure the persistent whirring and chirping of the teeming insects.

"I hope you make it," the District Commissioner had told us. But it is with anticipation, not fear, that I look forward to tomorrow and the beginning of our trip down the Kagera River.

Campsite above Kagera River. Jean Laporte (left) and André Davy.

Hippopotamus amphibius

The hippopotamus is a most peculiar creature—a
cartoonist's delight. Although its name in Latin
means *river horse,* its nearest relative is the pig.
It is the third largest animal of Africa, after the
elephant and white rhino, with a length up to
fourteen feet and a height of four or five feet at
the shoulder—the largest of all nonruminating
animals. Its enormous jaw spread is not exceeded
by any other land mammal. Both its canines and
its incisors never stop growing and therefore
become immense.* The hippo is insulated by a
two-inch thick, almost hairless skin, which is
sensitive to certain biting insects.
Hippos live in herds of twenty to forty, feeding
mainly at night on a vegetarian diet of grass and
aquatic plants, self-indulgently wolfing down as
much as 300 pounds of fodder in one nocturnal
orgy. Small wonder an adult sometimes reaches a
weight of four tons, the second heaviest of all
land mammals. Yet a hippo is surprisingly agile
in spite of its great bulk, and tremendously
powerful. Both the male and female can be
fearless and ferocious when wounded or

---

*During a visit to Zanzibar, I was offered, for $300, a monstrous
deformed hippo canine tooth a full forty-eight inches in length.
It was transformed into a coiled hooded cobra by an ingenious
Indian craftsman. He cemented to the great tusk a beautifully
molded head and tail of pure silver, with two flawless rubies for
the eyes.

defending their young. Old bulls often become
ill-tempered rogues, attacking anything or
anyone without provocation, as we so well
discovered!

An extraordinary demonstration of one species'
concern for another occurred in South Africa's
Kruger National Park. A wildlife enthusiast,
Dick Reucassel, photographed a hippopotamus
actually rescuing a young female impala from a
crocodile. The antelope was about to drink at
the edge of a pond when an eight-foot croc
lunged from the muddy water, seized a leg and
dragged her into the river. The hippo, less than
100 feet away, immediately came charging over
and chased the croc away. He nosed the injured
animal ashore and stood watching as she
staggered up the bank, then followed after for a
closer look. The impala struggled to evade her
frightening new companion as he twice gently
took her head into his great mouth and released
it. The mortally wounded doe collapsed from
loss of blood, and the hippo began sniffing her
body and licking her torn abdomen and broken
leg. Finally the impala died, but for a quarter of
an hour more the hippo continued to stand over
her as vultures began to appear, departing only
when the fiery heat forced him to return to the
pond. As the vultures converged on the body,
the crocodile appeared, drove them away, and
reclaimed his prize.

November 11: *On the Kagera River*

Morning came hot and clear, and we were so anxious to get under way that we dispensed with breakfast. We assembled our boats, carefully fitting and locking the various sections together and then inserting the frames into the canvas skins. We carried the slender shells down the deep bank and through a jungle of towering emerald green papyrus to the river's edge, and several more trips sufficed to load the four hundred pounds of equipment in the waterproof bags, four to each kayak.

I gave André my Luger pistol and Jean the .22 caliber rifle, keeping the 12-gauge shotgun, so that each of us would have a weapon for emergencies. Then, with everything securely lashed inside, André and Jean set their boats into the silty water, jumped in, and pushed off into the brown flood while I filmed their departure from the bank. The Kagera, one of the swiftest rivers in Africa, swept them downstream and out of sight before I could pack my camera away.

Eager to catch up and excited to begin the river journey, I pushed off into the river—and then was startled almost out of my wits by the sudden violent splashing of a huge bull hippo bobbing to the surface, blowing and snorting, forcing me to swerve close to the papyrus to dodge him. My private opinion that an unmolested hippo was not dangerous to man was refuted when this great barrel-shaped hulk plunged after me in a vicious charge that left no doubt as to his intentions. He was nearly as long as my kayak and must have weighed well over three tons, yet his rage drove him through the water at an incredible speed. His nostrils blasted spray with every snort, and his yellow tusks were, to say the least, awesome.

Fear set my arms flailing like a windmill in a gale, and the double blades of my single paddle churned the water to froth. I pulled ahead slowly until, at last, he broke off his pursuit and dropped back, content that he had evicted the intruder from his domain. I trembled with adrenalin and relief—and then noticed that downstream about a hundred yards a whole family of hippos were strung across the river in a formidable blockade. At the rate I was being swept along by the current, I couldn't avoid them; but I chose the widest gap and hoped I could get through before any of them closed on me. With a few quick, hard strokes I was able to streak through, leaving behind a group of startled hippos.

At the head of a stretch of rapids I at last caught up with Jean and André, who were also nervous from their hippo encounters. André had counted 112 of them.

And then we encountered the rapids, a short and tricky stretch that provided a chilling new experience for André and me—one that quickly taught us how little we were prepared for white water. André and I had gone on a shake-down cruise in our kayaks on the Marne and Seine rivers in France, but hadn't met any white water; Jean, on the other hand, was a skilled paddler with years of kayaking experience on all the prominent rivers in France. Prudently, André and I let Jean lead, and we tried to imitate his techniques.

Wearing heavy dark glasses, with his nylon hat jammed on tightly and strapped securely around his chin, Jean appeared supremely cool and confident as he stroked along, correcting his course with expert little dips and pulls of his paddle. By contrast, André and I were ham-handedly awkward—too often over-reacting in our nervous maneuverings. My kayak was so tippy I had the sensa-tion of being on a tightrope. To keep from listing, I repositioned the bags and sat squarely on the hard rubber seat. The heavy cargo made the boats sluggish and hard to maneuver around the masses of rock in our path; but at last we were through the rapids with only a few minor tears in the rubber hulls.

Just past the rapids the hippos began appearing again, and for twelve miles their unpredictable actions kept me in a state of hypertension. One monstrous old bull snorted and submerged as I glided toward him. A moment later I swept by his position, hugging the green bank as close as I dared, every nerve in my body jangling. Just as I began to relax, he reared to the surface only a few feet behind, lunging along in my wake in an obvious attempt to finish me off. I had read graphic accounts of hippo attacks in which boats had been smashed and paddlers mangled beyond recognition. My frail kayak seemed ri-diculously vulnerable, and again I raced for my life, whipping the little craft over the water as fast as my aching arms could paddle.

For twelve miles I dodged hippos, discovering that while they're merely amusing as seen from the deck of a large launch or from the shore, when one is in a fragile midget boat among them, they can be terrifying. At times it seemed as if I were in the water with them, positioned as I was with the seat of my kayak below the waterline and the top of the cockpit a scant eighteen inches above. The only amusing moment was when I passed a trio of hippos lolling in the shade of the papyrus. They raised their heads in amazement as I swept by, and I stared back in equal fascination, for one of them was a rare freak—an albino—not white, of course, but a light glowing pink. The exhilaration I felt at being whisked along on the sweeping current changed to alarm as it oc-curred to me what a precarious position we were in: the three of us racing single-file down a slender, hippo-infested corridor framed by impenetrable twelve-foot walls of papyrus, with no place to land and no way of stopping without capsizing. It was like a ski-jump—there was no stopping until the end. And for us the end came almost as a stark catastrophe.

Soon the wind blowing ahead of us carried the lusty sound of a big cataract ahead. I couldn't see it, however. Instead, all that was visible was a thick wall of scrubby vegetation that seemed to block the entire river. Yet the current seemed to head straight into the cul-de-sac. As I came closer, I saw that it was really two little islands, though the vegetation bridged the gap between them.

Could I possibly plow through the ivy-choked channel between the islands, or should I try to squeeze between the right bank and the first island? A pile-up was inevitable if all three of us held to the same course. So I gestured with my hand and shouted back at them, "Take the right channel," trying to sound more confident than I felt. And as I headed straight into the jungle ahead, I lay back as far as I could to avoid the tangle of vines and limbs clogging the gap.

The most hellish moments of my life began then. I had just flattened myself when the kayak crashed to a halt deep in the growth. Submerged roots snagged my boat, causing it to heel over sharply. Instantly the torrent rushed over the tilted craft, filling and engulfing it. As the kayak settled, it turned turtle and broke free of the vines.

I found myself being dragged along upside-down in the seething water. I tried to break free, but my legs were ensnared in the lashings that held the bags. Though I had been a skin diver from the age of twelve, with good lung capacity, I was in poor condition for the heart-bursting ordeal that followed. For several days I had been suffering from an attack of dysentery that had sapped my vitality, and what strength remained had been squandered in the exhausting escapes from the hippos. Worse, the shotgun, which had been wedged between bags of equipment in the bow, broke free and struck me in the face.

When my senses cleared, I forced myself to make one last try to break free, and with all my strength finally managed to escape. As I kicked away from the kayak, I was seized by the madly swirling water, which buffeted and bowled me along with such overwhelming force that I was completely powerless and too disoriented to determine the direction of the surface. I was swept along like a straw, rolling from one turbulence to another, scraping over reefs, colliding with rocks—desperately fighting to get my head above water.

The raging current tore at my hat, and the strap, still tightly fastened around my chin, was strangling me. With both hands I tore it off, fleetingly regretful as I thought of myself bareheaded under a burning African sun.[1]

---

1. Our hats had been specially designed and made for us at Gelot's, the most fashionable male chapeau shop in Paris, world famous for its illustrious clientele, including nobility. The establishment was once the official hattery of the late King Edward VII. Monsieur Gelot, Jr., a gracious, soft-spoken French-

Then it occurred to me that was the least of my worries right now. My heavy boots were dragging me down like lead weights. I clawed at them frantically to tear them from my feet, but I couldn't do it. I was drowning. "So this is the way I go," I thought, "like a fly sucked down a drain."

Then, as I silently cried out, "Dear God, please help me!" my head broke the surface just as my lungs were ready to explode. For a glorious moment I breathed in delicious gulps of air, then was sucked under again; but the brief respite was all I needed. I was angry and determined to survive, and I fought back to the surface again, using only my arms—kicking my feet only seemed to make matters worse—and I managed to keep from going under again.

The water was becoming less turbulent, though the current was still brutally strong, and I began to wonder how long it would be before the crocodiles came after me. Just then I glimpsed the river behind me and saw the dangerous stretch of rapids I had just come through. Jean and André were nowhere to be seen.

I worked my way out of the current toward the right bank, and after several attempts, I was finally able to grip stalks of papyrus and haul myself out of the racing water. I collapsed on a floating mass of decaying vegetation, gasping, half dead.

Through waves of nausea I felt a jolt, then heard an anxious French voice asking if I were all right. It was Jean. I rolled toward him and replied, "I think so. Where's André?" His only answer was to hold up a sodden hat and one dripping bag. André had capsized, and we could only assume he had drowned. We had lost one of our company and two-thirds of our irreplaceable equipment. The ambitious French-American Nile expedition appeared to be ended at its very beginning—and after only one month in Africa. "Send me a report," the district commissioner had said; but the report we'd have to send him now would only confirm his dire warnings.

When I had enough energy, I floundered through the jungle of papyrus and undergrowth to the steep bank, crawled on hands and knees to the top, and began searching for our lost comrade, while Jean crossed the river to do the same on the opposite bank. I shucked off my water-soaked boots and shirt to make the going easier and then picked up a game trail along the bank and followed it upstream toward the roar of the rapids, stumbling and nearly fall-

---

man, had expressed keen interest in the expedition and had personally designed, fitted, and constructed our headgear, refusing any compensation for all his trouble. Mon. Gelot had handled his creations in a tender and affectionate way, almost as if they were beloved living pets. Now I wondered what he would say if he knew that one of them was probably giving a stomachache to a gullible crocodile.

ing several times as I fought to throw off the effects of my ordeal. Like a post-operative patient, I scarcely had control over my body. My ears, clogged with water, rang and throbbed. I had trouble focusing my eyes. I had to stop and vomit up the stomachful of silty water I had swallowed, further closing the stricture in my throat that was causing me to gasp for air.

I staggered along back to the two islands where the ordeal had begun without finding any sign of André.

And then, exhausted though I was, I felt a quick sense of elation as I spied my kayak at the foot of the cascade, bottom up against a reedy bar. It seemed largely intact; we might be able to go on after all.

Ignoring the boat for the moment, I joined Jean in shouting to André. We called and searched for more than an hour. André had vanished. The only sounds were from the clamorous rapids and the monkeys chittering in the trees. Nothing could be seen but the boiling flood sweeping through the papyrus below us and hundreds of black swallows milling over the surface of the river, making little splashes as they skimmed and darted. The evidence pointed to a dreadful certainty I couldn't bring myself to accept—that André was dead and his body had been swept away downstream.

We postponed the search temporarily to salvage my kayak before it could break away from its resting place. I was on the right bank; the boat was on the left. To reach it I would have to swim the river, a prospect that, understandably, filled me with terror. But, steeling myself, I slipped into the river upstream of the boat and used the current to help me across, alert for a crocodile attack.

Jean and I splashed to the islet, righted the boat, and drained out the water. I opened the "waterproof" camera case and found it half-filled with water and my two cameras—the 16mm Ciné Special with five lenses and the Rectaflex—soaked. And 500 feet of exposed color film containing irreplaceable footage lay ruined under inches of murky water. One of the primary objectives of the expedition had been to make the first complete photographic record of the Nile Basin. Now our first effort was spoiled, and the movie camera, one of the finest available, was out of commission. The nearest place we could have the camera and lenses cleaned and renovated was Nairobi, Kenya—more than 700 miles away.

After our salvage operation, I forced myself to climb into my kayak and pushed off, heading downstream to where Jean had beached his boat at a hippo wallow. But I still didn't trust the river. By snatching hold of the solidly rooted papyrus every few yards, I was able to control my speed and prevent the current from capturing the kayak. I had a scare when my nervous grabbings nearly caused my delicately balanced craft to tip over. At last, with pounding heart, I nosed into the gloomy runway in the green sedge.

How could I face André's family and tell them what had happened?

At that moment I heard Jean crashing through the thick brush above the reeds. He bounded up to me with a whoop of joy, announcing that he had found André. He rushed to his kayak and we ferried across the river, then left our boats and hurried up the very trail I had taken in my fruitless search for André. After reaching the rapids, we plowed our way through the morass to the water's edge, where I looked out over the thunderous cascade and saw André nonchalantly waving to us from a mass of rock a hundred feet from shore, where he had crashed his kayak.

It was a tremendous relief. I had been blaming myself for the whole disaster, because it had been my idea to start our journey from the headwaters of the Kagera rather than at the Victoria Nile. But the disaster hadn't been so terrible after all—no loss of life.

We hadn't seen André before because he had smashed into a rocky islet in the center of a blind spot, where the right bank forms a horseshoe curve around the rapids. He hadn't heard our shouts over the roaring water and, as he told us later, he was afraid *we* had perished when we didn't show up. At last he had seen Jean searching for him—but Jean hadn't heard *his* shouts, either, and André attracted his attention only by tying his blue bandanna to a long stem of papyrus and waving it in the air.

But now we had to get him from his rock in the middle of the rapids. We had him tie a rock to the end of his kayak mooring line and throw it to us, and then we anchored the line firmly around a clump of papyrus. André settled down in his badly damaged boat and gingerly pushed away from the rocks, and we reeled him in as the racing torrent washed over and clawed at the frail craft.

We had pulled him almost to shore when his kayak, its back broken in the collision with the rocks, folded at the center, allowing the rushing water to flood in and engulf it. André was spilled out but made a lucky grab for the rope in time to keep from being carried away. While Jean plunged through the dense papyrus to help André out of the water, I held fast to the line, my arms nearly pulled out of their sockets by the swamped boat. When I couldn't hold on a moment longer, André heaved himself out of the water and began helping Jean with the kayak.

We tried to rest, then, lying on a mattress of cushy reeds; but a hotbed of hungry insects soon stung us into activity. We stamped a path through the forest of obstinate papyrus, then wrestled the battered boat and the baggage up the rocky wall of the gorge to the dry land above. We were exhausted by the exertion of wallowing and staggering with our loads in knee-deep muck, but the real misery came from the countless squadrons of kamikaze insects. It seemed that every creeping, flying vampire in the area had come to prospect our bodies for a meal, stilettoing us from ears to ankles until we were a mass of stinging, itching welts. It was the longest and most painful day of our lives.

We built up the fire with heavy branches, laid out all the damp equipment on the coarse grass around it, then collapsed in a stupor onto our sleeping bags. We were covered with chigger, tsetse fly, and mosquito bites and smarting from scratches caused by thorns and saw grass. André and I had numerous painful bruises from our capsizings in the rock-bound rapids. But though our first taste of kayaking in Africa had been nearly fatal, the single most overpowering emotion we felt was a tremendous gratitude to be alive.

November 12: *Beside the Kagera*

We slept as though drugged until late this morning, then arose to finish drying our gear. Lunch was leftovers, but during the meal André gave us a description of his adventure in the rapids. As he approached the white water, the stern of his kayak had become snagged on a boulder. The boat began to heel over and fill, but he concentrated all his strength in a great heave with his paddle and shoved free.

A startled hippo threatened him at the head of the rapids, sinking out of sight as he approached, and then suddenly appearing directly in his path. With a flurry of strokes he was able to swerve around the huge animal, but the effort caused him to career sideways and capsize into the white water. He, too, had almost drowned as the rough current held him captive, administering a savage beating as it swept him over the rocks and through the boils. The kayak bounced along, keel up, just out of reach until it fetched up in the throat of a narrow cascade and snapped in two from the pressure.

Though exhausted, André floundered toward the battered shell, grabbed on, and worked it off the reef. Holding to the stern, he managed to guide it to a safe landing on the tiny rock island, where Jean spotted him.

Our drying-out was interrupted by a heavy rainstorm that burst on us so swiftly that we had to scurry around camp to snatch up our drying clothing and equipment and fling them to shelter inside our tent. An hour later the rain stopped as abruptly as it had started. The sky cleared, and we were able to spread our things again under a brilliant sun.

Inventory of our equipment shows that André and I have lost several almost indispensable items to the river: our two canvas spray covers, so essential when shooting rapids to seal the cockpits against the water; my two-wheeled boat carriage for portage (carrying boats around difficult spots in the river); our chief weapons, the luger and the shotgun; and my broad-brimmed hat, an article more important to me than a gun in Africa where, under certain conditions, the sun can paralyze a bareheaded man in a matter of minutes.

But with the loss of our major weapons it will be a simple matter for me to keep my vow against killing animals during our trip. True, I hedged in the promise with the stipulation, "except in an emergency to protect ourselves or to get food when regular sources fail." But what can I bag with our only remaining weapon—a five-shot .22 rifle with a bent front sight? In an emergency, the luger and the shotgun could have stopped a good-sized animal with sharp aim at close range; but the .22 might as well have been a peashooter, and the only big game we could shoot would be rodents and birds!

November 13: *Beside the Kagera*

Today, unlikely as it seems, we have come to regard our calamity as a lifesaving event—a miraculous, though painful, reprieve from certain death. This afternoon as André and I were hiking through the bush along the river, intent on assaying the unknown character of the upper Kagera, we came upon a sight that chilled us—a murderous, impassable rapid, where the river churned through a narrow defile in an avalanche of angry water that sucked and leaped around several big boulders strewn over its course. Here nature had created a treacherous booby trap, camouflaging the wild, rock-choked rapids with snarls of lianas and creepers that hung down from tall trees and danced on the brown flood. So perfect was the concealment that a man approaching this deadly ambush in a kayak would not have recognized it in time.

If it hadn't been for our accident, which had so abruptly terminated our Kagera trip, we would have swept on unsuspectingly and would have been smashed against the boulders, sucked under, and finished off. Ironically, the only way our lives could have been protected was for us to have stopped, abruptly and decisively, where we had been—at the islands. Thus our mishap, though dangerous, had been a godsend in disguise.

November 14: *The Kagera*

Since the moment I awoke on the morning after our accident, I have been luxuriating in the delicious feeling of being alive. I feel as if I have literally been "born again."

Several times in my life I have had near fatal mishaps, but none have given me such a sense of *joie de vivre* as did my intimate flirtation with death on the Kagera. Never before has the fundamental fact of existence—to be alive and in full possession of my faculties—seemed such a blessing. The discouragement I felt at our setback has evaporated under the flush of this new inspiration. I have resolved to nourish it through the remaining years of my life and, like the Africans I have come to love and respect, live each day to the fullest, with optimism and deep awareness, as if it were my last.[2] The famous poem "Look to This Day," from the Sanskrit, captures the essence of my feelings:

Look to this day, for it is Life, the very Life of Life;
In its brief course lie all the verities and realities of our existence,
    The bliss of growth,
    The glory of action,
    The splendor of beauty,
For yesterday is already a dream, and tomorrow is but a vision;
But today well-lived makes every yesterday a dream of happiness,
And every tomorrow a vision of hope.
Look well, therefore, to this day.
Such is the Salutation of the Dawn.

From now on such will be the salutation of all my dawns.

November 15: *The Kagera*

For four days we have remained encamped by the Kagera, spending our time getting our gear back in order and exploring our great wilderness surroundings. We have found no human beings, but have observed herds of zebra, the far-ranging "sports model" of the horse family; also, white-bearded wildebeest, a species of horned antelope that looks like a combination pony, cow, and bison; and a small herd of impala, the champion athletes of the animal kingdom—beautiful golden antelope with long lyre-shaped horns, capable of clearing a ten-foot barrier or of leaping twenty-five feet in one bound.

Late this afternoon, as I tramped through the tall grass near our tent, I suddenly came face to face with a grazing hippo. He gave a surprised grunt, wheeled around, and headed for the river at a fast jog. Every year hippos kill quite a few people in Africa, a good percentage of them on land, so it seemed a wise idea to keep my specimen on the run before he got any pugnacious ideas and reversed his course. I let out a blood-curdling whoop and charged after

---

2. The people of some tribes in Africa believe that when they go to sleep at night, they experience death, which is overcome each dawn as long as their souls remain in their bodies. As a consequence of this belief, they live a day-to-day existence, enjoying each day of their lives as if they had seen the dawn for the last time. Thus they don't waste time in brooding over the troubles of the past or the doubts, worries, and fears of the future.

him at top speed. I already knew that hippos were marvelously fast swimmers, but it seemed incredible that on land, with no water to support their ponderous bulk, they could also be swift runners. Yet pounding after him all the way back to the river, I couldn't keep up with him—much less close the gap between us.

I didn't give up the chase until the hippo, his stumpy legs driving like pistons, plunged headlong into the river and disappeared under the waves. It was a foolhardy stunt, I know, but with a certain poetic justice to it. And how refreshing it was to be the pursuer for a change, rather than the pursued!

November 16: *Last day at the Kagera camp*

While rambling through the countryside alone, downstream from our camp, I came upon a hippo runway about 100 feet long—a passageway forged through dense papyrus and reeds, leading straight to the river. Thirstier than usual, I followed the shadowy tunnel to the water's edge for a drink. The vegetation closed above the runway, and it was a relief to be out of the sun, though the air was heavy with pungent hippo musk. I drank deeply, scooping up the flat-tasting water in double handfuls until I was satisfied.

Suddenly I heard a frightening sound as I turned to go back—a hippo entering the tunnel and tramping rapidly toward me. Perhaps my scent had alarmed him as he grazed nearby, sending him dashing for the security of his more natural environment, the river. I felt trapped, fenced in by the solid walls of growth on either side, with the swift river at my back and a charging hippo bearing down on me like a giant bowling ball racing toward a single pin.

Just in time I spotted a gap in the dense vegetation near me and dived through to safety as the excited animal swept past and crashed into the water.

Every afternoon the short rainy season has manifested itself around 3 p.m., with clocklike regularity, in a brief but torrential electric storm that drives us to the dubious shelter of our fragile tent until it thunders on to the west.

The huge drops fall with such shattering force that soon our tent is filled with a fine mist. We watch the storm as it sweeps over the undulating veldt toward us from the direction of Lake Victoria. A violent wind precedes the rain by several minutes, sometimes reaching such intensity that we have to hold the tent down to keep it from being carried away. As the cool wind and the black clouds from the lake clash with the hot, humid atmosphere around the Kagera, booming thunderclaps resound across the angry sky in great fluttery rips and crashes that cause the ground to tremble beneath us. The jolting rumble of the thunder sounds like a ship being ground to pieces on a rocky reef during a hurricane.

This afternoon, as we sat on the rubber floor of the tent patiently waiting out today's storm, I was intent on a vivid mental picture of a great sailing ship in distress on the rocks when I heard the sound of a human voice. It was so faint that at first it seemed part of my daydream—a phantom cry from my dying ship. But when my companions suddenly sat upright, I knew I had not imagined it. We listened, heard the sound again, and then, despite the downpour, we scrambled out of the tent and immediately located the source of the voice. Across the river, huddled together under a thorn tree and happily waving at us with wide grins, were five rain-soaked Africans—our "rescuers"!

The District Commissioner had become worried when we failed to appear at the next village, sixty-five miles downstream. The swift current should have carried us there easily the day after we left, and so he had dispatched a rescue team. We signaled the men to stay where they were, and then I ducked back into the tent to scribble a quick note to the Commissioner, assuring him that we were alive and in good health and that we hadn't been gobbled up—though both the river and the hippos had certainly tried. I told him we had met with a setback that prevented us from continuing on the river to Lake Victoria; we would have to portage back to our starting point, and planned to leave the next day.

I tucked the note into my shirt, got in my kayak, and crossed the rain-dabbled river. It took me three minutes to leave Tanganyika and enter Uganda, since the river was the boundary between the countries for thirty-five miles. The Africans chattered away in a strange dialect; I handed the note to a tall, muscular young man and said, "For your bwana." He understood, and a few minutes later the men, eager to return with the news of their successful quest and assured that we were safe, trotted off single-file into the bush. The rain had stopped by the time I returned to the camp. I regretted that we had caused the Commissioner anxiety—but was reassured to know of his concern about our welfare.

We celebrated our last night on the Kagera by squandering all our remaining food supplies as André surpassed himself as a chef—bouillon, rice, onions, potatoes, bully beef, and cocoa laced with powdered milk. It tasted especially good to men who had been on short rations for a week.

However, we weren't able to enjoy our last night in peace. The stillness of the night was fractured by the roar of a lion just as we were preparing for bed. I know how deceptive a lion's roar can be; even when he's half a mile away, he can sound as if he's about to walk into camp. André chuckled nervously when he saw my hand reach out to our little rifle leaning against the tent pole. "Let's hope he finds a nice, fat zebra before he catches our scent," he said.

It isn't easy to drop off to sleep with a lion prowling in the neighborhood. I'm aware that a lion will rarely make an unprovoked attack on a man. Generally, only incapacitated and aging lions that can't hunt regular game become a menace to humans. It is comforting to remember what a white hunter once told me: A lion, young or old, if given a choice between a man and a zebra would choose the zebra every time. I sincerely hope our prowler has conventional lion tastes.

November 17: *Breaking camp on the Kagera*

We started breaking camp in heavy morning mist, but by ten a.m. the fog had cleared and we sweltered under a brilliant sun. The three of us formed a relay to carry the twelve heavy bags and André's battered boat from our camp to the moored kayaks, so we could cross the river and enter Uganda. I assigned myself the job of lugging the baggage through the papyrus. André would meet me halfway down the bank with a single bag; then I would struggle through the towering green stalks to the spot where we had drawn up the kayaks from the river.

Occasionally as I plunged through the spongy mat of humus, my foot sank into cold slime; after extricating my leg, I had the distasteful chore of prying off the slimy black leeches that had immediately fastened themselves to my bare legs.

Whenever I paused to rest, I became entranced with the insect life around me. The mosquitos, gnats, ticks, and tsetse flies I was already too familiar with, but there were also preying mantises and walking sticks so perfectly camouflaged that I didn't see them until they moved, stalking gorgeously tinted butterflies. Inch-long black ants milked their herds of fat aphids, and a gaudy yellow and purple spider with a triangular body covered with sharp spikes labored industriously on a web that was at least six feet across.

When we had all the equipment down by the boats, we ferried it across the river; then, sweating like pack horses, we tramped down another trail from the river's edge through the papyrus to the base of the gorge wall. At last we manhandled the boats and baggage through to the grassy field above the steep banks. Then we piled everything precariously on top of the two little boat carriages that had survived the river. The loads were too heavy; we hadn't traveled a hundred yards when a thorn punctured the tire of one carriage, and the axle of the other bent under the burden.

We carefully hid everything in a well-marked clump of brush, and carrying nothing but the .22 rifle, we set out to hire some Africans to help us. Five hours and twelve miles later, we reached the familiar brick home of Monsieur

Klaus. Soaked to the skin and ravenously hungry, we found that the Belgian had gone to a beer party at the District Commissioner's house to celebrate the news of our being found safe and well. His manservant, Uto, welcomed us and fed us as if we were long-lost relatives.

Later Klaus burst into the house, his face flushed and beaming, and greeted us effusively. "You boys really had us in a rash when you didn't show up at Kyaka on schedule. The D.C. thought you had cashed in your chips for certain and sent out ten of his askaris to bring in the remains. And when the head office at Entebbe heard you were missing, they were going to have their plane come over for a look too!" After we had described our Kagera river episode to Klaus, he brightened and said, "Well, the Fates were with you this time and you're the wiser for your ordeal. Your luck has got to change now."

November 18: *Kakitumba revisited*

After a refreshing sleep on real mattresses we were ready to return to the cache. We had breakfast shortly after dawn; then with the help of Klaus, we hired five Chiga tribesmen who were willing to go with us to bring back our outfit.

Following a direct course, we worked our way toward the river with the Africans padding along behind, each man barefoot and carrying a long, slender staff. Only one was dressed in the typical costume of the region—a brown cloth wraparound; the others wore British khaki, though some had eccentric touches, like an old-fashioned vest or a rumpled British Army waistcoat.

As we neared the Kagera, the air sweetened suddenly with the fragrance of tropical flowers. A small band of chattering vervet monkeys swung daringly through the tall acacias in madcap acrobatics that filled me with admiration and envy. Across the river a herd of zebras grazed in the thick grass, and just beyond them a pair of reed bucks stood statue-still in contemplation of us as we marched along.

The cache was untouched, and we apportioned the loads as equally as we could. The Chigas bore their burdens on their heads, steadying them with one hand, while André and I loaded the boat carriages, this time with a burden they could bear. Jean carried a bag under his arm and another on his shoulder. Even the one bearer who had a kayak (André and I had the other two) jogged along smoothly with the awkward sixty-pound bundle neatly balanced on his bare head. The men bore their cumbersome loads with a grace and dignity that would have done credit to a fashion model. With regal posture they flowed along over a twisting trail through the trees.

I was already hot and exhausted when the second tire on my boat carriage was punctured, slowing me down even further. I fell behind the others and

Chiga tribesmen, André (foreground), and Goddard arrive at the cache of their expedition equipment.

was soon left to myself with only a swarm of maddening tsetse flies for company. With my free hand I stripped off the red bandanna that had been protecting my bare head from blistering sun, and, using it as a swatter, I tried to keep the insects at bay. They were not bothered in the least by my flailings but dodged past to probe my exposed anatomy, even insolently crawling into my nostrils and mouth. One nearly drove me to madness when it buzzed into my ear and refused to emerge. It took several minutes to route him out with a splinter without puncturing my eardrum. While I stood there, the flies began feeding in earnest, causing me to twitch violently each time they scored a hit, which stung like a hot needle and bored so deep that a speck of blood tipped the wound.

My anger erupted when they squeezed under the gauze bandages covering a painful eruption of eight small boils on my right leg. The infections had been ripening for several days until now they were exquisitely tender and tumid with pus: the searing bites of the insects were intolerable. I jumped to my feet, ignoring my weariness, and stomped along in exaggerated strides to keep the little saber-toothed devils off me.

A hippo, ash-gray with dried mud, decided not to get excited about my passing by and only ambled off into a thicket. And soon I found an ancient, worn hippo promenade, which their wideset legs had worn into a perfect highway for my boat carriage—two smooth ruts with grass growing between. When the path angled off toward the river, however, I left it and struggled on again through the brush.

I caught up with André and the Chigas just as we came to a steep, scraggly arroyo. Jean had taken a different course than the others and was nowhere in sight. We formed a column to relay the burdens across the arroyo, and at last reached the other side, giddy from the heat and exertion. During the strenuous climbing, one of my throbbing sores erupted, releasing a thick discharge that trickled down my leg and lured another cloud of vulturous flies. By then I was eagerly watching for the onset of the afternoon storm as a relief from the heat and the insects, and sure enough the magnificent thunderhead was building up a few miles away, an immense cumulo-nimbus shaped like an atomic explosion, promising imminent relief from my tormentors.

Just beyond the ravine Jean intercepted us, breathless and shaken after a harrowing encounter with a wild boar[3] that had attacked him without provoca-

---

3. Based on the details of Jean's description, he was probably charged by a giant forest hog (*Hylochoerus meinertzhageni*), a member of the African pig family *Suidae,* which ranges from Kenya to Cameroon. It weighs up to 600 pounds and has a thickset body covered with long, coarse black hair. Both sexes have a

tion as he crested a hill. With no weapon for protection, Jean dropped his burden and fled. But the boar gained on him, and finally Jean was forced into an undignified scramble up the nearest tree, where he sat safely out of reach until the irritable animal left.

The storm overtook us within about two miles of Klaus's place, drumming down with such blinding intensity that we gave up trying to hike in the rain and instead fled to a thicket to wait out the downpour, huddled together on our bags. The Chigas didn't like the storm at all, and mumbled worriedly to themselves, their eyes rolling with superstitious fear at the ghostly lightning and explosive thunder.

The downpour continued longer than usual, and it was in the dim gray light of evening that we continued on our way, splashing to the cottage over a flooded landscape, all the trails now hidden under inches of tepid brown water. It was a strange sensation to be soaking wet, tramping along in the rain in ankle-deep puddles, yet still feeling intense thirst. None of us had had anything to drink all day, and though I walked along with my parched mouth open to catch the water still dribbling from the sky, the few drops that I caught merely tantalized me.

It was dark when we reached Klaus's house, and we dropped our burdens and immediately drank our fill from the rain barrel. Water has rarely been so delicious. Then we paid our helpers a better-than-average wage and they returned to their huts, talking with a cheerfulness and animation we didn't feel. Instead, exhausted from thirty-five miles of trekking through rough Ugandan bush in two days, we each took a sponge bath from two old-fashioned pitchers of hot water brought to us by Uto, taking turns washing the mud and grime from our tired bodies in Klaus's small concrete bathtub. Then our sympathetic host gave us supper. Famished as we were, we were more interested in sleep than in food; it was a close decision, and food won, for the moment.

Other decisions were harder. We were tired and discouraged, and Klaus forced us to discuss the question uppermost in our minds when he said, "Well, what now, my friends? Do you still think you can do the Nile?" I answered quickly, "The Kagera is out of the picture, of course, but personally I'll never be satisfied until we give the big river a fair try." André translated to Jean, and I was relieved when they both expressed a desire to go on with the expedition.

---

double pair of well-developed tusks that are formidable weapons and huge wartlike swellings below the eyes that give them a dissipated appearance. Normally shy and nocturnal, they can be savage when aroused. Jean was downright lucky to have reached that tree in time!

Kampala

In 1862 two English explorers,
John H. Speke and James A.
Grant, penetrating from the
south in their quest for the
source of the Nile, became the
first Europeans to reach Rubaga,
the capital of Mutesa I, the
Kabaka or king of Buganda.
Rubaga was the site of present-
day Kampala. Emulating the
example set by twenty or more
of his ancestors (his royal line
going back at least 400 years),
Mutesa was an unmerciful
tyrant who held absolute power
over a realm that extended for
about 150 miles along the
northwest shore of Lake
Victoria and included, at the
time of Stanley's visit in 1875,
some three million subjects. His
royal court included a prime
minister, a cabinet, innumerable
nobles, courtiers, servants, and a
harem of two hundred fawning
wives. The Kabaka's powerful
army of 150,000 warriors and a
formidable fleet of 230 great war
canoes on Lake Victoria enabled
Buganda to dominate the entire

surrounding regions.
Through the encouragement of
Stanley, Mutesa welcomed the
first English missionaries into
Buganda in 1877, then French
Roman Catholics in 1879.
Christianity was expanding
steadily when the shrewd king
died in 1884 and was succeeded
by his unstable, anticlerical son,
Mwanga, who replaced his
father's tolerance with the
persecution and murder of
missionaries and their converts.
In 1894 Great Britain, in an
effort to bring peace, established
a Protectorate over Mwanga's
kingdom, which in 1896 was
extended to the other provinces.
These were included in the
present "Uganda," and this
name has ever since applied to
the entire country. The Kabaka
was designated the paramount
chief of the four kingdoms
included in the Protectorate, all
subservient to the colonial
administration, with Buganda
the largest and most powerful.

But it was not surprising that they both had very different ideas about how to do it. André, always impulsive and imaginative, was ready to give up the kayaks and have us make our way down the Nile as best we could in dugouts and feluccas. "We've found out our kayaks aren't strong enough for the Nile, so I think the only thing to do is to sell them in Kampala and continue by native means. We can always find people along the river who will rent their boats and services to us," he said.

Jean, as conservative as André was impetuous, disagreed with this scheme, proposing instead that we stick with our own craft and at the first opportunity send a wire to Jean Chauveau, the kayak manufacturer in Paris, and have him ship us new sections of framework to replace those broken on André's boat.

"Our kayaks are our only hope of getting through the cataracts," Jean declared confidently. "They're light, narrow, and maneuverable. They'll get us through places where a pirogue would drown. Besides, it would probably take us weeks longer and be twice as expensive if we traveled in heavy African boats." I was in full agreement. Our mishap would have been much worse if the three of us had been paddling together in one large boat, and we undoubtedly would have lost all our equipment and perhaps our lives.

But my agreement with Jean ended when he next suggested that we should have Chauveau send the kayak framework to us at Malakal in southern Sudan, "the first point of civilization," Jean said, "where we can be reasonably certain of receiving the shipment safely. It will probably take two or three weeks for the parts to come from Paris, and we can spend the time traveling to Malakal."

"And how do we get to Malakal if we don't go by kayak?" I asked.

"There's a dirt road from Kampala to Juba. It shouldn't be too difficult to arrange a ride with someone, and from Juba we can take the steamer to Malakal."

I looked down at the travel-stained map. It was at least a thousand miles of river from Lake Victoria to Malakal—a thousand miles that we would miss, or only travel by steamer, unable to stop and explore and produce on film, journal, and sketch-pad a detailed record of everything we encountered. I felt that if we did that, our expedition would have failed, for we had set out to explore the *entire* Nile.

But once again I was faced with the problem of reaching a decision with Jean and André. I have a genuine affection and respect for my companions, and if I hadn't trusted their judgment and abilities I would hardly have begun this expedition with them. But living with them has schooled me in diplomacy: they are polarized in temperament, personality, and tastes. Whenever a major issue arrives, invariably a dispute arises, varying in intensity according to the importance one or both attaches to it. Though I am the junior member of the partnership—twenty-six years old, five years younger than Jean and ten years younger than André—I often find myself in the role of arbitrator, with the responsibility of casting the deciding vote. But we had not faced a decision as important as this one before, and this time I was not satisfied with either viewpoint.

I studied the map and finally arrived at a solution that would keep us on the river. I said, "We have two good kayaks. All we need is another boat for André until we can repair his. We can buy a small dugout for him to use. And why can't we have the parts for the kayak sent to Juba instead of Malakal? It's only half the distance, and we'd have to paddle only 500 miles using the dugout."

At first Jean and André hesitated, but they brightened when Klaus declared, "I don't know much about the Nile, but I do know that there are several tribes living along the banks, and they all use pirogues. You shouldn't have any trouble getting one, and I don't think it would be too dear."

And I knew we were back in business when Jean said, "It's worth a try, anyway," and André responded, "A pirogue will be slower than my kayak, but I think I'll feel safer in one with hippos and crocodiles around."

Defeat is never really bitter, I thought, if you don't swallow it.

The last problem to be solved this evening was that of getting our water-soaked cameras and lenses in working order again. We wouldn't consider continuing down the Nile without cameras in perfect condition to film the rare sights and experiences. We decided that I should go to Nairobi, Kenya, 700 miles away but the closest place where the delicate job could be done. Jean and André would wait for me in Kampala, the largest town in Uganda.[4] And as Klaus launched us all to our beds with a well-timed sigh, we could see that our goal of traveling the length of the Nile was still possible to achieve.

November 25 to December 2: *To Nairobi, Kenya Colony*

There were times when I remembered the Kagera River adventure with fondness—as when I took my life in my hands riding with speed-crazy Africans

---

4. "Uganda is a fairy tale. You climb up a railway instead of a beanstalk, and at the end there is a wonderful new world. The scenery is different, the vegetation is different, the climate is different, and, most of all, the people are different from anything elsewhere to be seen in the whole range of Africa. . . . Here an amiable, clothed, polite and intelligent race dwell together. . . . There is a regular system of native law and tribunals; there is discipline, there is industry, there is culture, there is peace."
—Winston Churchill, *My African Journey* (1908)

in rattletrap cars and with a sleepy Italian truck driver who kept dozing at the wheel. I lost my camera and spent two days tracking it down; and I rode to Kampala in a British Austin sitting on a pair of elephant tusks that reeked so powerfully that I was nauseated all the way.

But in M'barara my hosts were Bryan Kirwan and a prior guest of his, Archie Tucker; and I could only conclude that I had been led to them by a divine providence. For Bryan Kirwan was more knowledgeable about Lake Victoria and the Albert Nile than anyone I had ever met, and Archie Tucker was an ethnologist and professor of African languages from the London Museum and an outstanding authority on the Sudan and its Nilotic tribes. No two other persons in Africa could have given me better and more pertinent information about what we would encounter during the first thousand miles of our Nile journey.

Other kind people extended friendly hospitality, including an Indian merchant who gave me a day-late Thanksgiving dinner of authentic Indian food and a geologist, who woke his seven-year-old son to tell him a real, honest-to-

John Goddard makes friends with two rare white rhino.

goodness American had come for a visit. Evidently picturing a native American, the little boy's delighted response was: "Oh, wonderful! Has he got his feathers on?"

In Nairobi, unqualified repairmen repeatedly turned me away, refusing to touch my 16mm Ciné movie camera, until finally Jack Yowell, the proprietor of the new Eapex Camera Shop, said, "Well, I might be of some help here. I've fooled around with enough movie cameras to know where I'm at with one."

For the next several days Jack and his wife, "Freddy," devoted hours to the painstaking job of dismantling, derusting, oiling, and recalibrating the delicate mechanisms and lenses until they were in perfect working order again. We talked as they worked on the camera, and I confided my dream of someday exploring the great Congo, the world's second largest river; and the conversations were joined by Geoffrey Lawrence-Brown, a famous white hunter recovering from a case of sleeping sickness he had contracted while on safari.

When the camera was fully repaired and I asked Jack for the bill for his services, I was overwhelmed when he refused to accept one shilling for all his time and effort. He just said, "You can't very well put a price on doing a favor for a friend, can you? If you really want to make me happy, just promise that someday we'll do the Congo River together."[5]

While in Nairobi I met Colonel Mervyn Cowie, the director of the National Parks of Kenya, who had met my parents while visiting in California only the month before and had learned from them about my Nile expedition. Cowie explained a great deal about his great work in protecting and preserving Kenya's incomparable wildlife, and along with Ken Beaton, the game warden of the Nairobi National Park, Cowie gave me a complete tour of the sanctuary.

And yet, though my associations in Nairobi have been rewarding, I am eager to get into action again and feel the water of the Nile beneath me.

------

5. Five years later Jack Yowell and I teamed up on an ill-fated project to explore and film the length of the Congo (Zaire). After paddling in kayaks 400 adventure-filled miles downstream from the source, we capsized in a violent stretch of white water, and Jack was drowned.

André Davy in a papyrus jungle along the Kagera River.

John Goddard, with Oumu and Gabrini, paddling in a dugout on Lake Kyoga.

A mother hippo with her baby.

A sunning crocodile (its mouth open to dissipate the heat).

An elephant herd.

Murchison Falls, where the Nile thunders through a narrow gap and drops 130 feet.

Madi bearers, Akim, Ogone, and Sabi, accompanied the Nile explorers on the 125-mile foot safari from Nimule to Juba.

Nuer herdsman.

A Dinka village.

Dinka men — their bodies coated in wood ash.

A Nuer father takes his son into the Nile for a fishing lesson.

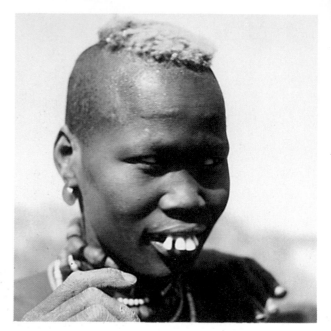

A Dinka girl.

The shoebill stork, one of Africa's rarest and strangest birds.

A Dinka girl and jewelry.

A Sudanese souk at Tangasi.

Moslem villagers at Renk (note tribal scars).

A Nubian riverscape at El Kab.

John Goddard and a temple at Naga, once an important capital of the kingdom of Kush.

The Kiosk at Naga, a temple blending Egyptian and Roman characteristics.

Kushite pyramids at Napata.

Pyramid tombs at the royal Kushite cemetery of Nuri.

A Nubian boy carrying fodder to his pet camel (note amulet on his right arm).

A Hadendowa herdsman—a member of Africa's oldest nomadic society.

A Nubian home and an old gentleman who served as a guide with Lord Kitchener's army in 1898.

John Goddard explores the Temple of Philae underwater.

One of the huge temples of Karnak, with a statue of Ramses II.

A graceful felucca under sail.

From
Victoria
to Albert

December 4: *Kampala to Jinja*

When I rejoined André and Jean in Kampala, we decided to spend two days driving and exploring along the grassy shores of Lake Victoria, the Nile's head reservoir and the world's second largest freshwater lake. The dimensions of this fresh-water sea are astounding: 200 miles long and 170 miles wide with an area of 26,700 square miles, half again as large as Switzerland! Because of its size, it actually has a tide of several inches—which the Africans have long explained by saying that the lake drops several inches when the hippos come out to feed!

As a teenager I had made a list of 127 life goals, and number 68 had been to swim in Lake Victoria. I fulfilled it with a refreshing dip in the slate-colored water of a calm bay—but I didn't stay long. The chief game warden of Uganda had warned us about the incredibly high crocodile population and the fact that they kill dozens of people every year, usually fishermen who wade in the water to set their nets.

Occasionally we saw massive termite nests of red clay, some easily fifteen feet tall and representing thirty or more years of chewing, digesting, and excreting the earth. Jean and I cut into one of these insect apartment houses—a vivid contrast against the deep green shoreline—to examine the occupants and architecture. Suddenly an aggressive soldier termite bit Jean on the forearm with such ferocity that its pincers pierced the skin and overlapped. To free Jean, I had to split the head and pull out each mandible separately.

When we left Kampala, we took the train to Jinja, a cosmopolitan community at the northernmost extremity of Lake Victoria, almost on the equator—

and where the Nile, called the Victoria Nile all the way to Lake Albert, is formed in the lake's only overflow. At Jinja we had our first good look at the river that would give us some of the most miserable along with some of the richest and happiest experiences of our lives.

We hiked along the hilly banks beside the Nile, a majestic river from the moment of its creation at the mouth of the lake. Once the banks had been heavily forested, rank with jungle growth; but the terrain is now barren of everything but grass, the aftermath of efforts to eradicate the breeding ground of the tsetse fly, carrier of sleeping sickness, a deadly disease that killed more than 200,000 people in Uganda in just six years near the turn of the century.

A Baganda fisherman weaves a fish trap beside his home adjacent to the Victoria Nile.

34

Half a mile downstream from the lake we came to the first barrier of the Nile, Ripon Falls, where the river has pierced a narrow reef of granite in three places to plunge fifteen feet down, where it begins its long spectacular march through Uganda, Sudan, and Egypt to the blue Mediterranean. It was also here that John Hanning Speke, the peerless English explorer, solved one of the most ancient geographical mysteries—the source of the Nile. A plaque marks the place and gives the date of his discovery: 28 July 1862.

Though the Nile takes many twists and turns in its northward passage, the two mouths of the Nile are on nearly the same lines of longitude as the two places considered to be the Nile's head: 30° at Kasumo Springs and 30°50' at Rosetta; and 32°58' at Ripon Falls and 32°30' at Damietta.

The hippos grazing and bathing along the edges of the river have forced the human residents to make a few concessions. The Jinja Golf Club on the eastern plateau above Ripon Falls is probably the only golf course in the world to have the rule that if a ball comes to rest in a hippo footprint the player may lift it out and drop it behind the print without any penalty!

A mile and a half farther on, we came to Owen Falls, where construction was beginning on what will one day be one of the greatest hydroelectric schemes in Africa. (It was completed in 1954.) Ripon and Owen falls should by rights be called the First and Second cataracts of the Nile; but the early geographers began the count from the river's mouth. So the last two cataracts incongruously are called the First and Second.

Phillip Juleins, a young Austrian engineer, led the three of us across the wooden foot bridge suspended over the river at the dam site. Midway we paused and looked down, watching the barbel, a big, carplike fish called *kisinja* by the locals, struggling upstream like salmon in the Pacific Northwest in order to spawn. A good number of them are able to leap the falls and continue upstream to the lakes.[6]

Those that didn't make it, however, were often caught in the hand nets of Baganda fishermen; the Baganda women washed their brightly colored *pangas* in the clear gray-green water as their men dived and pounced from the rocks

---

6. Only a few of the determined fish seemed to successfully hurtle the surging barrier and reach their goal. Yet the barbels were driven to endless bruising attempts by a mysterious instinctive force. The fish would speed forward with powerful lashings of their tails, make a sudden leap upwards, clear the foaming current for a split second, then fall back, some crashing with stunning impact on the rocks, thus providing a meal for a waiting crocodile or cormorant.

There are numerous species of barbel with a world-wide distribution. Members of the great carp family, they vary in size from that of a minnow to giant races that grow to be one hundred pounds in weight.

Owen Falls Dam

Owen Falls Dam is 2,500 feet long and eighty-five feet high, and has now obliterated both Ripon and Owen Falls. To ensure even power flow and maximum water storage for irrigation in Sudan and Egypt, the dam will raise the level of Lake Victoria three feet. This may not seem an impressive figure, but because of the lake's vast area it will mean an added accumulation of billions of gallons. Water impounded here will help prevent another "seven lean years" in Egypt, in case of a rainfall deficiency at the river's source. Forty hydroelectric power generating turbines here now produce 150,000 kilowatts of power to supply mines and mills that draw on abundant local raw materials.

As far back as 1907, Winston Churchill, with his usual acumen, realized the potential benefits to be derived from damming Lake Victoria and tapping the enormous kinetic energy produced by the outflow. In his stimulating book, *My African Journey,* he suggests that "it would be perfectly possible to harness the whole river" by constructing a dam and hydroelectric plant at its source, and "nowhere in the world would so little masonry be needed to control such an immense amount of water."

He was Prime Minister in 1954 when Queen Elizabeth opened the $61,600,000 project, which produces virtually all Uganda's electricity and almost half of Kenya's.

with their open nets, braving the turbulence of the rapids in order to scoop up thrashing fish too preoccupied with getting up the falls to dodge the fishermen. As we watched, one slender young diver brought up three barbel in his net at once, the biggest of them at least a twenty-pounder!

After spending the night with our obliging Austrian host, we set out on foot and investigated the river for several miles below Owen Falls, struggling through rank jungle growth and high grass that became increasingly impenetrable as we traveled downstream.

We had intended to start our expedition directly below Owen Falls, but after surveying some of the ugly stretches of rapids that churn the Nile for its first forty miles, we decided to travel by rail past this unnavigable stretch and put our kayaks into the river below it.[7] Why exhaust ourselves carrying our boats, when the point of having them was for the kayaks to carry *us*?

December 5–8: *Namasagali, north of Jinja*

A miniature train took us from Jinja to the hamlet of Namasagali, a little steamer port on the east bank of the Nile a few miles downstream from the last impassable rapids. Here, through the courtesy of the only white resident, the port captain, we stayed for three days, living aboard an ancient decommissioned steamboat reminiscent of the nineteenth-century Mississippi sternwheelers. We turned our attention to the most important task—renting a dugout to transport André on the river with us to Masindi, our first stop downstream.

The captain's young African clerk, Korfu, an educated Basoga, took us around nearby Basoga fishing camps to help us overcome the language barrier. André and I had studied Swahili, the *lingua franca* of East Africa; still, it was comforting to have an interpreter along who spoke the local dialect.[8]

The Basoga are a proud tribe of water-lovers, some of the finest boatmen in Africa. On the riverbank we watched several husky tribesmen, naked except

---

7. Just a year later Jean returned to the Nile to produce a motion picture documentary and to navigate this stretch and the 125-mile section between Nimule and Juba, which he had been forced to miss because of illness. He was accompanied by a French ethnologist, Jacques Blein.

The two launched their kayaks in the rugged stretch below Lake Victoria. Eight miles below Ripon Falls, both crafts capsized in the rapids. Blein was lost, apparently eaten by crocodiles. The siren Nile had lured another victim to his doom. A few days later Jean was hospitalized in Kampala, completely debilitated and feverish, with a serious case of typhus. After prolonged treatment, he reluctantly returned to his home in Paris, where he endured months of quiet convalescence before regaining his normal health.

8. More than 300 tribal dialects have been recorded in Uganda, a country slightly larger than Utah or West Germany.

Peoples of Uganda

The native peoples of Uganda can be divided into
three primary groups: Bantu, Nilotic, and Nilo-
Hamite or Hamite, although complex tribal
migrations through the ages have produced a
considerable intermingling so that few, if any, tribes
are of racially pure origin. The Baganda, from which
the name Uganda is derived, is the largest of the
thirteen principal tribes of the country, and of the
Bantu groups. The people of the Baganda tribe have a
strong admixture not only of the Hamitic Bahima of
Western Uganda, producing the lighter-skinned
aristocratic type frequently noticed in the leading
families, but also of the virile Nilotic northerners.
Buganda is the largest, richest, and most populous of
the four provinces of Uganda (based on four ancient
dynastic kingdoms). Its people are called Baganda and
its language Luganda.
The second largest of the Bantu tribes is the Basoga,
whose country, divided from Buganda by the Nile,
stretches north and east from Jinja. In language,
customs, and appearance they are very similar and,
although entirely independent, at one time paid
tribute to the kabaka or king of Buganda. Like the
Baganda, the Basoga are primarily agriculturalists, and
their land is a rich cotton area.
Three fifths of Uganda's population can be classified
as Bantu and one-fifth as Nilotic; the balance are
mostly the Nilo-Hamites with a small number of true
Hamitic strain, namely the Bahima of Ankole.

for loincloths, at work putting finishing touches on a long, sleek, racing pirogue, skillfully carved from a single jungle tree and painted with festive green and red designs. Other men sat on the ground mending fishnets. And hardly pausing in their work, the fishermen politely but firmly turned down our most generous offers, informing us that they were much too busy with fishing to take time off for such a long trip to no purpose. And we received the same response from all the other rivermen we talked to around Namasagali. Though we offered three times what they could normally have expected for working for a white man, they simply were not interested. White men come and go, but the fishing must always go on.

We hadn't anticipated any trouble in locating a dugout to replace André's boat—and now after three days we hadn't found one we could rent. There was little chance of buying one—next to his wife, a Basoga considers his boat his most prized possession. It takes too much work to build them—weeks of chipping, burning, and chiseling—and money isn't half as useful to the Basoga as his dugout. But what surprised us was their unwillingness to accept our lavish offers and take us downriver.

When I questioned the captain about this, he explained, "It's unlikely that any of these chaps has been farther than fifty miles away from home before in his life, and I guess that's as far as they care to go.

"How contented can you get?" I mused. "Haven't they got any adventure in their blood?"

"Oh, they enjoy a good adventure as much as anyone," he replied. "What they really need is one of your big Sears and Roebuck catalogues—then you'd see some real ambition."

Though we were temporarily stymied, we made the most of our stay in Namasagali. We had plenty of interesting neighbors on the antique paddlewheeler—a family of inquisitive lizards, a horde of big cockroaches, and scads of miscellaneous species of woodwork dwellers. My favorite, however, was "Junior," a two-foot baby crocodile. Every so often I would creep to the stern of the boat and cautiously lower, inch by inch, a tiny loop of twine toward his head as he dozed in the sun. But though he seemed to be fast asleep, he always sensed the lariat as it hovered over his head; he opened his eyes suddenly and then flashed into the water and disappeared. An hour or two later I would find him again comfortably esconced on the narrow ledge, soaking up the sun in perfect peace.

But the pleasures of life in Namasagali didn't compensate for the frustration of already being two weeks behind schedule, and we were beginning to toy with the idea of doubling up in one of the kayaks, certainly the last-ditch alternative, when the port captain solved the problem by producing two grinning Jaluo Africans who were willing to make the 106-mile river safari to Masindi Port in their big m'tumbi—for a price. The owner of the dugout, a tall, gravel-voiced man with the Neanderthal name of Oumu and the appearance of a black pirate, acted as spokesman, while his short, mild-mannered partner, Gabrini, stood solemnly by his side. The asking price was beyond all reason by African standards, but after friendly haggling, during which my limited Swahili vocabulary was given an exhausting workout, we settled on a down payment of two khaki shirts, a two-cell flashlight, and thirty-five shillings ($4.90 in those days) cash, with a bonus at the end of the trip. We shook hands all around and they left, with the understanding that they would meet us for an early start the next morning. I spent the rest of the day buying supplies of rice, beans, and fruit for the trip.

December 8: *North of Namasagali*

We had an audience of two dozen Basogas, who watched, fascinated, as we assembled our two good kayaks at dawn and set them in the river next to the steamer. It didn't take long to load them with our supplies, and then we sat and waited for our new companions to arrive.

Our spirits sank as the morning wore on. The Africans were obviously not coming, and I resolved to find out why. With Korfu's help I located them at their camp two miles downstream. Why hadn't they come? Some of the fishermen had convinced Oumu that he was foolhardy to take the trip with us—white men just didn't do such things as paddle all the way to Masindi, especially with Africans, and we probably planned to kill him and Gabrini and steal their dugout.

After much reasoning with them and reassuring them, we managed to convince them that we had no daggers up our sleeves, and they consented to trust us after all and go through with their agreement.

Eruptions of lightning blazed across a leaden sky, producing loud thunderclaps as we transported André's battered kayak and the rest of the baggage into the dugout, then pushed off. The port captain and the dusky populace of Namasagali stood along the bank to watch our departure. Our small flotilla made a colorful sight on the river, the two little satellite kayaks, bearing Jean and André, nimbly leading the way for the sluggish m'tumbi, with Oumu steering in the stern and Gabrini and me paddling vigorously in the waist.

Oumu's rough-hewn dugout was a reflection of his easygoing personality. It was disreputable-looking, about eighteen feet long, and looked as though it had been hacked out of a deformed tree trunk by an apprentice carver with delirium tremens. A long, crooked branch jammed into a hole in the prow served as a mast, and two mismatched sections of cloth were tied on as sails.

The storm came abruptly, drenching us. It was a strange sight—the heavy downpour sweeping up the river towards us, the path of the pelting raindrops clearly outlined as it advanced over the calm surface. When it hit us it was intense but cooling for an hour, and then the squall ceased; we paddled on past banks enveloped in rank vegetation and bordered with dense masses of papyrus under a bright, cloudless sky.

At sundown we pulled into shore at an old deserted shed, a lonely incongruity in the utterly wild landscape. As we set up camp, several Africans materialized from the surrounding bush and shyly watched us from a polite distance. Such visitations, we would soon discover, were the normal event whenever we stopped in an inhabited region along the Nile. They watched us carefully, as if not to miss a detail, and we greeted them cheerfully. Easing in for a closer look, they satisfied themselves that we were harmless and squatted among us companionably; when we brought out our supper, they produced a blackened pot filled with plantains, topped it with water from the river, and set it to boil over a small fire near our own. Oumu and Gabrini preferred the visitors' pot to ours and added several more large green cooking bananas to the kettle from their food bag. While the main course cooked, they munched cold sweet potatoes. The tough, pithy fruit took a long time to cook; long before the Africans began eating, Jean, André, and I had finished our meal of bouillon, beans, and oranges, done up the aluminum utensils, and retired to the dilapidated shed, where we made comfortable if smelly beds on old sacks of musty cotton. We had opted for the shed because, upon opening our tent, we had found it mildewed and fouled with fungus. We left it out overnight to dry.

December 9: *North of Namasagali*

Today there was a light breeze, and Oumu rigged a crude sail on his pirogue, which measurably helped the dugout's speed. Even so, the kayaks, piloted by André and me as Jean took his turn in the dugout, were able to paddle circles around the heavier craft. We had little help from the river's current, which had settled down to a languorous two knots, but we made decent progress, and early in the afternoon we spotted a break in the solid green of the left bank. Happy for a chance to rest from the demanding river, we pulled into shore, where we found five crude dugouts anchored at the end of the narrow channel and a mud hut perched on a knoll beyond. Two sleepy-eyed Bagandas dressed in copper-colored togas of cloth beaten from the bark of a tree of the fig family emerged and came down to welcome us, more than a little surprised at our unprecedented visit.

While André started a lunch of fried bananas, I accompanied one of the men to his home, a larger hut a quarter of a mile away, to bargain with him for one of his scrawny chickens. He seemed deeply pleased when I accepted his invitation to enter his hut, where in the cool shade his two buxom wives, to-gaed and barefoot, tittered nervously as I sat on the soft antelope hide he had spread for me on the pounded dirt floor. The tribesman told me his wives had never been close to a white man before and had only glimpsed an occasional white man passing on the river steamers.

I wanted to make a good impression, so I started up a Swahili conversation with the women; but they only looked at each other, giggled hysterically, then turned away and covered their faces with their hands. And so I concentrated on their more sophisticated husband. As we talked, an old man joined us, smoking a strange pipe that gurgled. The bowl of it was filled with water, and dried plantain leaves smoldered on top, the pungent steam of which he drew into his mouth through a three-foot stem of elephant grass. He ignored us completely, feebly rocking to and fro in time to some unheard rhythm.

I overpaid the man—two shillings (28¢) for his plumpest "cuckoo" (Swahili for *chicken*) and returned to the river. When we set out downstream, the man and his neighbor at the riverside hut followed us for a few miles in a dugout before bidding us "Kwaheri" and turning back.

Oumu started working the boats over toward the right bank, seeking a stronger current, and I dropped behind to photograph a pair of Jacanas— strange little water birds, with nut-brown bodies and white heads, hopping with sprightly grace from pad to pad. Aptly named lily-trotters, their long grey legs and spidery toes carry them over the surface of even the flimsiest vegetation. Suddenly I spied the shape of a big crocodile floating belly up, its body bloated with gases and with spear wounds showing around its head and neck. Apparently it had recently died from a brush with local hunters, for there was no odor of decomposition about it.

Toward dusk the stillness of the river was broken by the sounds of male voices. Behind us, tearing downstream at top speed, was the trim racing dug-out we had watched being constructed at Namasagali. It was thirty-five feet long, a beauty with a pair of impala horns now affixed to the curving prow, the seven-man crew stroking their paddles in time to a rhythmical ditty chant-ed by the last paddler. In years gone by, when the tribes still warred with each other, it would have been a war canoe headed for battle. Even now it passed us

42

John Goddard displays the head of a thirteen-foot crocodile that had been speared to death by African hunters. King-size teeth spike the crocodile's powerful jaws.

43

as if we were anchored in place, the sleek craft lunging forward with each stroke of the coordinated paddles, and soon disappeared into the distant haze.

Evening was welcome as a relief from the heat; but we still hadn't found a break in the jungle of papyrus to get to the shore, and it began to look as if we'd have to spend the night in the boats. Still we strained our eyes in the darkness, and at last we found an opening in the towering wall—exposing an open bay and a campfire glowing on the distant shore. Our elation at penetrating the papyrus quickly vanished when, as we left the river and entered the backwater, we became enmeshed in a thick net of floating vegetation. We backed off, lined up in single file, and tried again. At last, by trial and error, I ferreted out a narrow passage through the labyrinth of water and floating weeds, and we advanced slowly across the 400-yard bay that separated us from our refuge. Halfway across, Oumu cupped his hands to his mouth and called out in his deep voice. He was answered seconds later by the muted blare of an animal horn coming from the direction of the glow ahead.

As we worked our way across the last few yards of open water, six men, clad only in bark loincloths, appeared on the bank, two of them holding flaming brands above their heads to guide us to an anchorage next to their two dugouts. As we climbed stiffly out of our boats, they greeted us like visiting relatives, with warm, lingering handshakes and broad smiles, chattering with questions as to who we were, where we had come from, and where we were going. When I told them we were heading for the very end of the river, they only looked puzzled; when I explained that we were going far beyond Masindi, the outer boundary of their little world, they brightened and shook their heads in wonder. To them the river did not end.

They were Banyoro fishermen, and twenty big, freshly caught catfish were racked and drying out over hot coals to smoke and cure. The fish must have weighed twenty pounds each, looking for all the world like monstrous shiny polliwogs. While André boiled the chicken for supper, Jean and I set up the tent, now cleansed of most of its mildew and mustiness from being laundered in the Nile and spread before the sun all day in the m'tumbi. The Banyoros watched avidly as we unloaded our gear and set up the tent; only when André lit our sputtering stove did they snap out of their concentration and begin to chatter and laugh over the wonder of our visit. Despite our vastly different backgrounds and a considerable language barrier, we were soon relaxed and enjoying a real sense of fellowship.

André called, "Re-dee!" and we set to eating our chicken and bouillon while Oumu and Gabrini munched on fish and sweet potatoes. During the meal the Banyoros serenaded us with spirited chanting. As I cooled my soup, I was surprised to find something floating in the small calabash I used as a bowl. As I scooped it out and examined it in the firelight, I remembered that it was an old French custom to flavor the soup with the head and feet of a fowl. Hungry as I was, I still couldn't work up much appetite for the chicken head, and I tossed the grisly tidbit into the fire.

Swarms of ravening mosquitoes drove us into the tent after we had eaten, and soon we fell asleep—until three a.m., when the mosquitoes awoke us again, buzzing around *inside* the tent and attacking our faces and arms. A breeze had sprung up during the night, blowing open a corner of the netting at the entrance. It took us about five minutes to close the tent again, weight the netting so it wouldn't blow open, and mash the mosquitoes on the walls of the tent, our own blood providing ample evidence of their hearty last meal.

André Davy, his kayak smashed, rides swampy Lake Kyoga in a dugout.

December 10: *Lake Kyoga—Lotusland*

I took another turn in the dugout today, leaving at dawn with Oumu and Gabrini to get a head start on the swifter kayaks. Even though riding in the dugout meant harder work rowing, it was more stable and better for taking pictures, and I was able to keep my camera bag at my feet, where I could get at it quickly.

We had camped near a hill, and beyond it we entered the marshes of Lake Kyoga, an amoeba-shaped body of water, thirty-five miles downstream from Namasagali. The Nile flows sluggishly through this shallow lake for sixty miles, losing millions of gallons of water in the marshes and swamps spreading out on either side. The average depth of the lake is nine feet, and nowhere is it deeper than twenty-five. Discovered in 1875 by the American explorer Colonel Chaille-Long, it had first been named Lake Ibrahim.

As we entered the lake, Jean and André caught up with us. Soon we found ourselves confronted with a limitless expanse of glossy-leafed lily pads and densely matted lake weed that cut us off from open water. To my surprise, Oumu and Gabrini hesitated and seemed unsure which direction to go. They had assured us that they had been to Masindi many times and knew the way through Lake Kyoga; now they cheerfully admitted that Oumu had never gone any farther than the fish camp where we had spent the night, and while Gabrini had once gone to Masindi, it had been years ago. Our supposed guides now seemed perfectly content for us to figure out a way through the labyrinth. And as I realized that we were fully on our own, I visualized our little party wandering hopelessly in a boundless world of water and papyrus, challenged by angry hippos and hungry crocodiles.

But we were at the point of no return. We had to go on. And so I surveyed the four distinct skeins of narrow channel that filtered through the aquatic wilderness and decided that the widest and straightest of them might have the strongest current—and the least chance of dead-ending on us. The others agreed with my suggestion, and we launched ourselves in a dense liquid jungle, where for hours we labored with all our strength, heaving and shoving with the paddles to make headway through the weed-choked water, our progress held down to a snail's pace. We felt trapped, but the route proved successful. The cramped causeway soon ended, but not before we found a side channel, where we turned off and miraculously found another channel, and then another—continuing until we joyfully found ourselves in clear water, where we were free to glide along unhampered.

We passed many islets of sudd, heavy rafts of papyrus and reeds drifting on the sluggish current. Wind and rain detached them from the banks of the riv-

With Oumu acting as helmsman, André and Gabrini paddle a crude dugout across swampy Lake Kyoga.

er, and they often clumped together as they moved downstream, forming great living dams of vegetation that impede the current and completely block the navigational channels, a major problem farther down the Nile in the great Sudd Swamp of the Sudan.

Now that we were in open water, I consulted our charts, supposedly excellent survey maps that I had purchased in Kampala. They proved totally inadequate, as did all our Nile maps. The scale was too vast—the maps had no detail where we needed it, and whole areas were grossly distorted. However, they did provide some general bearings, and we found our next heading, a diagonal course across the lake that I judged would enable us to reach the north shore, ten miles distant, by dusk.

I was gradually winning the friendship of Oumu and Gabrini, and they relaxed and became more natural. Working side by side, "Gabby" and I chanted little duets together to keep time with our strokes. Neither he nor Oumu could speak a word of English, but he picked up melodies quickly. Gabby's favorite was the "Song of the Volga Boatmen," and he lustily "yo-ho-hee-hoed" in his quavering tenor as I sang in my tenuous bass. Oumu never joined in our songfests, but sat in the stern as helmsman, grinning in appreciation.

Gabrini was Jeff to Oumu's Mutt, a humble little man where Oumu was tall, an impressive figure of strength. Though Gabrini was older, with his hair graying, he was so much smaller that he seemed to be Oumu's son. However, his slight-seeming build was deceptive; he kept up a murderous pace at the paddles, rowing with strong, swift dips of his heart-shaped oar while I panted beside him, using the detached half of my spare aluminum paddle. At one time it occurred to me that he might prefer using a lighter paddle, and I called to André to bring him the other half of my spare from his kayak. But I had created a Frankenstein monster, for he now rowed even faster, forcing me to work much harder to keep up; and all the time his face was a study in joy, like a kid with a special birthday present. I was already tired and sore, and this added demand made my muscles twitch with strain. My derriere and legs, too, had taken a beating, particularly from the kayak, where I had had to sit for long hours in a cramped position on a hard seat. The kayak cockpit is only 2½ feet wide, and the seat is a thin wafer of foam rubber that feels like a slab of cement after an hour or two.

Paddling along with Oumu and Gabrini, I no longer felt like a creature of the twentieth century. I was a kindred spirit to stone-age man, borne by one of the most elemental and ancient forms of transportation ever conceived—a ponderous, muscle-powered, carved-out tree trunk directly descended from the oldest boat yet discovered—an 8,000-year-old dugout exhumed from a bog in Holland.

Even the kayaks gave some of this feeling, as we moved along quietly in complete harmony with nature, powered only by our own strength, polluting nothing. We stroked along without conversation for hours, with only the soft rhythmic splash of the paddles dipping into the lake, and I became aware of every sight and sound of the life on the lake—the flight of vultures gracefully riding a thermal, the flash of red and iridescent green as a sunbird darted past, the breeze dancing over the lake's surface, creating a kaleidoscope of patterns, the whir of dragonflies around us. I have never felt more at peace with myself or the world in general.[9]

---

9. Though physically it would have been far easier to have traveled down the Nile by means of an outboard motor boat and by river steamer, I had no doubt that in using our own small, individual hand-paddled kayaks we would have an infinitely richer experience and would become a part of all we encountered. My boyhood dream had been to explore the Nile in native river craft—dugouts, papyrus rafts, and feluccas. It had been Jean's idea to use the kayaks—an idea I wholeheartedly supported.

In the kayaks we traveled silently and unobtrusively, approaching river people and wildlife without undue alarm. A motorized boat—noisy, intrusive, and frightening to all—would have changed everything.

The Vulture

Most people regard vultures as the ugliest of all birds—ghoulish, unclean symbols of death. But these maligned scavengers fill an ecological niche by purging their territory of carrion and of refuse, from corpses to rotting garbage.

No creature in the animal kingdom should be regarded as ugly or repulsive looking. These terms are anthropocentric, often misapplied to various other forms of life besides vultures, such as snakes, crocodiles, sharks, and hippopotamuses. Their physical appearance may not be attractive, but each feature represents a successful adaptation to the demands of their special environments.

On the wing, vultures are a symphony of smooth, coordinated motion. They soar for hours on thermals rising from the sun-warmed earth, with scarcely a flap of their great wings. Their telescopic vision is possibly the keenest of all birds, including the eagle, enabling them to perceive the foot-long body of a dead rat from an altitude of half a mile.

Lake Kyoga fish camp with two of the fishermen who hosted the Nileteers for the night.

We reached the far shore of the lake in the late afternoon and skirted it for miles without seeing a sign of life. Once we heard human voices coming from beyond the papyrus and called out, but they fell silent and we heard no answer. At last we saw smoke and found a sanctuary, a small fish camp occupied by three nude Africans, the most primitive looking we had seen.

We followed a tight, winding corridor through the papyrus and tied up next to a leaky dugout. To reach the bank from the water, we had to pick our way carefully across a broad floating mass of papyrus and fermenting swamp vegetation.

Loaded down as I was with the heavy tent bag, I misstepped into a thin spot near the middle and sank with a yelp of surprise over my crewcut into the black water. I bobbed sputtering to the surface in a stinking effervescence of marsh gas and laboriously hauled myself out. A few staggers farther on, I repeated the whole ridiculous exhibition.

No one enjoys a comic situation more than an African. He'll laugh at the drop of a hat—not to mention the drop of a white body. My impromptu splashes were apparently regarded as first-rate slapstick. The three fishermen watching me snickered when I first plunged into the drink but burst into uncontrolled laughter the second time, particularly since I emerged from the water festooned from head to sunburned toes with garlands of slimy lilies and lake weed that gave me a rather dashing, festive air.

My clumsy but entertaining entrance broke the ice with our new-found friends, and they abandoned reserve and treated us to a real make-yourself-at-home hospitality, sharing their food with us and offering us the shelter of their crude mound-shaped huts of papyrus stalks. I wondered if the first rule of making friends with Africans was "make 'em laugh"—and then realized that this was the first rule for making friends anywhere in the world!

We accepted their offer of fish—their staff of life—but when one of our hosts, a skinny, shy lad of about seventeen, gave us fat roasted locusts, an African delicacy, we risked offending our hosts by politely ignoring them. (Later, out of necessity, we became less fussy and no longer examined the menu so carefully. Once, while partaking of African hospitality, I gingerly sampled some well-cooked locusts, and with hunger as a sauce I found them surprisingly palatable.)

The vegetation was a thick carpet on the shore, too, and we found we couldn't pitch our tents. We refused the offered huts: they were so small that even one person could sleep only in a cramped fetal position, and we would rather brave the insect vampires than the pungent smell of the huts.

December 11: *Lake Kyoga*

We awoke peppered with mosquito bites, and today Jean took my place in the m'tumbi. We established a line-up that was to become our daily pattern throughout the long months ahead—me in the lead, André next, usually half a mile behind, and Jean trailing in the m'tumbi, almost out of sight.

An overwhelming feeling of isolation enveloped me as I stroked along in my kayak. I was alone, surrounded by the vast swamp, with the sweeping immensity of sky overhead and only the whisper of the wind and the occasional haunting cry of an ibis to break the eerie stillness. To add to the somber atmosphere, a rainstorm swept over in the afternoon, whipping great black clouds across the clear sky, obscuring the sun. With the voice of the wind rising often to the verge of a scream, the gruntings of nervous hippos, and the ominous, racing shadows driven before the clouds, I was oppressed by a foreboding of disaster.

But an hour later the skies cleared, and so did my melancholia. I was soon dripping with sweat again under the hot sun, my eyes squinting against the dazzling glare off the water. But the effects of my exposure to the equatorial sun since leaving Namasagali were not all negative. The sunbathing of my right leg had accomplished what poultices and penicillin ointment had failed to do; it had dried up and healed the last of the stubborn boils that had broken out nearly a month earlier while we were on the Kagera. Five of the eight abcesses had healed in a week, but the three largest had resisted all medication and developed into nasty running sores, the kind that are so difficult to clear up in the tropics. The sticky heat and bugs had made walking with the sores pretty grim. I was grateful they were gone.

I experimented with the plants we were passing, using one giant lily pad three feet broad as added shade, plopped on top of my wide-brimmed Australian Army hat, called a sloucher, which I had bought in Nairobi to replace the hat I had lost in the Kagera. The lily shriveled up in fifteen minutes, however. I tried a papyrus stalk for a while; it worked pretty well, until a host of tiny red mites decided to abandon the papyrus for more succulent fare—me!

The birds on the lake were the best show, particularly to a lifelong bird-watcher like me. Cattle egrets, grey herons, ducks, and plovers were common sights, along with hawks, kites, and vultures. I was able to approach a flock of pelicans to within a few yards before they lumbered into the air, and while I paused for a lunch of a banana and an orange, a fish eagle (cousin to the American bald eagle, with the same white head and neck and shiny black body and with yellow beak and talons) soared by, seemingly oblivious to a pair of heck-

Landing in the dense papyrus lining Lake Kyoga. Two fishermen paddle by in their dugout.

ling sparrows pursuing, diving, and harassing the grand bird like two fighter planes making passes on a bomber.

I passed one island of sudd with five cormorants riding it. They had their ragged black wings stretched out and were placidly warming them in the breeze to dry out after a morning of diving for fish and eels. King fishers were frequent companions and created a striking sight with their dark blue wings, cinnamon bodies, and red legs. They would hover like toy helicopters fifteen or twenty feet above the water, then arrow down in a splash of color and spray to seize a small fish swimming too close to the surface.

From late afternoon on we sought in vain for a landing. We stopped briefly at a small camp where several fishermen had hacked out a clearing in the papyrus just above the water line. They were friendly and wanted us to stay the night, but there was no room for the tent, and we didn't want to spend another night in the open as a free meal for the mosquitoes. We would have enjoyed getting to know the fishermen, but we decided to get back on the open water, where the hungry insects were sparse enough to be endurable.

Paddling on into the setting sun, we found a wide creek mouth, with smoke curling above the sedge from a campfire upstream. We searched for a landing path through the papyrus, but found none, and apparently our shouts of greeting frightened whoever was at the encampment, for no one answered our calls.

And so we moved on into the darkness of a moonless, hippo-haunted night—tightening our formation, hoping for safety in numbers. A bolt of fear shot through me as a shadowy apparition materialized out of the gloom—a lone hippo moving through the dimly lit water toward us, rending the night with sepulchral bellows.

We laid to with our paddles as fast as we could, but the m'tumbi moved at a maddeningly slow pace, and André and I had to force ourselves to slow down and stay with our companions, hoping that by staying together we might confuse or intimidate the hippo. But he was evidently more curious than anything, for he tagged along behind us at a respectful distance and after a few minutes vanished as abruptly as he had appeared.

In the daytime we had been able to see hippo herds far in advance and skirt around them, but in the night we felt vulnerable. We cocked our ears this way and that, trying and failing to get an accurate fix on the location of the many hippos in the lake and along the shores. We could hear them splashing around us, uncomfortably close, sometimes blowing noisily as they surfaced after a long dive. Their grunts and snifflings reverberated through the dark as though amplified through an echo chamber. Some of them were inconsiderately silent, and André, a few yards to my right, suddenly exclaimed in fright as a hippo bumped into his kayak, splashing water over him. As he described it later, "I thought it was all over for me. I could hear his noisy breathing directly behind me, causing my heart to beat like a trip-hammer. Large drops of sweat stood out on my forehead. I opened my eyes wide in a useless attempt to pierce the gloom. I sensed his presence within a paddle's reach. The hippo grunted menacingly, and I could imagine his huge jaws closing over my tiny boat—and myself along with it. I therefore raced ahead, and was able to leave him behind. But I have never felt such fear in my life."

Before coming to Africa, I had thought of everything about a hippo as comical. But all the charm disappears on a dark African night when you are in a fragile boat in the midst of a hippo-studded lake.

Two hours after André's encounter, a quartet of hippos decided to challenge our right-of-way. Moving in close, they threatened Jean and the two Africans first. In their unmaneuverable boat they seemed helpless; André and I returned and attracted the hippos' attention, drawing them off, but having to paddle as fast as we could to keep beyond their reach. Three gave up the chase quickly, but the fourth followed us closely for more than a mile.

At last, exhausted, we tied our boats to the papyrus of a small island and fitted ourselves among the baggage in our boats to sleep. It was midnight, and we had been paddling almost constantly for fifteen hours.

December 12: *Lake Kyoga and Masindi Port*

I awoke early, shivering with cold, and had to open my personal bag and heap all my extra clothing over me to get warm enough to go back to sleep. When I got up at dawn, the m'tumbi had already left, with Oumu and Gabrini paddling and Jean still asleep in the prow. André and I, stiff and weary, would have preferred to sleep longer, but our destination, Masindi Port, was close by, and we were eager to arrive in time to catch the supply trucks that would come to haul away the boats' cargo to Masindi Town and Lake Albert. We cast off and moved on, cruising at our normal speed of four or five knots, and in an hour caught up with our friends.

We passed three early-rising fishermen as we neared Kyoga's western terminus, but when we cheerfully called out, "Jambo sana," they only stared at us long and hard, with frozen half-smiles on their glistening dark faces. Apparently we presented an unfathomable mystery, and with African equanimity they quickly returned to their work, laying a long floating fish net that hung down vertically in the water, suspended from woven papyrus floats.

A steady headwind arose shortly after dawn and developed in strength as the sun rose. By nine o'clock we were laboring like Trojans to make any headway, and for the last few miles to Masindi we had to yaw into the driven waves at a forty-five degree angle to keep from being capsized or washed into the lily beds.

At noon I passed a lone Banyoro watching me from a clearing on the bank, and I called out, asking him how far it was to Masindi Port. I had come to expect the reply, "M'bali sana sana!" (very, very far). But instead he grinned, pointed ahead and said, "M'bali kidogo" (just a little way). Generally, an African villager's conception of time and distance are baffling to a European or North American—sometimes he will answer a question about distance by giving the number of pipeloads of tobacco he thinks a man would have to smoke before reaching his destination. "Not far" could mean one mile—or twenty. And time means less than distance; villagers rarely make a direct trip, but instead take side trips or linger here and there to hunt or fish or visit.

In this case, however, the Banyoro had spoken accurately enough for any white man to be satisfied—I hadn't gone more than half a mile when I heard the faint muffled blast of a steamer whistle sounding above the wind. André heard it, too, and we paddled on into the stiff waves, much encouraged. The dugout had fallen far behind. But now the lake had narrowed into a recognizable channel; we were no longer on Kyoga but were instead on the Nile again, with the river reborn after a period of wandering benightedly in its marshy purgatory.

An hour later as we rounded a bend, we caught sight of Masindi Port, with a small wood-burning paddle-wheeler[10] resting at the dock. The captain, a solidly built Britisher of about forty years, barefoot and clad only in khaki shorts, waved to us from the upper deck. As we landed, at least sixty villagers stood along the bank to watch our arrival and to greet us with hearty "*Jambos.*"

My legs nearly buckled as I jumped ashore. Twenty-seven hours of sitting in the kayak without a single step on shore had left them stiff and rubbery, and I had little control over them. It took two days to get them back to normal. My paddling muscles all throbbed, I was painfully sunburned since my uniform of the day had been only khaki shorts, and I was a few pounds lighter—but altogether I was in fine shape and eager for the next adventure.

We had timed our arrival perfectly—the captain had been ready to leave, and we were able to persuade him to wait a half hour longer so that Oumu and

---

10. Steamer service on Lake Kyoga has now been abandoned because of the navigational difficulties imposed by the shifting sudd.

Gabrini in the dugout would have time to arrive, ship their dugout on board the steamer, and ride back home instead of having to paddle all the way back upriver to Namasagali. The captain invited us to his cabin, where he poured a brandy for André and himself and a lemon squash for me to toast our safe arrival. "How are you making out with the hippos, chaps?" he asked. When we described our adventures with them in the Kagera and on Lake Kyoga, he shook his head and said: "you don't know how lucky you've been up to now." He told us a harrowing hippo story—an experience he had had the year before while traveling in a small motor launch near the mouth of the Kagera. He and a white friend and three African crewmen were cruising downstream towards Lake Victoria when a maddened hippo attacked them, and before they could maneuver out of range began chomping away at the stern of the boat with his great yellow tusks. Unsatisfied, he submerged under the launch, then lurched upward toward the surface so violently that the craft heeled over and capsized, spilling everyone into the water. There was a frenzied scramble to climb on top of the overturned launch, all of them reaching it safely except one crewman. Somehow he was trapped underwater and drowned.

Oumu, Gabrini, and Jean landed a few minutes later, and our African traveling companions broke into smiles of happiness when we told them the good news about their trip back. We hurriedly loaded them and their heavy m'tumbi aboard, presented their well-earned bonus, shook their hands in farewell, and then waved them off as the little paddlewheeler churned upriver. There was a tinge of sadness to our abrupt and hurried parting—we had become genuinely fond of them during our days together, and it was with sincere regret that we watched them go, realizing that we would never see them again. But then, for me, this sadness on parting from African friends, black and white, has been a frequent emotion, and one of the real hardships of our journey. I meet and establish warm ties with special individuals whose friendship I could cherish throughout a lifetime—and then have to leave them forever only a short time afterward. I have never learned to accept this gracefully or without a wrenching sense of loss.

Because the government had emphatically forbidden us to kayak down the Somerset Nile between Masindi Port and Murchison Falls, impassable because of the steep-walled canyons and treacherous rapids, we planned to detour around by way of Lake Albert and continue on down the Nile from below the falls. Now we tackled the problem of transportation to Butiaba, Lake Albert's chief port, seventy-five miles away. Only one supply lorry was left at Masindi Port, and it was so heavily burdened with sacks and bales that we couldn't see much hope of there being room for our three boats and twelve bags. But the dispatcher, a burly Sikh wearing a neat, pale blue cotton turban and a magnificent black beard, graciously permitted us to squeeze in as much of our gear as possible. Two large bags and one small one were left over, and the Sikh offered to store them for us and send them on the next supply convoy to come through, but that would mean a delay of several days.

Good luck appeared again, however, in the person of Lawrence Wilson, a British police lieutenant, who offered to drive us to Masindi Town. While Jean and André drove off to Butiaba in the lorry with the Ganda driver, I rode to Masindi Town with the officer—and the three leftover bags—because I, the only one who spoke English well, had the best chance of arranging a ride from Masindi Town to Butiaba.

Herds of hippos and elephants below Murchison Falls.

On either side of the road to Masindi Town, large stretches of ground had been burned over recently, and the drifting ash and smoke blinded and choked us by turns. The villagers set the fires to burn off tinder-dry vegetation. The firing of the grasslands is an annual practice during the dry season in many areas of Africa, clearing the land of dead growth and leaving a deposit of rich ash to fertilize the ground. This helps produce luxuriant new grass for cattle grazing after the rains begin. The burning also helps control the tsetse flies, destroying the pests and their breeding grounds.

"This makes me homesick for old Smogville!" I gasped, as tears rolled down my cheeks. When the officer looked puzzled, I explained that the acrid air had reminded me of my hometown, Los Angeles, on a bad day with no wind.

We arrived at Larry's home, and I was invited to share cakes and sandwiches with him and his young wife and ten-year-old son Benjamin, served outside in a well-tended garden by a dignified African butler. And I gratefully accepted an invitation to sleep the night there. "In the morning we'll see what can be done about getting you to Butiaba," Larry said.

December 13: *Lake Albert*

The next day Larry himself drove me to Butiaba, forty-five miles away, tending to some official business en route. With us rode a husky *askari*[11] and we bumped along a bumpy sod track, stopping for an hour at a rubber plantation where Larry conferred with the manager, then continuing our tooth-rattling drive. Once a six-foot black mamba, a lethal member of the cobra family, streaked aross the road in front of us, narrowly missing getting crushed by the tires of our Austin.

Suddenly we broke out of the cool woods and found ourselves on a high escarpment, the edge of the Great Rift Valley overlooking a panorama of low, hot bush country sixteen hundred feet below us. The pale green waters of Lake Albert, the Nile's third source and western reservoir, gleamed in the distance. Through the shimmering heat waves we could make out the Congo (Zaire) Mountains across the lake, thirty-five miles to the west, which form a watershed between the Nile and Congo (Zaire) river basins. We carefully wound down the steep escarpment and drove the last five miles to the lake through increasing dust and heat. At Lake Victoria the elevation had been nearly 4,000 feet; at Lake Albert we had descended to 2,000 feet.

Jean and André were easy to find; they had set up a camp by the lakeshore and were having a late lunch of fish and beans as we drove up.

---

11. African policeman.

The Rift Valley

The Rift Valley is one of the most
extraordinary features of the earth.
Actually, there are two of these
massive troughlike depressions.
The Eastern or Great Rift is a
colossal fault that sweeps across the
earth's surface for more than five
thousand miles from southern
Turkey, across the Red Sea into
Ethiopia, through Kenya, and
finally through Mozambique,
where it penetrates into the Indian
Ocean just below the Zambezi
river. The Western, or Albertine
Rift, which extends from the
Sudan to Malawi, is an offshoot of
this gigantic fracture in the earth
several hundred miles away,
running roughly parallel for most
of its 1,200 mile length before
shifting eastward and uniting with
the Great Rift in northern Malawi.
Both rifts are from thirty to fifty
miles broad, with steep
escarpments that vary from
hundreds to thousands of feet
high. They form natural reservoirs
for the runoff from the bordering
high country, resulting in a twin
chain of long, narrow lakes. With
the exception of Lake Victoria,

which is situated in a shallow basin between the rifts, all the important and several of the small lakes of Central Africa lie within the two Rifts. Lake Albert, Edward, Kivu, Tanganyika, and Nyasa occupy the trough of the Albertine Rift. Geologists propound three main theories to account for rift formation. The most plausible one is that the rifts were created by faulting: it is evident that in geologically recent times the valley floors were contiguous with the top terrain, since the bedrock of both is identical even though in some places 3,000 feet apart. But the land fractured into two deep parallel faults, and the center gradually sank over a period of thousands of years to its present level. The second theory deals with continental drift. The creeping of the continental land masses on their underlying beds of molten magma caused splits in the surface. The third theory concerns pressure, or the rearing up of the land surface on both sides of a plain due to internal pressures.

"Charlie," a British fisherman from Nairobi, hooks a fifty-two pound Nile perch in Lake Albert.

Butiaba is Lake Albert's chief port, situated on a narrow hook of windblown sand that provides a good natural harbor for the lake steamer *Coryndon*. Port officer Captain Chimister gave us permission to establish our temporary headquarters aboard the first steamer ever to serve on the lake, the Lugard I, a moldering old relic of the nineteenth century. We spent the rest of the day getting our gear aboard, though we fervently hoped we would be here for only a brief stay.

December 15: *Lake Albert*

I spent today in the company of four jovial British fishermen who had driven up from Nairobi; I went along to photograph the southern reach of the lake, where they planned to fish. The youngest of them, Charlie, hooked and landed the day's largest specimen of the fish they were looking for—Nile perch, or *mputa,* the largest freshwater fish in Africa.[12] Charlie's catch was a fifty-two-pounder, half as big as the fisherman, and though the other perch caught that day didn't equal it, it was still far from the 280-pound fish caught the year before, not to mention the record catch of 376 pounds.

About thirty-five miles south of the port we sighted a Banyoro village nestled in a valley between the steep hills and the water and stopped to investigate. Thick bulrushes kept us from beaching the boat, but we waded ashore through clear green water, moving as quickly as possible to avoid any crocodiles that might have been lurking around.

The villagers were apathetic about our arrival, to say the least; they were far too busily engaged in an activity that at first made very little sense to us, until I remembered a reference in Emil Ludwig's *The Nile* to an industry peculiar to Lake Albert—the mining of salt from local mineral springs. Several Banyoro girls were channeling a fast trickle of water from the salty springs into a series of flat troughs formed of mud, and as each trough was filled, they directed the stream to another trough. Then the sun did the work of extracting the water, leaving the salt behind as a thin grey film, which was scraped off. So valuable is the "white gold" of Africa that periodically the mud of the brook bed itself is dug up and the salt is extracted in clay crocks filled to the brim with hot water. The salt dissolves from the mud into the water and slowly drips into the jar below to be evaporated, collected, and sold. The leftover mud is then piled onto chest-high walls that over the years have covered much of the ground,

---

12. In 1955 and 1956 several hundred Nile perch were transferred from Lake Albert to the Victoria Nile above Murchison Falls and to Lake Kyoga. These fish have now bred and established themselves and are being caught by local fishermen.

leaving the impression that the area contains the ruins of an ancient adobe village, with only the walls left standing.

We hiked up the narrow rocky gorge to the salt springs. The water bubbled up from fissures in the bottom of the pools, crystal clear and scalding hot. Sulphurous fumes rose like wraiths from among the rocks, overpoweringly pungent. They gave the canyon a weird, volcanic atmosphere. My companions, being enterprising businessmen, bemoaned the fact that the springs were so far from Nairobi. Had they been closer, they could have been developed into a profitable spa for rheumatic males who would come for the sulphur baths—and the pretty masseuses.

As it was, the springs provided the sole support and major industry of the Banyoro village, the inhabitants using the dirty gray mineral to trade with other tribes for all the necessities of life. The springs also explained, at least partially, why Lake Albert has a salty flavor, while Victoria, more than ten times larger, is completely fresh.

A quarter mile from the dock, as we were returning to Butiaba, I spotted a big crocodile sleeping on a sandspit, his awesome jaws spread wide and glowing pink in the sunlight. I pointed him out to the men, whereupon Allen primed his .404 rifle and motioned to the Acholi helmsman to cut his engines. As we coasted toward the island, I saw through the field glasses a black and white bird teetering audaciously on the croc's lower jaw, facing the "jaws of death." However, the small-bodied, long-legged bird, a species of plover, is the croc's only friend, serving him as a combination animated toothpick and alarm system in a unique bird-reptile relationship.

We got within fifty yards before the bird cried the alarm and the crocodile awoke; but Allen fired at the same moment, stopping the reptile dead with a bullet just behind his right eye. The animal measured fourteen feet long, and his teeth were worn down to gnarled stubs, with maggots writhing between them in the decaying gums. Though I find hunting for sport repugnant, crocodiles kill more people than any other creature in Africa, the larger specimens, like the one Allen shot, being the most likely to kill humans, and I felt no deep regret at the old croc's death. Their annual toll is more than the "big five" (Cape buffalo, elephant, rhinoceros, leopard, lion) combined—and while they primarily eat fish, all living things are fair game to them, and even lion's claws and buffalo hooves have been found in their stomachs.

The Acholi tribesmen with us quickly flensed the smooth, amber skin of the beast's underside, the only part useful for tanning, and rolled it into a neat bundle; it would make Allen and his friends a number of fine shoes, belts, and wallets.

The Crocodile Bird

The crocodile, unable to clean his own
teeth, sleeps with his jaws locked agape,
openly inviting the spurwing (*Hoplopterus
spinosus*) plover to enter and dine at his
leisure. The bird, happy to oblige and
grateful for such easy pickings, hops
around inside the jagged jaws,
industriously plucking juicy tidbits of meat
from the grooves between the fangs,
sometimes getting a bonus of a tender
maggot. Crocs have never been known to
snap shut on a feeding bird. The bird also
feeds on the persistent flies that swarm over
the croc's eyes and which, because of his
stubby legs, he cannot dislodge.
Fully as valuable to the crocodile as his job
as dental hygienist is the bird's function as
"lookout." The bird flies up with piercing
cries and warns the croc of approaching
danger long before he would otherwise be
aroused. This is mainly the reason why
hunters find it so difficult to stalk close
enough to a beached crocodile for a mortal
shot. In the 5th century B.C. Herodotus,
referring to the plover as "the crocodile
bird," described this amazing symbiosis in
which the bird contributes service in
exchange for food.

December 16–17: *Butiaba on Lake Albert*

I spent two days roaming through the nearby bush country, impatient for word about transportation to Murchison Falls. The government had forbidden us to use our kayaks through the densest crocodile and hippopotamus population in Africa. Instead we would have to take the government launch.

The only benefit while I waited for word was the chance to swim in the lake behind a crocodile-proof barricade of sturdy logs that Captain Chimister had had built near his residence. For the first time I had a chance to use my diving equipment of fins and face mask and to dive and swim at will without the fear of a crocodile attacking me.

On Sunday evening we were told that the government launch would not be available until sometime in early January. My friends accepted the news resignedly and settled down for the long wait in sultry Butiaba—but I fumed and ranted over the *mañana* complex we'd encountered from the beginning of our trip and decided to take matters into my own hands. I remembered that someone in Masindi Town had told me about the owner of a nearby plantation, T. P. Margach, who had a private boat. Maybe he could help us.

December 18: *Entebbe*

I picked up a ride on a lorry to Margach's coffee plantation, twenty-two miles to the east. Margach proved to be a grand old man. I found him sitting on his porch with a tall drink, quietly celebrating his seventy-ninth birthday. "I'd like to lend you my boat, lad," he said, "but it's only a small fishing sloop and won't hold more than two." And then, to take my mind off the problem, "T.P." began a fascinating account of his early days in Africa when he had made a precarious living as a white hunter.

We were thus engaged when the Colliers, close friends of his, dropped by to wish him a happy birthday and to say good-bye; they were moving to Nairobi after living three years on a neighboring rubber plantation. I took an instant liking to them, and when they told me they were driving to Entebbe before going on to Kenya, I asked for and received their permission to accompany them, hoping I would be able to talk to the government officials there and arrange, perhaps, for more immediate transportation to the falls.

After a beautiful trip—interrupted twice by a flat tire, which I fixed, and an empty gas tank, fortunately just outside one of the few villages in Uganda with a gas pump—we arrived at Entebbe at 8 p.m. We had traveled 180 miles, and now I was back at Lake Victoria. After a badly needed bath, a change of clothes, and an excellent supper at the Lake Victoria Hotel, I left my friends and went to the local police station, where I finally was able to get a phone call through to Major Bruce Kinloch, Game Warden of Uganda. "Stay right where you are," he said, "and I'll come round and collect you in fifteen minutes."

He arrived in ten minutes in a rattly little Land Rover, and we got acquainted at his bungalow. He had just fallen heir to the esteemed office of Chief Game Warden and at thirty-three years of age he was rather on the spot to prove himself.

December 19: *Entebbe*

I went along with Bruce to Kampala, where he had a case of illegal ivory poaching to try in the local court. Before the trial he found out for me that a hydrographical engineer, Malcolm Winny, was leaving for the falls in the regular launch the very next morning to measure the Nile's flow. He was going virtually alone; there was a good chance there'd be room for us to accompany him.

With no time to spare, I thanked Bruce for his aid and then rushed to the outskirts of town, where I parked myself on the Hoima Road and was picked up by the first vehicle to come by—a jeep driven by John Smith, a professional fisherman from Scotland who had been hired by the Uganda government to pioneer commercial fishing on Lake Albert. I had met Smitty on our first day in Butiaba, and we had become friends. "What in blue blazes are you doing here alone?" he demanded, and I explained that I had to contact Malcolm Winny as quickly as possible in order to get a ride on his launch. Winny was at Hoima, 150 miles away, and Smitty laughed and said, "I guess I'm the man your genie sent you. I'm just now returning to Butiaba—through Hoima! So I can drive you right to Winny's house and then back to your French buddies."

The trip could have taken days—with Smitty's help we did it in an afternoon. On the way the radiator boiled over—cars have a hard life in the African bush—and some Ganda women gave us water in an old petrol tin. That was for the car; for us they had pombe (fresh banana wine only slightly fermented, with a sweet, tangy flavor). However, a Gandan who came up to the car had a different idea of an interesting drink—he wanted some of Smitty's kerosene. "He seems to think it would make a great highball," Smitty told me. The African gave the impression he couldn't get through the rest of the day unless he had a good swig of the fuel. I attempted to distract him with the offer of a banana. He accepted gravely but only to use it to give emphasis to his supplicating gestures toward the tantalizing kerosene. We drove off, feeling like cheapskates, leaving him standing in the middle of the road, crestfallen and still thirsty.

Good fortune was still with me—we found Winny's house quickly, and he was at home. Best of all, he was completely agreeable to having our Nile expedition travel with him to the Falls. He had read of our project and was happy to be the one to get us back on the river. With only himself and two Africans in a boat built to hold eight, there would be more than enough room to hold us and our gear, and we arranged to meet the next morning at 9 a.m.

On the way back to our camp by the shore, Smitty took me by his new headquarters six miles from the port on the escarpment overlooking the rift. It was a long, low structure that had been set up years ago as a hunting shack for the Prince of Wales; we stopped long enough for a snack and then reached the Lugard just after sundown, where I casually broke the big news, producing sunburst smiles on the faces of my brooding companions. We'd be on the river again tomorrow!

December 20: *Murchison Falls*

Everything was loaded in a half hour, and we left dull Butiaba without looking back. We reached the mouth of the Nile, where the river flows into the lake, at about one p.m., then turned eastward and for the first and last time in our voyage went upstream through narrow, winding channels choked on both sides with dense papyrus and marsh grass.[13] From the mouth on we found ourselves in an African Coney Island, with huge herds of hippos lolling in the water, literally hundreds of crocodiles baking in the sun along the sand bars, and numerous elephants browsing dreamily in the meadows beyond the river. This, my first glimpse of elephants along the Nile, was a big moment for me. I had always regarded elephants with awe and reverence. Next to man, the anthropoids, and the marine mammals, they are the most intelligent creatures alive and, for me, the most fascinating of all African wild life. But this El Dorado of nature was dominated by hippos. They swarmed everywhere around us, in the papyrus and in the Nile, yawning and napping, swimming and cavorting, a few feeding greedily on shore.

For once it was the hippos that moved out of *our* way, instead of our avoiding *them,* and one hippo that didn't regard us as a serious threat was struck a sharp blow by the prow of the boat. It would have killed a less-padded animal, but the hippo only bellowed and swam off in terror toward his herd.

---

13. The discoverer of Lake Albert and Murchison Falls, Sir Samuel Baker, and his lovely blonde Hungarian wife, Florence, covered this twenty-mile stretch to the Falls in a dugout canoe in 1864, but had to abandon their boat when a bull hippopotamus attacked and knocked them overboard. With so many crocodiles around they were fortunate indeed to have been able to swim to safety.

Sand banks, dark with the massed bodies of dozing crocodiles, came alive when alarmed by our approach. The sinister reptiles roused and hurled themselves into the water toward us. We counted twenty-three on one beach, crisscrossed like driftwood, not one under eight or nine feet in length. And we spotted a pair of wary cape buffalo loping away from us as we rounded a bend. Many consider the cape buffalo to be Africa's most cunning and dangerous animal. "A bloody awful beast!" said Winny, pointing toward the retreating pair. "Wound a buffalo, and he'll either run off to hide so he can ambush you as you come looking for him, or he'll charge on the spot, and you can't even be sure a heart or brain shot will drop him before he's on top of you. Killing's not enough for the ruddy brute—he butts, kneels, and tramples his victims into porridge."

"Can't really blame him, can you?" I answered. "I'd probably feel like doing the same thing to anyone who had just shot me!"

Bird life was abundant and incredible, ranging from brightly plumaged sunbirds to Goliath herons and carrion-eating marabou storks. Two of the storks along the banks looked like a pair of dignified, bald-headed old judges in frock coats strolling along, their hands clasped behind them, discussing weighty points of law. Iridescent blue king fishers hovered above the river as if fluttering on an invisible perch. Brilliantly colored red, green, and yellow bee-eaters flashed past us as we chugged along. Orange weavers clambered around their long swinging nests suspended high in the acacia trees.

The next bend brought us into view of the majestic falls, roaring hugely and enveloped in a pink gossamer mist that glistened in the late afternoon sun. While my friends made a landing well below the falls in the launch, I pushed off alone in my kayak and paddled farther upstream against the powerful current to take pictures. When the current would let me go no further, I beached and picked my way through dense undergrowth until I reached a finger of granite jutting out into the madly swirling waters. Balanced on the tip of the rock spit, I shot a lengthy scene with my movie camera pointed directly into the maw of the mighty falls. Then I slipped and slid along the mossy rock to another perch and shot another scene. No sooner had I finished than a crocodile lunged into the river only a few yards away. He had been dozing on the far side of the ledge and because of the noise of the water hadn't heard me approach until I was almost on top of him.

Then, with the camera in its case strapped to my shoulder, I clambered to the top of the falls, a far more difficult feat than I had expected, especially since the greedy tsetse flies regarded my slow progress as an open invitation to dine. At last, covered with sweat, dust, scratches, and bugs, and with a few creepers draped artistically about me, I reached the top and discovered that it was well worth the ordeal of climbing. A vista of violent beauty spread before me. At my feet, framed by two cliffs of solid stone, surged the spectacular Murchison Falls, the only major waterfall on the Nile and one of the most dramatic sights of Africa.[14] Upstream the river frothed over a series of heavy rapids, then swept toward me with increasing speed, swooshed into the narrow chasm, and plunged with a roar 130 feet to the rocky channel below. (According to Winny it surged through at the rate of 500 tons of water every second.) I gazed down at the great flood storming through the gap, held spellbound by the river's power. Just above the falls the Nile shrivels to its narrowest width, a scant eighteen feet across, a distance I had broad-jumped in high school. "Imagine being able to jump the Nile!" I thought to myself. For a moment I toyed with the idea of attempting it, but one hard look at the steep, slippery wall on the opposite side and the raging torrent below changed my mind.

Jean, André, and I bathed in a spray-fed pool next to the falls, then headed back for the landings. I worked my way down the cliff through the luxurious vegetation to the tree-lined bank where my kayak rested, while my companions returned over the trail high above the river. After one last backward glance to etch the spectacle of the falls on my mind, I pushed off into the dark green river, cutting through masses of foam riding high on the surface. I worked out to midstream where the current was swiftest and where the chance of being ambushed by a hippo was least. The day had been blazing hot, but in the freshness of evening the air was soft and cool as silk. The river calmed and became broad again, and I was swept along its widening channel through a lovely setting of hills that gradually gave way to savanna. It was exciting gliding through the shadowy twilight as I hurried to reach the launch. The banks and the river pulsed with animal and insect life, their resonant voices reverberating through the balmy evening in a symphony of exotic sound.

My passing didn't go unnoticed. Hippos bobbed up and down around me, often snorting indignantly at my brazen intrusion. I paddled nervously past them, expecting to be charged at any moment.

My anxiety became more intense when I noticed a crocodile trailing me with sinister persistency, his long body a ghostly outline dimpling the surface. I couldn't help imagining how it would feel to have his viselike jaws crunch down on my arm or leg. It was a critical situation since I had only a .22 rifle for protection, and he could easily overtake my kayak and crush it with one snap

---

14. Abnormally heavy rainfall in 1961 created two permanent lesser cascades 100 feet high, making the falls even more impressive.

of his fang-spiked jaws. On impulse I suddenly raised my paddle high and smashed it down with all my strength on the water toward my gruesome shadow. Startled by the sudden loud splash, he disappeared beneath the water with a lash of his tail, and I lost no time paddling away before he could surface again and renew his stalking.

It was almost dark when I reached the motor launch, where Jean and André and Winny were waiting. Winny had completed his survey of the river's flow and volume below the falls, and they were ready to go as soon as I swung aboard and pulled my kayak up after me.

For hours we followed the shimmering, moonlit waterway, stirred up now and then by hippos thrashing out of our way. Then we finally broke from the river and cruised across Albert toward the lake's northwestern limits. Our plan now was to set up a camp on the far shore and find one of the local fishermen with a dugout, who was willing to go with us as far as Pakwach.

It was nearly midnight when Winny left us camped on the sandy shore, taking his leave after warm and grateful farewells. Hordes of mosquitoes inspired us to set up the tent in record time, and the ceaseless murmur of the lake wind sound soon lulled us to sleep.

December 21: *Lake Albert*

We were wakened by the giggles of bare-bosomed Banyoro women who came to fill their ponderous waterjars at the lake—we had inadvertently camped by the watering hole of a local village. The women went about their business, loudly speculating as to who we were and where we had come from, and we ate our breakfast surrounded by a circle of wide-eyed children, their little round shaven heads gleaming in the morning sunlight.

I decided to take a swim in the lake, and fished out my face mask from my bag. Clad only in my undershorts, I walked to the water with the young Banyoros trailing behind, donned the underwater gear, and put on a one-man aquacade, to the delight of my young audience. As they waded timidly into the water after me, I swam under the surface to the first two and grabbed their ankles, sending them scampering back to shore, whooping with alarm. But they quickly caught onto the game and, shouting in glee, began dancing about in the water, dodging me, the stalking *lutembi*—crocodile. I got bored before they did and changed the game, playing "torpedo"—swimming under them and then suddenly rising with a child perched on my shoulders.

Afterward I let them try out the fins and diving mask; but they fit badly, and they spanked the water furiously but ineffectually with the fins and sputtered and gasped as water leaked through the mask. When the fun was over, we set out to arrange for a dugout. But the men in the nearest village politely told us they had to fish; no one accepted our offered payment for going only twenty-five miles to Pakwach.

Hoping to find someone with less sales resistance, we went off into the bush toward the next village. On the way we found a huge old tree with long liana vines looping down from its top branches. It was too good a setup to resist; so I tucked one end of a long vine under my belt, climbed up the trunk to a branch ten feet above the ground, then shouted to André, "Look, this is the way Tarzan does it in the movies!"

With that I swung vigorously out into space, clinging tightly to the creeper with both hands. Things went well until I heard a sickening crack and at the same time felt the vine go limp. The branch had collapsed under my weight, and I came down heavily in a stand of low-lying shrubbery, the breath completely knocked out of me.

Children of the Alur tribe prepare to launch Goddard's kayak into Lake Albert for a trial ride.

As I lay there wondering how many bones I'd broken and whether I'd ever walk again, André came running over applauding enthusiastically, and said with an impish grin, "Truly a magnificent performance! What daring! What grace! Encore, if you please!"

It took only a few minutes for me to recuperate, and as we worked our way through the undergrowth, we heard voices coming from the direction of the lake. Hopeful of finding men who might help us, we soon broke out of the bush and spotted three dark heads bobbing in the tall marsh grass near the lake. We started forward; they saw us coming. I raised my hand in a gesture of friendship and called out a greeting, but for some reason our appearance frightened them. They dropped what they were doing and vanished.

When André and I reached the spot where they had been standing, we found the mutilated remains of a hippo that had been dragged out of the lake

Excited youngsters dare crocodiles to give Jean and John a proper send-off into Lake Albert.

to a clearing in the reeds. The Africans had been hacking the carcass into portable sections, probably to be carried to the Banyoro village.

A half hour later we came upon two men sitting before a simple lean-to a hundred yards from the lake. They showed no inclination to run, but they had obviously been warned we were coming. After our rebuff at the village we were cautious now, fearful of making a botch of things. André and I sat on the ground crosslegged beside the Africans and took our time getting around to Topic A. I spoke to them in short, simple sentences of Swahili, supplemented with some elaborate sign language, and we were heartily gladdened when they seemed agreeable to going with us to Pakwach.

But there was a catch to it—they had no dugout. "This isn't our day for luck, I guess," I said to André. "Let's start back." Before we left, I explained to the men:"*apana m'tumbi veve apana quenda safari. Aksente sana. Kwaheri,*" which, roughly translated, means: "Without a boat you can't go on the journey, but thanks very much anyway and good-bye." As we headed back, we began to discuss our plight, which had now reached a crisis. "Let's stay for one more day," I urged; "then if we still can't get help, we'll have to travel on our own. We can each take a turn hiking along the banks while the other two paddle the kayaks."

Jean had spent the day collecting entomological samples—and guarding the camp. We were sitting on the sand around a small fire, analyzing our situation, when I looked out on the lake and spied a boat far out on the dusk-tinted water. "Look!" I cried excitedly. "Isn't that a steamer?" We leaped to our feet, and I ripped the binoculars out of their case and, yes, the boat was a steamer—the *Lugard II,* in fact, successor to the old craft we had lived on at Butiaba. There was only place she could be headed on this part of the lake—her home port of Pakwach! "We must stop it!" said André fervently.

I had my kayak in the water in a moment and paddled out with all my strength to intercept the approaching paddlewheeler. A stiff wind whipped the water into sharp, choppy waves that kept me bobbing like a cork and soaked me completely. I nearly tipped over several times as waves broke over me from all sides, but I reached the steamer just as it came bearing down to intercept my course—I had timed it just right.

Many black hands pulled me aboard, and the incredulous captain, the only white on board, listened as I explained our situation and asked him to take André and his kayak—along with most of our baggage—to Pakwach. "Why, I'd be delighted to have him!" said the rotund, bespectacled little Englishman, and within a half-hour we had ferried André and a big load of equipment out to the steamer on a large Banyoro dugout. We said good-bye to André, promising to meet him at Pakwach by the following evening, and Jean and I spent the evening sitting before the tent under a pale moon, reminiscing about war experiences until we grew drowsy.

December 22: *The Albert Nile to Pakwach*

We pushed off this morning under a leaden overcast against a gusty headwind but made steady progress as the lake narrowed into the Nile. On the left bank we spotted some Africans and greeted them, but on the right bank we saw no sign of human life: extending eastward from the Nile and covering many hundreds of square miles into the Sudan is a vast, virtually uninhabited region, abandoned by all but a few villages because of the scourge of the tsetse fly. The shoreline was grassy and low, with only an occasional hill covered by forests that had parched to yellow in the dry season.

A few miles before reaching Pakwach I sighted four dark isolated specks against the green and yellow shoreline far in the distance. They moved as I watched them, and the binoculars confirmed it: elephants. I turned to alert Jean, but he was far behind, so I moved as close as I dared in my kayak, then pulled into the papyrus. A crocodile slid into the water not far away as I crept out of the boat and sat crosslegged in the reeds beside my kayak, watching the huge elephants peacefully feeding, their spinal columns massive and prominent. I knew that once they became aware of my presence they would probably move off. Fortunately, their vision is poor, and while their hearing and smelling are more acute than a dog's, I was downwind and trying to be very quiet.

My patience was rewarded when they began to drift toward me. They had sprayed themselves with water, which made them darker than the elephant I had seen in the Tsavo Forest. Their trunks snaked down to scoop up grasses, and though three of the elephants ambled away, one of them wandered toward me—so close I could hear his stomach rumble as he ate. With baggy knees and extensive wrinkles, his immense body appeared enclosed in a loose gray robe that he had slept in. His trunk was marvelous in action: a fusion of nose and upper lip, the trunk weighing upward of 400 pounds and moved by 40,000 tiny, separate muscles to make the trunk serve as a combination hand, arm, nose, suction pump, trumpet, and snorkel, able to tweeze a berry or toss around a ton-heavy log. The bull elephant coming toward me also had three tick birds and two large white cattle egrets balanced blithely on his broad back, looking like five dignified commuters on their way to work.

The elephant turned, finally, and started up the bank, giving me the chance I had been waiting for; I wound my Ciné, adjusted the settings, and then cautiously stalked my quarry, creeping forward at a half-crouch. I was afraid that at any moment the birds might give the alarm, but they remained silent, and as I stood tensely watching, the elephant turned broadside providing a more photogenic shot of his anatomy than the enormous hindquarters had been presenting.

Then the elephant caught the sound of the camera whirring and faced me squarely. His trunk tested the air, swaying like an aroused cobra. He had not yet caught my scent. When I started to retreat, the great triangular ears moved forward, then flapped back along his head; he rocked nervously, shifting his weight from his left to his right legs and back again in a funny little shuffling dance. Then he made a short rush at me in what amounted to a sham charge, taking several quick, short steps forward and stopping suddenly, raising a small cloud of dust. There was nothing vicious in this action; it was like an old farmer shooing a trespassing chicken out of his garden. I could almost hear the elephant say, "Scat!"

He tried a sham charge twice again, giving me ample warning and time to escape. I kept eyeing my boat, figuring the fastest getaway—but still whirring away with the camera. Because I was holding my ground, the elephant's sense of privacy was completely outraged, and the charge he began this time was no sham. His ears fanned out wide, wing-like, his trunk went down and curled back in the danger signal position, and he came for me.

I rushed to my kayak just as he charged, cold fear now lending speed to my flight, dropped my camera in, and wrenched the boat into the river almost in one motion, scant seconds before the elephant came thundering up. His momentum carried him knee-deep into the oozy shallows, where he stood shaking his great head and lashing the air with his trunk.

I was riding safely on the river a few yards from the tusker when Jean caught up. He picked up my camera and filmed a scene of me with my irritated friend, who pulled himself out of the weed-choked water and lumbered up the bank, turning our way every few feet to see what we were up to.

African elephants weigh up to six tons and stand as tall as eleven feet; yet they can move murderously fast. They have been clocked at twenty-five miles an hour. If I had been twenty-five feet farther from my kayak, I would never have reached it alive. As some consolation, however, if the elephant had trampled me to death, he would then probably have provided me with a decent burial under twigs and leaves. For included in the remarkable practices of elephant etiquette is the paradoxical custom of burying a freshly killed enemy. Because of his cunning, speed, and strength, many authorities consider the African elephant to be the world's most dangerous big game animal.

When we reached Pakwach, Captain Barnes of the quaint *Lugard II* took us under his rather corpulent wing, and after we were reunited with André,

Barnes asked, "How would you chaps like to meet the king of the Banyoros? He's really quite a fellow, and if anyone can get you a boat, it would be he."

"Tell us where he is," I said, "and we'll go see him right now!"

"I knew you'd be keen about this, so I've asked him to stop by this evening," our host said. "He'll be here by and by."

We managed a makeshift bath from a wash tub and were seated around the comfortable living room when we heard a cough at the door. "Villagers don't knock," Barnes pointed out. "They just let you know they're there by a cough or a sneeze." He arose and admitted three solemn-faced Banyoros who stood ramrod stiff as the captain made his introductions. The first of them, a handsome, medium-sized man in a brown toga, was King Oubidu; the other two were his top aides.

An enraged elephant mounts the banks of the Albert Nile after charging the author and chasing him into the river.

I shook the king's hand and noticed he was wearing a bracelet similar to my own, woven from the thick tail hairs of an elephant, a good-luck amulet equal to a giraffe-hair charm in potency.[15] Oubidu handled himself with great dignity, querying our host in Swahili about us, and finally giving his consent. "What did I tell you?" Barnes said. "Our friend here says to be happy because he will have a dugout and two of his own people ready to go with you tomorrow morning."

December 23: *On the Albert Nile*

The king himself supervised our purchases of rice, bananas, eggs, and a chicken, plus a supply of maize flour for the journey. And our boatmen, Okelo and Oliyo, were waiting for us at the river in a small bark whose bottom was already covered by two inches of water, seeping in from a crack in the starboard side of the stern. Okelo, to my surprise, spoke some English, and his brother Oliyo understood Swahili. A crowd from the village saw us off.

About five miles downstream we met a big dugout ferrying fifteen men and women of the primitive Joanam tribe across the river to the west bank. As so often happened, the others went on by without stopping, but, eager to visit with the people, I stopped and followed them to a landing in the papyrus. Conversation was impossible—my best Swahili got no response—but sign language served for all we needed. Three elderly grandmas, thin and gray, with flabby breasts like deflated footballs, rode in the prow of the boat; the others, four men and eight young women, were splendid physical specimens, the handsomest people I had seen in Africa. The men wore loin cloths and the women were attired in nothing but kirtles of fresh green grass tied to a waist cord fore and aft, and a few bits of beadwork. Their ample breasts swung free and erect. One of the old ladies and two of the men smoked pipes of native tobacco mixed with elephant dung. A comely young mother bore her sleeping baby on her back in a clever harness consisting of a wooden crossbar and an antelope pelt sling, while a great half-dome gourd, like an outsized G.I. helmet, acted as a sunshade over the infant.

As soon as the boat touched ground, several of the Joanams dashed off and never returned. Those remaining were very timid until I brought out my movie camera for them to examine. They crowded around me, patiently taking turns at squinting through the lens viewer, curiosity replacing their fear. The

---

15. Ideally a bracelet should not be purchased but should be presented by a friend as a gift. Mine had been given to me by Ken Beaton, Warden of Nairobi Game Park. It had been created by one of his African scouts from hair confiscated from poachers.

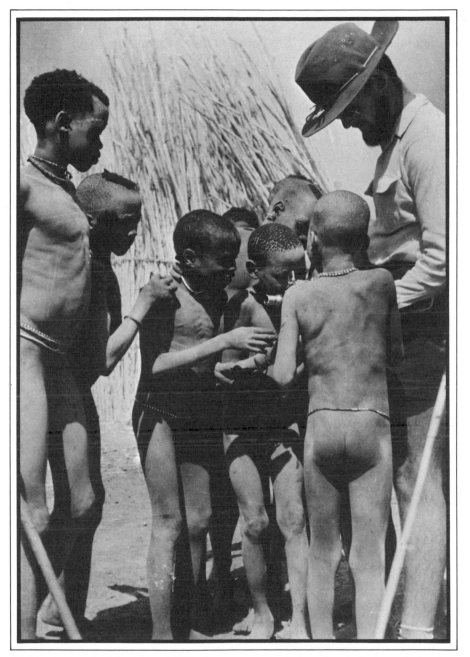

Goddard wins the friendship of Shilluk youngsters by letting them look through the view finder of his movie camera; to look down and yet see straight out amazed them.

79

viewer completely astounded them. Everyone had to peek through again and again. Each in turn would stand close as I held the camera and, screwing up his or her face, would bend over to peer through the small opening, then would step back for the next in line, laughing and marveling over the wonder at being able to look down and see something in front of them.

Suddenly, after taking pictures of the group for some time, I realized that my companions would be far ahead, and I'd have to paddle hard to catch up. I hated leaving such happy, completely unaffected people; as a present I opened a tin of toffee and passed it around. It must have been their first experience with white man's candy; I had bought it to give to Jean and André on Christmas day, but they could not have appreciated it as much as the Joanams, who waded out into the water and clustered around to shake my hand as I left.

I caught up with my friends after several hot hours' exertion. Jean and I dawdled along, easily keeping ahead of the heavy m'tumbi, exerting more energy fending off a cloud of tsetse flies than in paddling. High overhead a dozen vultures wheeled lazily, gliding the thermals billowing over the parched countryside.

Toward dusk immense storm clouds obscured the sky, and a strong wind swept over us. I took off my hat and shirt and stowed them in a bag to enjoy the cooling rain on my sweaty body. The storm developed swiftly and with overwhelming force. We were amazed to find ourselves enveloped in a furious northerly gale with torrential rain and wind of almost hurricane force. Our placid waterway was transformed into a maelstrom that threatened to engulf us. The churning river slammed us against the papyrus, where we tossed helplessly. For an hour we fought to keep our plunging prows headed into the huge waves sweeping upstream. Several times we nearly swamped as large swells crested over us. Because of its load and waterlogged condition, the dugout rode low in the water and took the waves more smoothly than the light kayaks. But the three men had to bail and paddle constantly to keep it from capsizing.

At last the storm abated as our strength gave out, leaving us soaked and exhausted, but free to continue. (We didn't realize at that time that this was the last drop of rain that would fall on us during the remainder of the expedition—it was ironic that it was a violent cloudburst that all but drowned us!)

We bedded down on a grassy knoll, but were wakened by the sudden throbbing of big drums not far away. Immediately forgetting our fatigue, we scrambled out of the tent, heading toward the hypnotic sound.

We picked up a thin trail that twisted and turned through tall elephant grass until we reached a small Madi village, where the people were ecstatically leaping and cavorting in time to a concert emanating from three drummers and a cymbalist.

The festivities stopped abruptly when they spotted us. Frightened-eyed women and children edged away as we approached, and the men stood stiffly in place. But after a brief palaver we convinced everyone we were not enemies. The three of us sat engrossed before a hut, watching while the drummers heated their instruments before the fire to make them more resonant. With the drums warmed up and thundering out the irresistible rhythms, the dancers quickly recaptured the mood, the men dancing with grotesque movements around the four musicians, their oiled, naked bodies glinting in the moonlight. The women stood just outside the circle of dancers, jigging in time to the drums, from time to time uttering piercing shrieks. Fascinated, we watched the hopped-up jam session until far into the night, then left quietly for camp, where we dropped off to sleep with the riotous noise still in our ears.

December 24: *Rhino Camp*

A fast paddle of thirty miles brought us to Rhino Camp, the most prominent settlement on the Albert Nile and a trade center for all the local tribes, even though it is little more than a village in appearance. We set out to look for a white trader we had heard lived in the town—the only white in the area, besides Captain Barnes—and found an unpainted ramshackle house that we assumed was his. If it was, he wasn't in. And then we passed through the marketplace, where in wooden stalls, called *dukas,* Africans of the Banyoro, Joanam, Madi, Alur, Lugwara, Acholi, and Moru tribes dickered and traded.

Our coming aroused no particular excitement, but a mob of curious youngsters tagged along as we canvassed the market for foodstuffs. I was completely captivated by a Lugwara carving from the two lower tusks of a hippo. One figure was a crocodile with jaws agape; the other had been carved into seven little elephants linked trunk to trunk. I had vowed not to buy souvenirs because of the limited space on the kayak; but I couldn't pass these up. After a bargaining session in sign language and a few words of Swahili, the Lugwara traded them to me for a khaki shirt.

I had just reached my kayak and was giving the Lugwara his shirt when a green lorry came clattering down the dusty track from the village. It was driven by a Persian just about my age, who introduced himself as Ali Khalfan, a merchant from Arua, a town bordering the Belgian Congo (Zaire) forty-two miles to the west. "We heard about your expedition in Arua over the wireless, and when I stopped for petrol at the souk just now, they told me you had reached here, and I very much wanted to see you."

The Upper White Nile

The upper White Nile is created by
two distinct river systems, one that
drains into Lake Albert and includes
Lakes Edward and George, and the
other that drains into the Victoria
Nile and includes Lakes Victoria and
Kyoga. Most of the water draining or
falling in Uganda ends up in Victoria
or Albert. Lake Albert is the great
receptacle for all brooks and rivers
flowing down the slopes of the
Ruwenzori. The rain and snow water
draining from both the eastern and
western slopes of the Ruwenzori are
carried to the Nile through Lake
George and Lake Albert. An artificial
boundary cleaves Lake Albert directly
down the center, so that the western
half lies in Zaire and the eastern in
Uganda. The deepest part of Albert is
only 140 feet, but it has an area of
2,000 square miles and is more than
100 miles long and 30 miles at its
widest point.
The four lakes with the English royal
names belong to the *Nile*. Those with
the African names, Lakes Kivu and
Tanganyika, to the *Zaire* river.

When I introduced Ali to Jean and André, the Persian impulsively said, "Why don't you come back to Arua with me and spend Christmas at my home? You can't be traveling on such a holy day!" My first reaction was that we should keep moving, but Jean and André both expressed a desire to accept the generous invitation, and I decided, too, that it would be wonderful to relax one day and observe Christmas in a more meaningful way. It surprised me that Ali, a devout Moslem, would attach such importance to a Christian holiday; he explained that Moslems revere Jesus as a divinely ordained prophet of God and celebrate his birthday, too.

Ali drove us the thirty miles to Arua through a moonlit wilderness over a rocky, spine-jolting track. Halfway from Rhino Camp to Arua the headlights picked up a column of dark figures tramping down the road. We stopped the lorry and found they were a party of Lugwara hunters returning to their village after a day of hunting with bows and arrows. Their game, slung over bare shoulders, appeared to be huge guinea pigs with bristly dark gray fur. Upon closer inspection I recognized them as hyraxes, a species of cony—queer little animals, snub-nosed and tailless, with an eerie, pathetic cry like that of a human child in distress. In size, appearance, and habits, they seem to be rodents, but zoologically they are grouped with the ungulates or hoofed mammals. The bony formation of their blunt-clawed paws and the wrist bones overlying them are similar to those of the true hoofed beasts. According to mammalogists they are, of all things, the nearest living relative of the elephant. The Lugwaras boil and eat them with great relish.

Ali's own home was too small to hold us, so he took us to the home of his brother Ahmed, who greeted us as if we were long-lost relatives. I was already feeling a glow of "Christmas spirit" from the beautiful night drive, and the feeling increased as we ate a delicious curry and listened to Ali and Ahmed as they told us of their background. Their father had been the first white settler in Arua more than forty years earlier, after years of restless wandering as a nomadic merchant. He married a beautiful African girl, started a family, and found life in Arua so idyllic that he never left it again.

And that night, after talking until the small hours, we slept unmolested by mosquitoes for the first time in weeks, since there were no standing bodies of water near Arua for them to breed in. It was a wonderful Christmas Eve.

December 25: *Arua*

This morning I wished André and Jean a *très Joyeux Noël* and presented them with two sodden, misshapen chocolate bars that I had cached away with the toffee. At ten o'clock Ahmed drove us to the only Christian church in the settlement, but the British minister was speaking in the local dialect, and, unable to understand a word, we left to pay our respects to the district commissioner. His name was J. D. Gotch, and he and his young bride were amazed to find us on their doorstep. "Why, we've just been to Rhino Camp looking for you!" said Mrs. Gotch. "We got up at four o'clock this morning and drove there to invite you to be the guests of honor at our Christmas party tonight. We saw your boats there but couldn't imagine where you had gone."

"But how did you know we had reached Rhino Camp?" I asked.

"We heard a rumor last week that you had arrived and were planning to stay for several days. We felt certain you would spend Christmas there, at least."

The news came as a pleasant surprise to us; we hadn't dreamed that people as far away as Arua would be following our expedition's progress so closely. But thanks to the African grapevine, swift and far-reaching (but rarely accurate, as even in this case!), we had a rather involved social calendar for Christmas day; though we had to turn down the Gotches' invitation to Christmas dinner because we had already accepted Ahmed's, we did accept the invitation to their party.

Dinner with the Khalfans was certainly the most remarkable Christmas feast I have ever eaten—and one of the tastiest. Before eating, we washed our hands in table bowls of scented water, then ate only with the right hand, according to the Moslem custom. The table was loaded with Persian delicacies: fluffy wheat chappaties, wild rice with chunks of succulent kebab, two kinds of mahig (stewed fish), topped off with a special fruit pudding and tall glasses of lemonade.

We were not quite as comfortable when we entered the Gotches's house for the party: everyone there was in an evening gown or a tuxedo. But at least our khaki was clean and neat, thanks to Ahmed's personal servant, who had washed and ironed them during the day. And everyone was so cordial and informal that we soon lost our self-consciousness.

The party could have been taking place in Europe, and we were much impressed that an isolated hamlet in the heart of Africa could produce such a charming assemblage. After our weeks of primitive living, this party with cultured and fashionably dressed people seemed like some kind of happy hallucination. Unfortunately, we were rigidly locked into the habit of rising and retiring with the sun; at 10:30 we were too drowsy to be of any use to anyone, and we thanked our host and hostess, bid everyone "Cheerio," and departed to our cots.

December 26: *Rhino Camp to Obongi*

On Tuesday morning Ali made a special trip to return us to Rhino Camp. A few miles before reaching the village, we encountered a group of women clad only in bustles of green twigs with bulbous jars balanced gracefully atop their shaven heads. I asked Ali to stop so I could take pictures, but the moment I stepped from the truck, the girls jettisoned their loads and fled in terror into the tall grass.

Ali explained they were frightened because of a rumor that had been sweeping northern Uganda, alarming thousands of gullible villagers. A new brand of bully beef had appeared on the shelves of the local dukas, bearing a picture of a grinning Negro as its trademark. Some mischief-maker had spread the word that the cans contained the flesh of Africans captured, killed, and canned by evil whites! It was no wonder the women fled in such panic. They probably viewed our approach as an attempt to grab them and throw them into a cooking pot.[16]

"I have a great feeling we will meet again someday," Ali said as we parted. "We will be praying for your safe journey."

By nightfall we hadn't found a break in the dense papyrus lining the river, and we decided to push on to the next village, Obongi. André was in my kayak, and I was taking a turn in the pirogue; while Jean and André pushed ahead to set up the tent and prepare supper, Oliyo and Okelo and I dodged hippos in our unmaneuverable craft. What had started out as a lovely tropic night now became sinister as hippo after hippo challenged or pursued us.

Most of the time we could hear only their grunts and splashes as they came toward us, but on two occasions a lone hippo caught up with us close enough to be plainly seen. The two men were terrified of them and paddled furiously to get out of their way. For two endless hours we ran a gauntlet of river-hogging hippos; then, with great relief, we sighted our campfire, a cheery oasis in the dark. Okelo told me later that neither he nor his brother could swim. If the boat had been upset, they would surely have drowned. The men had lived all their lives beside the Nile, spending much of their time on the river, yet,

---

16. In her book written on a trip through East Africa, *The Sorcerer's Apprentice* (Chatto and Windus, London 1948), Elspeth Huxley describes a similar experience that ended in tragedy. An entomologist was stabbed to death only a few miles from a large town because he just happened to be driving a red car, which villagers associated with an unpopular brand of tinned meat with a red hand on the label as a trademark. They were convinced the red hand symbolized the contents of the can and mistook the entomologist with his butterfly nets for a hand hunter.

typical of people in Africa, had never learned to swim because of the danger from crocodiles.

When we joined Jean and André, they told me that the "canned African" tale must have reached Obongi—the village fires that had guided them through the dark were quickly extinguished as they approached. All the Madi went into hiding immediately, and as they walked through the village it was completely deserted. "We found just one person, a young boy crouching behind a tree. We shook hands with him and gave him a shilling to show our good intentions." With confidence thus established, the lad signaled the others it was safe, and within two minutes the entire village surrounded the Frenchmen, jubilant to find the whites friendly.

The situation struck me as ironic. "What a laugh," I said to André. "There was a time when it was the explorer who worried about ending up in the cooking pot; now it's the poor African!"

Footsore
and
Fevered

December 27: *Obongi and Northward*

We joined a hippo hunt this morning. We were wakened by the chatter of villagers as they passed our tent. I ran to the water as nine men pushed off in three dugouts. One of them held up a long spear and shouted to me, "Kiboko!" (hippo). We needed no more explanation, and with no thought of breakfast, Jean, André, and I soon had the tent pitched and were on the river paddling downstream to catch up.

When we found them, they were floating near the bank, intently watching a group of hippos clustered in the middle of the river. One of the animals became separated from the others in the milling of the herd—immediately a dugout started toward it. But the hippo saw them coming and submerged. The pirogue stopped, pulled back to the bank, and the hunters waited. The Madi are famous for their skill and bravery in hunting, but to attack the herd as a group, even with nine men, was inviting death and disaster. The hippos refused to cooperate today, staying drowsily in the middle of the river, finding safety in numbers, and at last Jean and André and I had to leave, unable to wait and see the outcome.

When the hunters get close to a hippo, one of them spears him with a sturdy iron-tipped harpoon attached by a length of rope to a heavy log. The log slows down the animal and also serves as a marker buoy. When necessary a hippo can stay submerged up to six minutes, but the hunters can follow his underwater movements by means of the float, then finish him off with a barrage of spears when he surfaces for air.

We passed other hunters farther downstream, but found no settlements. The parklike countryside was deceptively lovely, yet it is regarded as the most dangerous sleeping-sickness region of East Africa. We slapped at tsetses constantly, twitching with pain each time their tiny daggers stabbed our skin.

Late in the day, André and I stopped on the left bank to check out what looked to be a good campsite under a granite cliff, but there was too much brush, and the slope was too steep. Coming back down to the river, I was so grimy that I decided to swim for a moment and dived off into the water.

"Angalia mamba!" Oliyo called—"Look out for crocodiles." The reminder was enough. I scrambled back to my boat and we headed on downstream.

Hugging the right bank in the kayaks, André and I were far ahead of the others at sunset when we heard queer noises emanating from the other side of a bend in the river. We rested on our paddles and coasted, straining to identify the sounds—then recognized that they were the trumpetings of elephants. We edged closer to the bank and, stroking quietly, rounded the jutting shoreline to behold a timeless scene: thirty-eight magnificent elephants grouped in a grassy meadow, grazing and watering beside the Nile. The rays of the setting sun, filtering through a bank of low-hanging clouds, bathed the scene in a golden radiance.

"I would have paddled one hundred miles to see this," I said to André.

"It wouldn't be too far for me, either," he replied.

We beached the boats and crouched behind a brush shelter to watch a baby elephant suckle between its mother's front legs, a perfect miniature of its parent. The proud bull stood in front of his contented mate, gently caressing her face and head with his trunk.

Nearby stood an ancient bull, seeming ageless and indestructible, scraping its shoulder against a tree and making contented purring sounds. His companion fed silently, great ears languidly fanning the flies away, his sensitive trunk rolling tufts of succulent grass into bite-sized balls and sweeping them into his mouth with a flourish. As I watched them, it occurred to me that the contentious family of man could well profit by emulating these animals, who live together in affectionate companionship, with a deeply engrained sense of community, an enemy to no other living thing so long as they are unmolested.

A few miles farther on, we came to a Madi village on the east bank—the first human habitation we had seen on that side of the river since leaving Butiaba. André and I had been gliding along when we noticed a prominent waterway leading into the papyrus. We followed the rocky corridor past the jungle of sedge and came out into a tree-lined pool below the village, with a few huts nestled in a picturesque setting of trees and granite hillocks. It was beautiful;

Elephants graze beside Albert Nile.

the men were friendly and talkative, though we understood nothing; and if the mosquitoes hadn't been murderous, the campsite would have been perfect. As it was we had to kill quite a few of the insects before sleeping—and then the idyll was complete.

December 28: *Uganda-Sudan border*

Before we left the village this morning, I looked around and noticed that interspersed among the huts were five granaries, finely woven containers of creepers and reeds set on a platform with a cone-shaped lid, each containing one of the crops or food staples produced by the people: cotton, peanuts, millet, manioc, and durra. Okelo told me that babies and young children were often hidden in the glorified baskets at night when there were leopards or other dangerous animals about.

And besides the human population, the village was heavily populated with fat, gaudy orange and purple lizards that scuttled out of my way wherever I walked or sat blinking at me with heads engagingly cocked.

The village turned out en masse this morning to see us off, and everyone stood on a granite outcrop to watch us as we floated through the papyrus tunnel to the river. Our visit was probably the biggest thing that had happened to them in many a year, and they wanted to savor it to the end.

Today I took another turn in the m'tumbi. Okelo moaned and said, "I happy with you, Bwana, but you make me work too hard and I get pains in heart." This from a man who had twice my stamina in rowing.

"My friend, you're just a twenty-four carat goldbrick," I told him, to his bewilderment. To distract him from his cardiac problems, I taught Okelo a little rhyme to paddle by that I had composed, using the names of African places that we had visited beginning with the letter *k*: Kitale, Kabale, Kisenyi, Kigali, Kitega, Kampala, Kagera. He soon had the syncopation down fine, but had trouble saying them in the right order.

As we neared the Sudan border the country became more hilly and rocky, and for the first time we began seeing date palms. We had another brush with hippos when we blundered into a dozing herd submerged next to a rocky island. We didn't see them until they reared suddenly from the water. Okelo forgot the pains in his heart and nearly broke his paddle in his mad efforts to escape. But they were sleepy, and as startled by us as we were by them. By pulling on the paddles with all our might we got away without incident. (I tried to keep count of the hippos I saw on the Albert Nile but lost track at around 450.)

Jean Laporte and Madi women at a village along the Albert Nile.

André and Jean, anxious to collect the accumulated correspondence they knew must be awaiting them, left us and raced ahead to Nimule, hoping to arrive before the post office closed. They were in for a let-down. Though prominently labeled on our maps, Nimule turned out to consist of an outsize customs shed and a few scattered huts beyond—rather a humble gateway to the largest nation of Africa, the Sudan.[17]

When we arrived at Nimule, only three villagers were waiting to greet us. Jean and André had apparently gone inland, so barefoot and dressed only in

---

17. With an estimated 19,000,000 people (1978) dispersed over an area of nearly one million (967,491) square miles, Sudan, though Africa's largest nation in area, is one of the most thinly populated countries of the world. Nine out of ten Sudanese live in the countryside as farmers and herders. Sharp racial and political differences exist between the citizens of the northern and southern provinces. Arabic-speaking Moslems, culturally linked to the Arabic world, particularly Egypt, make up almost three-fourths of the population and live in the upper two-thirds of the country in the six northern provinces. In Sudan's three southern provinces live four million Negroid Africans, culturally related to the peoples of Zaire, Uganda, and Kenya. They speak some eighty tribal languages and are largely pagan in religion, with a sprinkling of Christians and Moslems.

The Sudan

The Sudan got its name from the Arab term, *Bilad as Sudan,* meaning "country of the Blacks," or, simply put, "Negroland." Originally it applied to a vast 1,000-mile-wide sweep of savanna and desert between the Sahara on the north and the forests to the south and extending all the way across Africa for 4,000 miles from Dakar on the Atlantic to Djibouti on the Red Sea.

The people of the northern Sudan, numbering approximately 14,000,000 (1977) are composed of largely brown or black Arabic-speaking Moslems, who identify with the Arab World. The Sudanese "Arab" defies accurate racial classification because he is a complex blend of Arab, Negro, and Caucasian. Arab migrants first entered the Sudan either from Egypt after the Arab conquest in the seventh century A.D. or directly from Arabia across the Red Sea. As with the earlier Hamitic invaders, they intermarried with the indigenous populations of the land, but gradually drove the Hamiticized Negroid tribes southwards.

The inhabitants of the southern Sudan, nearing 5,000,000 (1977), are ethnically and culturally of Black Africa, with affiliations tending southward to Uganda, Zaire, and Kenya, rather than northward. They belong to predominantly pagan, preliterate, pastoral tribal societies with their own languages. The southerners have descended from Sudanic peoples who, in ancient times, were of pure Negro stock, one of the original African races, but who intermingled

with successive waves of Caucasian
invaders from Asia and northern Africa.
Throughout most of the 19th century Arabs from the
north preyed upon the southerners for cattle, ivory,
and slaves. They justified their practice of slavery and
the acquisition of black concubines on an erroneous
interpretation of the Koran, which led them to
continuous raiding of the southern tribes. They
captured hundreds of thousands of slaves and took as
many concubines as they could support. This practice
resulted in miscegenation, which continues to this
day, so that the citizens of the Sudan are a mixture, to
widely varying degrees, of Caucasian (Hamitic and
Semitic) and Negro.
Many northern Sudanese still look upon the tribal
people of the south with condescension and consider
them inferior, and the southerners still harbor deep-
seated resentments and distrust against the Arab
Sudanese, a distrust stemming from the days of slave
raiding. This mutual antipathy, plus the southerners'
fear of political domination of the Muslem north, was
the foundation that produced Africa's longest war, the
Sudan's seventeen-year civil war, that extended from
1955 to 1972. This bitter conflict resulted in more
than 500,000 deaths and forced 200,000 southerners to
take refuge in neighboring countries. A peace treaty
was signed in March, 1972, but the issues involved,
particularly political autonomy for the southerners,
have still not been resolved.

khaki shorts, I followed the road they must have taken. I had gone only two miles when a car appeared, driven by James Dodson, an engineer for the Sudanese government, and carrying Jean and André. By coincidence he had been driving to his home in Juba from a visit in Jinja, and had happened to see Jean and André walking along a road where cars passed only rarely.

Jim Dodson was a godsend. Along the 125-mile stretch between Nimule and Juba, the Nile surges swiftly over a solid granite bottom—a narrow rapids-ridden torrent that would have been death to our thin-skinned kayaks. We had previously decided to cover this expanse on foot, since following the river along the banks was the best alternative to paddling.

Since Dodson's wife and son were staying in Jinja for a few weeks, he offered the hospitality of his home—and we gratefully accepted. We paid Okelo and Oliyo and left them at a Madi village near the river, commending them for their courage in coming the 120 miles with us from Pakwach, a distance farther than they had ever traveled. We like to think that they are now probably regarded by their family and friends as globetrotters.

Tonight we are sleeping in a rest house thirty miles from Nimule.

December 30: *Juba, in the Sudan*

We drove to Juba yesterday, and today we called at the two-room post office where we picked up a month's accumulation of mail—a real bonanza from our families, friends, and girlfriends. André and I caught up on correspondence most of the day, and Jean returned to Nimule in Jim's work lorry to bring back the kayaks and equipment. Tonight was the New Year's Eve party for the forty-five Britishers in town—a costume party. Among the clowns, sailors, geishas, and bullfighters we fit right in: André and I went dressed as explorers.

We met all the officials of the province of Equatoria, of which Juba is the capital, but at last the heat and clamor and closed-in feeling were more than I could bear, and mumbling something about being the outdoor type, I went outside for air. I could immediately hear the throb of drums in the distance, and started toward the enticing sound. Three miles later I found it—farther than I had thought to go. But it was worth the hike, for I spent the next hour watching an ecstatic moon dance executed by several strapping Mondari warriors, their leaping figures grotesque in the firelight. I sat in the shadows at the edge of the village and enjoyed the performance unnoticed.

Then, because it was getting late, I slipped away and returned to the clubhouse, marveling at the limitless energy that enabled the Africans to dance for hours without ceasing. The white people's party, too, was still going strong; but it was one a.m., Sunday morning, and so I retired.

December 31: *Juba*

The British party last night was enjoyable enough; but tonight I spent the most cosmopolitan and interesting New Year's Eve of my life. Jim Dodson is the only Englishman who is accepted by the Greeks in Juba as one of them; their invitation to him was extended to us, as well, and we had a marvelous Greek dinner that began with a prayer from an old bearded patriarch.

The next part of our New Year's Eve was spent in the company of twenty-five German fräuleins at the British Club. They were nurses stopping over-night on their way from Germany to Johannesburg, where they had jobs waiting for them at a hospital. So I welcomed in the new year with a bewitching petite blonde from Fribourg named Gabriella—the first feminine companionship I had had in ten weeks.

And then some of the British men piled us all into their pickup trucks and drove us to a big Scottish party down the road. We spent the remainder of that night and part of the first day of 1951 watching sprightly Scottish reels, listening to phonograph records of bagpipe music, and singing old Scottish ballads.

At midnight, it was a touching experience to stand in a circle with these exuberant people—Scottish, English, German, French, and American—arms linked together, singing "Auld Lang Syne" with real feeling. It was, all in all, a United Nations in miniature.

January 1–3: *Southwest Sudan*

We spent the first three days of the new year on a side-trip: a 400-mile safari with Jim in his light truck, visiting some of the primitive areas of southwest Sudan, going as far as Aba in the Belgian Congo (Zaire). The countryside was tinder dry, with trees and scrubby vegetation ready to ignite at any moment. Fires were frequent, and at one time, while riding in the back of the lorry, I received a mild scorching when we had to make a dash through one big blaze. I pulled my sloucher hat on tight, tucked my head between my knees, and held my breath as we raced down the narrow dirt track with giant flames crackling furiously on either side.

The first night we slept in a neat little Fajulu village 150 miles from Juba, and I took pictures of the local residents, including several Azande (Niam Niam) men, who were cannibals until recently. Other tribesmen we saw on our safari were Lukyia, Mondari, Moru, Kakiva, Logo, Abukiya, and Dinka: the Dinka men never wear clothing, even on the main street of Juba, though sometimes they wear a string of bright beads around their waist. The Dinka didn't seem to mind our cameras, but whenever we stopped to photograph people of other tribes, they would run off into the bush. As we had discovered

The Dinka

Generally, at six feet one inch, I would be considered tall, but among the Dinka I was only average in height.* The majority of the men stand more than six feet tall, and many are almost seven feet tall. The height is a great advantage in the marshes of their homeland. With their spindly limbs and angular bodies, the Dinka seem human counterparts of the cranes and herons living there. Their posture and their exaggerated walk are strikingly similar to those of a water bird. They raise their large feet high off the ground and thrust them well forward with each step. A Dinka in repose, with one leg resting in the crook of the other, bears an uncanny resemblance to a big crane in the same attitude. Centuries ago this characteristic earned them the title, "stork men of the Nile."

Dinka men walk around in unashamed nudity, "barefooted up to the eyebrows," a situation that created a problem whenever I wanted to photograph them. Women go topless but wear skirts of soft, tanned goat or sheepskins. Except for special public occasions, such as dances and ceremonies, the men generally disdain wearing clothing, considering it unnatural and unnecessary. Jean, André and I had quickly become accustomed to the sight of naked villagers along the Nile, but I knew that filming them for television and lecture audiences would pose a serious problem.

I made a half-hearted attempt at persuading some of the men to gird themselves in loincloths made from my trade bandannas, but they were offended at being asked to cover up their well-endowed manhood. All I could do was aim my cameras high and settle for torso shots.

*See January 31, page 124 and following, for more information about the Dinka.

The men convey an image of graceful beauty with their broad, muscular shoulders, narrow waists, feminine hips, and slender, well-proportioned legs. They frequently wear attractive body decorations, including strands of red and white beads around their waists and necklaces made from giraffe-tail hairs. Many wear metal coils or thick ivory bracelets around their biceps so tight they cut into the skin and impede circulation, though no one seems to mind. The most essential and useful item of their ensemble, one they would really feel "naked" without, is the spear they carry everywhere, usually at least ten feet in length and possibly the longest used by any tribe in Africa.

I saw many men with war clubs of heavy purple wood and shields of buffalo hide. Attesting to the slimness of the men, I couldn't fit my hand into any of the shield grips I tested. The coiffure of the Dinka male is similar to the hair style of the Masai of East Africa—the hair done up in little plaits and smeared with ochre. It seems a comical contradiction when they wash in the Nile until their dark skin gleams like polished ebony, only to daub globs of thick red ochre over their heads and smear wood ash over their bodies.

Though essentially peaceful cattle raisers, the Dinka sometimes become involved in bloody battles with their neighbors or among their own clans. Hussein* described a skirmish that took place last month in which the Afak Atwot Clan disputed the rights to some pasture land of the Cic Clan. Thirty-eight members of the Afak Atwot Clan were speared to death by members of the Cic group, and four Dinka warriors of the Cics were killed in the violent hand-to-hand fighting.

*The Assistant District Commissioner at Bor.
(See February 10, page 131.)

before, villagers rarely cooperate with our picture-taking when we come upon them suddenly; only when we go to their villages and win their confidence do they trust our cameras.

On our second night, which we spent at the town of Yei, we were about to retire when we heard a big dance in progress at a nearby village. Two miles from Yei we found that a funeral was in progress at a Lubari village. The dead man had been buried beside his hut, and his three wives and seven children sat on the mound of dirt wailing over their loss. The rest of the villagers were grouped around three drummers in the center of the clearing, solemnly dancing in place, the women clapping and the men beating time with a handful of arrows rapped on their bows. From time to time a woman would utter a shrill cry and fling out her arms.

I couldn't help comparing this somber ritual with the happy-go-lucky, unrestrained dances the villagers usually indulge in. Both their joy and their sorrow find cathartic expression in dancing and chanting and I'm convinced that

A Madi fisherman hunts dinner in the turbulent Fola Rapids.

we moderns could eradicate many of our anxieties and neuroses if we would occasionally express ourselves as villagers do, without inhibitions or self-consciousness.

Jim let me drive the lorry home to Juba, a mixed pleasure—it was fun to drive again, but hard to keep the vehicle on the narrow track that passes for a road. Jim has been the most helpful host we could have met in the southern Sudan. At a time when gasoline is rationed, he took us on this marvelous and eventful safari, and now, having lived with the Arabs and speaking their language fluently, he is teaching us Arabic, along with giving us priceless information about the Sudan and Egypt. At forty-three and rather portly and balding, Jim isn't a romantic type—yet his life has been full of romance and adventure. And for us, this expedition has exceeded our wildest dreams. Each day presents us with some unexpected beauty, scenic wonder, or novel adventure, and the trip would have been worthwhile simply for the people we have met. And I expect the next phase of our journey to be the most adventurous and eventful yet.

January 7: *Juba*

For the past three days André and I have been bedridden with attacks of malaria, with the typical symptoms of weakness, nausea, and paroxysms of torrid temperatures and wracking chills, despite the quinine we had been taking as a preventive measure.[18] Jean, however, has bronchitis, brought on by the temperature extremes between the heat on the river during the day and the damp cold among the reeds on the shore at night. Dr. Obbid, an astute local Sudanese doctor, has been indispensable in getting us on our feet again.

However, shaky as we are, we're eager to get started on our foot safari from Nimule to Juba. This hike will take us through a beautiful unspoiled land of thinly forested bush abounding with wild life and populated with a few small villages of "shenzis"—isolated villagers living in a primitive hand-to-mouth, "survival of the fittest" kind of existence, virtually untouched by civilization. We're taking only the minimal gear for the trip. With the help of Jim and his half-Arab foreman, Abdullah, we'll be at Nimule tomorrow evening.

---

18. Malaria is an acute infectious disease caused by several species of a parasitic protozoan belonging to the single genus *Plasmodium.* It is transmitted into the blood from host to host by the bite of an infected female anopheles mosquito. The infection is produced by four specific parasites known as *Plasmodium vivax, P. malariae, P. falciparum,* and *P. orale.* The doctor diagnosed André's and my malaria as an attack of the benign tertian type caused by *P. vivax.* He felt that since our symptoms were less intense and more irregular than the usual clinical pattern, it was likely that we had developed a partial immunity from a build-up of quinine in our blood resulting from the prophylactic doses we had been taking over the past three months.

January 9: *Near Nimule*

Jim and I stopped at the village of Zelindo late yesterday afternoon and talked with the paramount chief of the Onadi tribe, a tall man with the bearing of a Roman senator, who wore a rather unusual headdress—a splendid new khaki sun helmet and a khaki uniform to match, just sent to him by the provincial governor. Jean and André had already arrived and talked to him, with Abdullah's help, and had arranged for three of his tribesmen to accompany us on the hike. Unfortunately, Jean became ill again during the night and was too weak to go with us—he has returned to Juba with Jim.

André and I, with Akim, Ogone, and Sabi, our near-naked, spear-carrying Madi bearers, left from an embarkation point near Nimule, and I took the lead, carrying the .22 rifle and a pack that included the movie camera. The five of us made a colorful procession as we trekked along in the traditional African safari style, single file, through the dense ten-foot-high elephant grass and acacia woodlands. I set a steady, even pace and tried to pick out the game trails that would keep us near the river. At Nimule the Nile changes course ninety degrees and plunges to the northwest. From this point to Lake No, a distance of 450 miles, it is called Bahr-el-Jebel, Arabic for "River of the Mountain"; and for at least a quarter of the way, that is just what it is, a swift, vigorous, rapids-filled torrent pouring downhill over a solid rock bottom through a narrow valley almost all the way to Juba. Less than 300 yards from the Nimule customs shed the rapids began.[19] I took a picture there of a fish trap set down between the rocks near the shore by the local Madis. A great catfish was caught in the clever contraption; we left it undisturbed.

About four miles downstream, we came to the magnificent Fola Rapids, where the Nile narrows to about seventy-five feet and crashes over a series of reefs. From here we saw a fine specimen of white rhino grazing on the western bank.[20] He must have caught our scent, for he suddenly jerked up his ponderous head, faced in our direction, then lumbered off into the forest. He looked like an animated tank and could be just as deadly: we had recently heard that a Uganda game warden was killed by a charging black rhino near Murchison Falls, and on our drive to Entebbe the Colliers and I had come

19. In the past, great rafts of water plants have accumulated here, jamming together in a compacted mass to form a natural bridge solid enough for people and even elephants to cross over to the opposite bank.

20. Game authorities are unable to explain why white rhinos are found only on the Nile's west bank and black rhino on the east. Because of over hunting and poaching, white rhino are now found in only two general areas of Africa—one in Uganda's west Nile district and southern Sudan, and the other 2,000 miles away in Zululand.

upon an overturned Austin that had been rammed and tipped over by a black rhino. White rhinos, which are only a shade lighter than black ones (their name comes from the Boer word *weit,* meaning "wide" and refers to their wide mouth) are also much more docile and bovine. The black rhinos have weak eyesight and a highly emotional temperament, which frequently causes them to charge any unusual sound or movement near them, from a fluttering butterfly to a passing truck. Their charges are often sheer bluff, but a black rhino can be deadly when enraged, rocking along in a charge at a speed of thirty miles an hour, like an armor-plated locomotive.

Both species and sexes have double horns, which are densely compacted, hairy, fibrous extensions of the skin. Poachers slaughter rhinos solely for their horns to sell to traders for as much as fifty dollars a pound. Orientals create an inexhaustible demand, believing erroneously the ancient superstition that a pinch of powdered horn in food or drink is a potent aphrodisiac. This fallacy is producing a steady decimation of the rhinoceros wherever it exists, and has made the white rhino one of Africa's rarest animals.

We were able to stay close to the river by following game trails. These were our salvation in penetrating the dense jungles of otherwise impregnable elephant grass and thorn bush. But there was an aura of menace whenever we entered one of these narrow corridors through the tall grass, with only a few feet of visibility and no escape on either side. What if we should come upon something dangerous, like a buffalo or a spitting cobra? We always closed ranks and stepped along cautiously without speaking, making as little noise as possible.

We kept flushing impalas and kob antelope out of the bush all around us, and the Africans couldn't understand why I didn't shoot them. I tried in vain to explain that a .22 rifle is no gun to be used on an animal as large as an antelope. To them a rifle is a rifle, and no doubt one of the main reasons they came along with us was in the belief that with our gun we'd be bagging all the meat they could eat. They were to be disappointed.

Tonight, when we set up camp, the ground was so hard I could only drive in about half the stakes—and I bent several in the attempt.

January 10: *Near Nimule*

After we fell asleep last night, Akim wakened us with the disquieting news that a large animal was crashing around in the brush near our camp. André was so worn out from the long day that he rolled over to go back to sleep. I was curious, so I got up to investigate. I found the Africans huddled around a fire, although it was a warm night. They had built it up into a roaring blaze. Their eyes were saucerlike with fright, and each one had his spear stuck in the ground nearby for instant use.

Akim told me they were sure it was a cape buffalo, the most feared animal in Africa, but a few minutes later the beast came along a trail not a hundred feet from our tent—not a buffalo, but a full-grown black rhino. I had always been under the impression that rhinos, white or black, stayed put at night—yet here was this one, bumbling around in the dark with a bewildered look on his top-heavy face like a drunk trying to find his way home. He sized up our camp briefly, then ambled off into the bush. We turned in again and slept peacefully until morning.

The morning was chilly, surprisingly, but though we wished the chill could remain throughout the day, by 9 a.m. the equatorial sun was beating down on us unmercifully. André and I wore our hats. Our friends in Juba had warned us to wear our hats all the time outdoors because "your head is like a hunk of butter under the Sudan sun."

André and I were torpid from the heat, but our progress was more hindered by the heavy undergrowth slashing at our bare arms and legs. I marveled at how well our African companions endured everything. Each man was barefoot and clad only in a short loincloth and bore a heavy load atop his head, yet he accepted this and the considerable discomforts of heat, thirst, fatigue, tsetses, chiggers, and thorns without a word of complaint and in constant good humor.

We had a rest period at a Kuku village before noon and bought five eggs, three of which were "ripe" and had to be disposed of. The villagers were the sickliest we had come across in Africa. Aside from rheumy eyes, sores, and emaciation, I noted several pitiful cases of elephantiasis among the males of the tribe. I had an urgent desire to help alleviate the misery of these people, but the "shenzis" rarely trust modern medicine and usually prefer to put their faith in their witch doctors.

We crossed the Uma River by jumping from one big boulder to another. This was the dry season. As we approached the stream, a herd of beautiful golden brown impala bounded across ahead of us in great splashy leaps. We set up camp under a thorny acacia tree near the Nile. We almost camped a little farther upstream, but we noticed in time that a hippo run passed nearby, with fresh droppings. Occasionally Africans sleeping along the banks of lakes and rivers are stepped on and killed by hippos as they emerge from the water to graze at night; so we always choose our campsites with great care.

I set up the tent, as usual, while Akim and André prepared supper and Ogone and Sabi gathered firewood. When all the work was done, I set out for the river to fill the cooking pot with water. It was a beautiful evening, the sun just setting and the air, at last, becoming balmy. Dusk is always the finest time of day in Africa. The diurnal animals were bedding down, and the night creatures had not yet come out.

As I hunted for a passage to the river, I spotted an unusual shape offshore—a long dark blotch on the sandspit of a large island in midstream. At first it seemed to be a long outcropping of rock in the sand, but when I moved closer I saw it was an enormous crocodile, at least two or three feet longer than my sixteen-foot kayak and twice as broad.[21] I estimated he weighed nearly a ton, the largest crocodile I had seen since coming to Africa.

Nile and Congo River explorers of the nineteenth and early twentieth centuries had reported seeing twenty-five- and thirty-foot monsters, but in recent years even eighteen- and twenty-footers have become a rarity because of hunting to fill the heavy demand for crocodile hides.

The great reptile lay there like an immense prehistoric creature, showing no evidence of being alive even when I climbed down the bank and worked my way through an opening in the papyrus to the water's edge a stone's throw away. I stared at him until the light began fading, wondering about his age, which must have been great, and whether he had eaten many humans. (No one knows what a crocodile's maximum life span or size might be. These living fossils grow slowly until they die or, as is usually the case, are killed).

On the way back I found a perfect natural bathtub formed by the rocks in the river, completely croc-proof. So we all luxuriated in a quick but invigorating dip.

January 11: *Between Nimule and Juba*

Throughout the day we saw dozens of water buck, impala, antelope, and hartebeest. We flushed guinea fowl frequently and grouselike francolin occasionally. I managed to bag a plump guinea hen, which we had for supper. A deadly black mamba snake glided across the trail in front of me, a prime specimen about seven feet long. It was gone so quickly, however, that I couldn't take a picture.

Today we started the policy of having a ten-minute rest after every hour of hiking—we found that under the hot sun with our heavy burdens we quickly became exhausted.

After tramping through a deserted village, we came upon our first Bari settlement. Not knowing what else to say for a greeting, we shouted "Salaam

---

21. I found my kayak to be a useful gauge for measurement throughout the expedition.

Nilote Forehead Scars

Some Nilotes carve several horizontal bands on the foreheads of their young—long thin slashes for the Dinka, wider ones for the Nuer. But the Shilluk employ a skilled specialist to create these peculiar scarifications on the foreheads of their children at about the age of fifteen or sixteen.* He achieves this by lifting the skin with a fish-hook and slicing it off, making evenly spaced cuts from one ear to the other, then packing the incisions with cow-manure. When the forehead heals, the process is repeated. This continues until the artificial warts of scar-tissue stand out at least a quarter of an inch. Not only do the scars designate the wearer's tribe, but they symbolize his or her initiation into adulthood. They are also evidence of remarkable courage and self-control, since the cutting process is an agonizing ordeal that, in the case of the Nuer and Dinka, involves slashing the forehead to the bone four to six times from one side of the head to the other with a sharp knife, without benefit of any kind of anesthetic. Rarely does a young Nilote cry out during the operation, but an initiate's fainting from the pain is not uncommon.

When a boy has received the forehead scars, he is regarded as an adult, is eligible to participate in dances and hunts, and is given a share of his father's cattle.

Aleykum!"[22] In response the people either dashed off into the bush or dived into their houses. We must have looked like pretty sinister and desperate characters to them. Some kids who had been playing nearby ran away screaming and several emaciated dogs cut loose with yowls of fright. Even goats, chickens, and lizards became alarmed and scampered around, adding to the pandemonium. But at last, with the help of our African companions, the Baris began to trust us, though picture-taking was difficult: when they didn't flee at the sight of the camera, they hid their jewelry under their togas and struck stiff, unnatural poses. I was disappointed that I couldn't take pictures of the beadwork in their necklaces and in their tanned leather aprons.

The men had recently killed an elephant and were busy smoking the meat. Killing an elephant is an hours-long job. The elephant spears have two-foot heads of razor-sharp iron, and the first spear is thrown from a tree as the animal passes below. As the animal walks, the weapon works its way farther in; the hunters keep making small noises to make the elephant move. After the big spear is firmly embedded between the shoulder blades, the hunters show themselves, attacking the beast from all sides, harrying him with their spears as he tries to escape. Sometimes the fight will go on for hours, and the elephant may run for miles before he weakens, collapses, and is finished off.

The Bari people scar themselves more elaborately than any other people we have seen so far. Besides being tribal insignia, the scar designs are considered beautifying, and great pains are taken to make each scar neat and uniform. A deep incision is made in the skin in the pattern desired, and then wood ash is rubbed into the wound. I counted 125 bean-sized scars on one young warrior's face, arranged in rows, each having smaller scars at the bottom than at the top.

André had a rather bad experience this afternoon. We were moving along through thorny scrub when we stirred up a flock of guinea fowl. No matter how hard we chased these big game birds, they wouldn't take wing but would scurry away in abrupt zigs and zags and vanish into deep cover. It was tantalizing to come within inches of them without being able to grab one. André decided to make one last attempt at catching one for our supper. As I called for a rest stop he said, "Please to wait for me," and hurried off toward the flock, now busily absorbed in feeding on seeds and insects. The birds melted into a thicket as André approached, but he followed them and became lost to view. After we had waited for fifteen minutes, the Africans and I went in the direction he had taken, figuring to catch up with him. But after covering half a

22. "Peace be with you" – the standard greeting in Arabic, official language of Sudan and Egypt. Swahili was no longer useful, since only tribal languages and Arabic are spoken by people living along the Nile from southern Sudan to the Sea.

mile with no sight of him, I became worried. I had nearly decided to circle back when he suddenly appeared at the summit of a rise 300 yards away. He caught up, breathless, without his bush hat and drenched with sweat.

He told me that he had been chasing guinea hens without success; then, in trying to return, had lost his bearings. Suddenly he panicked and raced madly off into the bush. When he couldn't find us or even the Nile, he had visions of wandering through this uninhabited region until he died of thirst or starvation. As he plunged through the thorny thickets, he stumbled on a rock and gashed his knees. That was where he lost his hat, but in his terror he didn't stop to retrieve it.

Exhausted, he came to a stop and calmed down. Reason returned, and he decided we couldn't be too far behind him. He waited for us, and sure enough, we caught up. But it was a good lesson on the dangers of becoming separated in the interminable bush. Losing his only hat, a calamity that would have thrown some African explorers into a panic, didn't bother André. He merely draped a shirt over his head, took his place in line, and continued on his carefree way, looking like a little cowled and bearded monk.

We saw a small herd of elephants tonight, about fifteen; they sauntered away. Since it was getting late, we camped near where we had seen them. Because of the risk that they might return in the night, we began gathering wood for a large fire to keep them away. At last, darkness made us stop before we had gathered enough to be sure of our safety. And sure enough, we were awakened late at night by crashing limbs and rumblings. The camp was surrounded by elephants. The frightened Africans built up the fire, and André and I quietly left our tent to help them. We stood by the fire with our backs flat against a tree, listening tensely as the herd fed and watered just beyond us. The night was so dark our straining eyes couldn't make out a single elephant, but the noisy crashings as the animals ripped off branches or toppled trees to feed off the leaves conjured up a vivid picture of what was happening just beyond the flickering light cast by our campfire.

"If they come any closer," André whispered, "we're going to have to do some climbing."

"I doubt seriously if an elephant would have any trouble knocking this tree down," I answered. "Let's just hope there's not one in the herd that has a grudge against humans."

Actually, it was thrilling being so near the elephants, even though their proximity was a serious threat to our tent and equipment—and possibly our lives. After a very long hour, during which André and I offered up ardent prayers for safety, they gradually drifted off, enabling us to return to bed.

106

January 12: *Between Nimule and Juba*

We inspected the damage the elephants did and found the vegetation devastated over quite a large area. Twisted and uprooted trees lay everywhere, with bare patches where bushes and grass had been torn up. I took a picture of one tree only twenty yards from our tent that had been snapped in two and stripped. "I'm mighty glad our visitors believe in coexistence," I said to André.

More blistering heat all day. We are choked with thirst ten minutes after drinking our fill. Our stomachs can be full of water, but the air is so hot that it parches our mouths and throats, cracks our lips, and makes swallowing almost impossible. And though we are traveling beside a river, the banks are often too steep and the papyrus too thick for us to get a drink for miles on end. The Africans don't have such a hard time—they drink at any pool of standing water, no matter how thick it is, or green with scum. Sometimes I envy them their omnivorous tastes.

We spotted a large wart hog today, and the Africans wanted me to kill it with my rifle. We were no less starved for fresh food, and when André whispered, "Try to get him, John," I decided that my distaste for killing was outweighed by the need to supply five hungry men with fresh meat. I only wished I had the same trust in the .22 that the Africans had.

I had only a few seconds to aim and fire before he raced off. The little bullet whopped into him with a resounding smack, but it didn't seem to faze him. He was off at a fast clip, looking like a pygmy rhino, with André and me in hot pursuit. He ran a full 300 yards, his long tufted tail straight up, stiff as a ramrod, before dropping.

But the tough old boar wasn't ready to give up easily. The minute I came close to him, he lurched to his feet and came for me in a fast rush, squealing in rage and pain. I had just used my last bullet; I couldn't protect myself with the gun. So I picked up a big rock and hurled it at his head with all my might. The rock bounded off as if it had struck solid rubber, but it stunned him. He fell over, lay quivering for a few minutes, then quietly expired.

"Why didn't you give him the coup de grace?" André asked. I showed him my empty clip and said, "Now I can retire as the game hunter of this safari."

The Africans were ecstatic over the kill, happily performing an impromptu dance around the pig, then dragging him under a tamarind tree to begin the job of butchering, laughing and chattering with delight. The boar must have weighed more than 150 pounds, and would keep the five of us well supplied with pork for the rest of the trek.

Killing an animal this size with a .22 rifle is unusual. But I had hit him just over the left eye, and the bullet penetrated to the brain. I examined the body, particularly the strange wartlike protuberances that give the pig its name. There were a pair of four-inch growths just below the eyes and another, shorter pair above the sharp curving tusks on the snout. These "warts" protect the eyes and face as the pig digs for roots and tubers or enlarges its favorite home—a tunnel excavated by an aardvark in its quest for termites.

After plucking the coarse brown bristles from the warthog's neck and shoulders to weave into good-luck charms, the men dressed the pig in about an hour, and we were soon enjoying some delicious fried liver and steaks, the first fresh meat that André and I had eaten in almost two weeks. I was amazed at the absence of fat on the body; he was lean as any steer, and his meat was clean and red, with a rich flavor that seemed more like beef than pork.

The Madis carefully cleaned the entrails, boiled them, and then leisurely savored each mouthful like experienced gourmets as they lolled around in the shade. The vultures gathered, of course, waiting quietly for us to depart so they could scavenge our lunch site. Two black kites found the lure of food so irresistible that they couldn't wait for us to leave—they swooped down, trying to snatch morsels from our fingers. So André and I held up our mess kits containing pieces of raw meat, and they snatched up each morsel in such close passes that we felt their wings brush us.

The Madis were all in favor of calling it a day and eating for the rest of the afternoon, but since they had already devoured about five pounds of meat apiece, André and I didn't feel bad about making them come with us as we set out to make more progress today. We had to leave some meat behind; but we passed three Bari hunters soon after and directed them to the leftovers. They were very appreciative.

At our campsite the Madis built a large platform of green branches and laid the raw haunches and long strips of meat on it. Then they built a low fire from slow-burning wood and took turns feeding the fire all night. By dawn we had smoke-cured hams and pork jerky, tasty dried meat that would last for days without refrigeration. And since the last of our metal forks and spoons broke today, I had to improvise chopsticks out of thick, rigid elephant grass. The sticks worked well, but we had to guzzle our soup, and we ate the meat Arab style with our hands. But "fingers were made before forks."

While we were eating, a DC-6 passenger plane flew over us at about 15,000 feet, emphasizing our isolation. It gave me a nostalgic feeling to see this airship winging overhead, full of people who were going from one civilized place to another—passing over this primitive world but never seeing or understanding it. But I wouldn't have traded places with anyone aboard the plane.

January 13: *Between Nimule and Juba*

This morning we spotted a group of Baris across the river. They hid immediately, but Akim coaxed them out of hiding by shouting explanations of who we were. They shyly crossed over in two dugouts. Each of the women had a silver ring through her right nostril and wore a hide lappet edged with pale blue beads. I decided to break the ice by letting them inspect my Rolliflex camera. The oldest woman, smoking a fifteen-inch pipe, laughed so heartily at seeing André framed in the viewer that her high-pitched cackle brought the others crowding around for a peek.

Our lunch stop was next to a ten-foot termite nest that had enveloped the trunk of a sizable acacia so that the tree appeared to be afflicted with elephantiasis. And later on in the afternoon we spent an hour filming and visiting with twelve Bari fishermen who were on the way back to their village. Three of the men had grotesquely enlarged testicles—about the size of large mangoes. My guess is that this is a condition known as *hydrocele,* caused by an infection from parasitic worms.

Included in their catch were several twenty- to thirty-pound specimens of African lungfish. This amazing eel-like relic of the Paleozoic Era weighs up to 100 pounds and is a voracious predator that feeds on any kind of aquatic life, including members of its own kind and even full-grown ducks. Its four long, pointed pectoral and pelvic fins serve as limbs for propelling itself along the bottom of a lake or river and give it support when at rest. Fish absorb oxygen from the water flowing over their gills, but the lungfish has both gills and a primitive lung, by means of which it is able to breathe atmospheric air.

During dry seasons or droughts, lungfish burrow deep into the mud, form a leathery cocoon around themselves, leaving a few holes for air, and then curl up with their tails over their eyes to prevent loss of moisture. There they estivate until the water returns, living off stored fat and muscle tissue. In this way lungfish have been known to live for as many as four years out of water.

This afternoon André and I agreed that for the sake of variety and the possibility of seeing white rhino, we should cross over the Nile and travel on the other side for part of our trek. We were able to do this when we met two fishermen who were pleased to be able to ferry us in their dugout across the Nile to the west bank.

January 14: *Between Nimule and Juba*

Today was the hottest day of all. The heat seemed to have physical consistency, like fiery fog. My heavy hat was necessary, but it caused a steady flow

The Driver Ant

The highly carnivorous driver ants are the most feared
insects of Africa. Every living creature, from fleas to
humans, is potential prey to them. They can goad even
an elephant into a panicky dash for the nearest water
when they swarm into his trunk; and they can envelope
and consume a large python that has been rendered
helpless from eating an antelope or a pig.

A colony of the ants is composed of the queen, a few
male drones, female workers (the majority), and the
dangerous soldiers. More than half an inch long and
rapacious, the fearless soldiers function as hunters and as
protectors of the colony. Though they are blind, their
sensitive antennae can detect a potential threat or a meal
several yards away. The drivers live in underground nests
three or four yards wide, where the queen lays at least
100,000 eggs every twenty-four hours. In a month the
eggs hatch, triggering a mass migration to a new
settlement—usually within a mile from the old one—
where the process is repeated. Once a new camp is
created, the soldiers lead the workers on a reconnaissance
of their surroundings in search of food, moving in long
columns three or four inches wide. These hunting parties
attack and eat everything they can overwhelm (which
may even include crippled humans), first assaulting the
eyes so that their victims are blinded and unable to find
an escape. Once a prey is killed, some of the smaller
workers transport it back to the nest in small chunks
while the rest of the column continues its hunt.

of hot sweat to stream into my eyes and down my cheeks. I marched along at a steady pace, André following a few yards behind, and the bearers stepping along behind him. My body felt drained of energy, but my eyes and mind still responded to the abundant life stirred up by our passing: many vervet and blue monkeys and a lovely little bush duiker, a species of antelope only two feet tall with a pair of tiny horns, which shyly darted across the trail ahead of us and vanished in the dry grass the same color as its tawny coat.

One of the most painful episodes of the continuing battle between us and the insects, which they persist in winning, was an attack today while we were eating our lunch. A column of driver ants descended on us without warning, racing up our bare legs and biting us with their sharp, hooklike mandibles. We hopped around in a frenzy, trying to brush them off, but there was no defense against their numbers—we grabbed our loads and evacuated the area.

We passed more rapids today that would have been unmanageable in *any* kind of boat. And there were many fresh lion tracks along the banks. The beauty of a flock of green lovebirds with red heads took our minds off our miseries for a moment. This is a land of incredibly beautiful birds. One dramatic species was the Abyssinian roller, with wings of vivid blue that glowed in the sun and with two long, antenna-like tail feathers.

We noticed a colony of ants that had enveloped a ball of elephant dung with a thin layer of mud and were living just below the surface. "That's one way to beat the heat," I thought.

André has been an enjoyable companion on the trip. He can be impractical and forgetful at times, but his even and cheerful disposition more than makes up for any of his shortcomings. He is an inspiration in a tight situation or when the going is rough.

I can't remember ever feeling so utterly weary or yearning more for rest. I have had just two attacks of malaria during the trek, each lasting only about an hour, and they have come at night so they haven't delayed us. But it's difficult to distinguish between the symptoms caused by the infection and the normal physical reactions to this environment. Is the fever sapping my strength, diminishing my appetite, and giving me a splitting headache and rapid pulse? Or is it merely the effects of hiking twenty miles through rough country in temperatures that reach 110 degrees in the shade?

But at least my hand is almost healed. Last Wednesday I picked up a branch from an overhanging acacia tree that had fallen across the trail, blocking our way. When I tossed it aside, a thorn snagged my hand, paralyzing three fingers in my left hand as it drove deep into my knuckle. The hand has been so numb and tender that I haven't been able to use it normally for three days. But penicillin ointment and nightly soakings in hot Epsom salts have healed the puncture and restored feeling.

January 15: *Between Nimule and Juba*

We were awakened just before dawn by the cacklings and high-pitched shriekings of a hyena, one of the most chilling sounds in the animal kingdom, particularly when it jolts you from a deep sleep and is the first thing that penetrates your consciousness—even worse than the scream of a fire engine siren. Normally they avoid men, but when pressed by extreme hunger they have been known to attack humans sleeping in the open. And their attack is something to be avoided—their jaws are the strongest in the animal kingdom, able to crack an elephant's thighbone. Knowing this made it impossible for me to go back to sleep.

But I was in bad shape today, and it was an effort even to get out of the sleeping bag and into my clothes. All day I stumbled along in a daze, feverish, weak, and uncoordinated—barely able to keep up with the others. My head seemed to be detached from my body, floating above it.

During the afternoon we detoured around impregnable bush and tramped over a dry river bottom for a mile to return to the Nile. The glare and heat from the dazzling sand gave me the blind staggers and all but put me out of commission. At one point I found myself on my hands and knees in the sand, wondering who had bashed me with a baseball bat. I knelt there in a stupor, staring at my retreating companions as they threaded Indian file into the tall grass on the opposite bank. Stumbling along after them, I finally caught up as the remarkable conical hill of Rejaf loomed in the distance—a heartening landmark, since it is only thirty miles from Juba.

Since our food supplies were almost used up, we decided to test the hospitality of a Catholic mission across the river from the village of Rejaf. We crossed over in a pirogue at dusk and were landed upstream two miles from the mission. I was feeling so woozy that I started off immediately, while I still had strength to make it; André waited for the bearers, who had yet to be ferried over.

I don't remember much about the next hour except that I plowed along through almost impenetrable reeds, groping my way in the dark until I finally hit the sandy road leading to the mission and soon arrived, only to find everything dark. The first person I met at the mission was a Bari altar boy, who, after recovering his composure, led me to a room lit only by a candle, where I collapsed in a canvas chair with my pulse pounding in my head as the boy went to fetch the father.

After I waited for what seemed an age, my thirst was unbearable. And on a wooden table in the center of the room was a single place setting for dinner. In a pottery vessel beside the plate was fresh, cool limeade, and I shamelessly drained the entire contents—more than a pint. I felt guilty—but it was the most delicious drink I had ever tasted.

Suddenly the room brightened as my host, a young priest, stepped through the doorway carrying a kerosene lamp. He was an Italian from Naples named Father Paolo. Communication was difficult—I was in no state to be bilingual, and he spoke no English. But he shared his supper with me, and I recalled enough of my Italian to answer his stream of questions about who I was and what had brought me to his remote doorstep. I was so giddy that I committed the *faux pas* of inquiring whether the good father was married and had children. He passed it off with a laugh, apparently understanding that I was *non compos mentis.*

André and the Africans soon appeared, and since Father Paolo provided two empty rooms for our use, we were spared having to set up the tent.

January 16: *Between Nimule and Juba*

I felt weak but much improved as we set off from the mission early this morning. During the day we tramped past several Bari villages, ranging in size from a cluster of a dozen round huts to one of about fifty. Each settlement was surrounded by a field of pearl millet that towered over our heads. This tall grass produces a cereal that is ground up and made into Africa's most important bread, a thick, pliable porridge that is usually eaten dipped into a spicy stew.

The people, all Baris, were once a pastoral people, but Arab slavers in the nineteenth century forced them into agriculture. They have no single chief; instead local clan heads, rainmakers, sorcerers, wealthy men, and hereditary ritual officials lead them. At one village I was pleasantly surprised to find two girls willing to let me photograph them. They were bathing in the Nile, wearing small leather aprons, and they ignored me completely as they finished their toilette and returned to their huts.

It was a pleasant change to have the life of the village flow on without interruption as we passed through—usually everything came to a stop when we arrived as the villagers made much of our arrival. This time we were able to see normal life in progress, as the women carried out domestic work while the men were away hunting and fishing. They labored at hauling water or pounding millet and sorghum into powder by jamming a wooden pestle into hollowed-out spaces on the tops of logs. The women all wore a white splinter of ivory protruding from a perforation in their upper lip that jiggled erratically whenever they talked.

Beside each hut were several wicker and clay storage containers mounted on platforms and surrounded by piles of thorn bush to keep out predators. These vessels contained the staples of their diet: millet, sorghum, manioc, lentils, and peanuts.[23]

At the beckoning of an old gentleman, I stepped into a hut to sit for a few minutes as he delivered a lengthy monologue, undeterred by the fact that I couldn't understand a word of what he said. The hut was typically African in construction—a round structure built of sturdy branches and wattle plastered with mud. Its rain-proof thatching covering the roof consisted of a dozen neatly trimmed overlapping layers of grass. We sat on a smooth clay floor next to the cooking area with depressions of various sizes and shapes molded into the surface for holding food and utensils, and with soot-covered pottery pots and calabashes lined up against the wall. The air was pungent with the smells of smoke, fish, and perspiration.

Spears, hoes, digging sticks, and a fish net were stored on a shelf of branches above our heads. Opposite the kitchen and partitioned off from it was a single bed, consisting of a stretched hide resting on a log frame and covered with cut stalks of dried papyrus.

After I rejoined André and the others, we followed the broadest and best-defined trail we had seen since leaving Nimule. In the distance we could see billows of gray smoke from a rapidly expanding grass fire that had probably been started by Baris. These uncontrolled fires not only cause serious destruction of living trees and other vegetation, but they also kill wild life and occasionally even incinerate people.[24] Africans set the fires because they clear off excess vegetation, fertilize the ground with ash so the grass grows well the next year for their cattle, make hunting and traveling easier, and reduce insect pests—particularly the hated tsetse fly.

We had no choice but to pass right through the blaze, and Akim led us, picking his way along unburned areas. We hurried along, gasping and cough-

23. For those who still harbor the belief that the Negro is an intellectually inferior race and has never been able to make significant achievements without external help, it is worth mentioning that agriculture was developed independent of other races more than 5,000 years ago by the Negroes of West Africa in what is now known as Mali. They developed cultivated plants that have been and continue to be of monumental importance to all humanity, including cotton (*Gossypium herbaceum*), the leading textile crop, sorghum, among the top four cereal grains of the world, and sesame (*Sesamum indicum*), the world's principal oil plant and oldest herb.

24. An official at Juba told us that in December a small village had been overwhelmed by a grass fire and all its inhabitants burned to death.

ing from the acrid smoke, while flames crackled around us and fiery debris rained down, searing our skin and clothing. We soon emerged into clearer air and continued through a blackened landscape that steamed and smoldered in the brassy, smoke-filtered sunlight.

Late in the afternoon of this, our eighth day afoot, we stumbled into the outskirts of Juba. We were soot-stained from head to blistered toes, feverish with malaria, and our eyes were bloodshot and ringed in dark circles, our lips cracked, our beards scraggly and tangled, and our bare legs like raw hamburger from the lacerating thorns and saw grass. "Our own mothers wouldn't recognize us," said André.

We headed straight for Jim Dodson's house, paid off Akim, Ogone, and Sabi, and thanked them for their staunch and loyal service. Then André and I flipped a coin to see who would use the bathtub first. I won, and proceeded to enjoy the most sensually satisfying bath of my life, despite the sting from the multiple abrasions all over my body.

André and I had barely the strength to get dressed after our baths. Jim Dodson had arranged a special dinner to celebrate our successful trek, but we had no appetite and only picked at our food. Later in the evening we began feeling very sick. It was as though our bodies had been able to postpone the worst symptoms of our malaria until we had completed our foot safari and had reached our goal of Juba, where we could properly collapse. And collapse we did–right into our beds. Jim quickly summoned Dr. Obbid, who did what he could to reduce our fevers and sooth our agonizing headaches.

During the night I awoke in a panic, desperately gasping for air, with a feeling of being slowly suffocated under a great weight. Jim, sleeping in the next room, was wakened by my strangled breathing and came to sit beside the bed until the spasm eased off.

I was so weak I couldn't turn over or lift my head from the straw pillow. A terrible fear gripped me that if I went to sleep again, I would stop breathing completely. Finally, unable to fight off sleep any longer and comforted by Jim's presence, I drifted off into merciful slumber.

January 25: *In Juba*

For several days I was held captive in bed, flat on my back. Luckily André's symptoms were milder, and he was able to get back on his feet sooner than I did. Dr. Obbid stopped by every morning and evening to minister to us–but in the end he refused, with great dignity, any compensation for all his able ministrations as he said, "It was an honor to treat such unfearing explorers."

The Nilotic Tribes

No pure racial strains have been
preserved in Sudan. Racial
interbreeding has occurred for
millenia, and the tribes of the
south are not true Negroes but
merely Negroid, possessing
Hamitic and Semitic genes in
various proportions* During our
expedition we saw many
individuals with fine, almost
Grecian features—thin lips,
delicately molded noses, and high
cheekbones, attesting to this
ancestral intermingling.
Of the three major Nilotic tribes
in the Negro-dominated southern
Sudan—the Dinka, the Nuer, and
the Shilluk—the tall, slender, long-
headed Dinka, numbering more
than 1,000,000 is the largest. In
fact, it is the most numerous and
occupies a larger area of any ethnic
group of the southern Sudan. Like
the Nuer, who resemble them
closely in physical characteristics,
language, and customs, but who
have only half their population,
they are one of the tallest,
slimmest, and most dark-
complexioned of all races.

*See page 125 and following.

The Dinka, called "the blackest people of Africa," are composed of a number of independent tribes of between 1,000 and 30,000 persons, grouped on the basis of shared regional, linguistic, and cultural characteristics. These proud, dignified people are transhumant pastoralists, or seminomadic cattle raisers, grazing their extensive herds in pastures along the Nile during the December to April dry season. With the arrival of the rainy season, when the grazing lands and their temporary camps are inundated, they drive the cattle back to their permanent villages in the savanna forest. Here they grow millet, their most important food, and other crops.

Each Dinka tribe is fragmented into patrilineal, exogamous, and totemic clans that function with considerable autonomy. By tradition certain specific clans supply the spiritual leaders of the tribes, the priest-chiefs or "masters of the fishing spear," whose authority is verified by elaborate myth.

"Well, sorry to disillusion you," I said, "but I must confess that during the past three months I've experienced some of the most intense fear of my life!"

While André and I were recuperating, Jean, a skilled draftsman, had been able to help Jim with several of his engineering blueprints. Since the indispensable sections of the kayak still had not arrived from Paris, André and I had extra time to regain our strength and sightsee around Juba, which was spread out over an area far out of proportion to its population of only 12,000.

One of the sights was the government building, which looked for all the world like an oldtime hotel from the American West. Two poles side by side on the roof flew the British Union Jack and the Egyptian green-with-white-crescent flag, symbolizing the joint rule of Anglo-Egyptian Sudan.[25]

The most interesting aspects of Juba, however, were the people, particularly in the teeming marketplace. Here we happily mingled, shook hands, and bartered with individuals of half a dozen different Sudanese tribes, including one of the three main Nilotic tribes, the Nuer. While studying anthropology at the University of Southern California, I had done research on these fascinating cattle-raising, marsh-dwelling people and had been eager to visit them ever since. Now there were several Nuer men before us—tall, lean giants wearing short cloth togas rather than appear in their usual total nakedness in a "foreign" marketplace. As I watched, one of the men raised one leg and rested his foot alongside the knee of his other leg, and, balancing himself with a spear, relaxed comfortably in the way that gave the Nuers the title "stork men of the Nile."

In the market we also bought some food staples to help replenish Jim Dodson's larder, which he had been emptying for us for several weeks. In Kenya and Uganda the merchants had been dominated by Indians; here in Juba the storekeepers were either Arabs or mustachioed Greeks, and the conversational Swahili I had labored so diligently to develop was now useless, since Arabic is the official and most commonly spoken tongue in Sudan and Egypt.

January 26: *In Juba*

Our host, Jim Dodson, left today for a three-month vacation in South Africa. We said farewell to this kind and generous man with genuine regret.

---

25. This hybrid form of government was established by Lord Cromer of Britain and the Egyptian Foreign Minister in 1899 in what was called the Condominium Agreement, after the joint Anglo-Egyptian conquest of the Sudan in 1898. This dualistic rule was mainly a legal technicality; in actual practice Britain was the major power, and from 1924 until 1956, the sole power, administering the country. In January 1956 the Sudan achieved complete independent nationhood, but at the time of our expedition the country was governed by a corps of 2,000 British Civil Servants.

During the rest of our stay in Juba we were made the guests of the airport personnel at their new club headquarters just a half mile from Jim's home.

January 28: *In Juba*

The long-awaited shipment of new kayak sections to repair André's damaged craft arrived today from Paris. We cleared them through customs and raced back to the club, where Jean, our genius with equipment, spread the parts out on the lawn for a minute inspection. Everything was intact, but unfortunately one of the most integral parts, a spar for the cockpit framework, was for the right rather than the left side. This mistake caused us to delay our departure another day while a carpenter from the Public Works Department manufactured a usable spar.

We looked forward to being back on the river, this time with three swift kayaks, unhampered by the slower, more ponderous dugout that had been our necessary companion for so many miles.

Nuer "storkmen."

The
Sudd

January 30: *Back on the Nile*

After a big party last night, which the governor of the province himself attended, we ended our month of landlubbing when we carried our kayaks down to the steamer dock, loaded our equipment aboard, and set them in the clear olive green water. The many kind British, Greek, and Sudanese friends we had made in Juba crowded around to see us off, and, sporting our expeditionary flags (from the Los Angeles Adventurers Club, the French Explorers Society, the Museum of Natural History, the Geographical Society, and the Touring Club of France), we shoved off into the current. Our friends had filled every available space on our kayaks with gifts of fresh fruit, chocolate, and tins of tea biscuits, and they shouted "bon voyage!" A throng of excited and curious Baris lined the bank and chattered and giggled as we floated past, for they had never seen the likes of us or our tiny boats before.

It was stimulating to be back on the river again, headed toward our goal, the mouth of the Nile, which was still 3,000 miles away.

The winding river channel constantly fluctuated in width, at times narrowing to only about fifty yards, then in other places ballooning to over three hundred. The high clay banks were lined with thick grass and reeds.

Because it was the dry season, the river was often so shallow that we scraped the bottom and had to get out and drag our kayaks to deeper water, watching carefully for crocodiles as we splashed along. André had a scary experience when, as he was passing over a submerged bar, his paddle scraping the sandy bottom, his kayak was jolted with such force that he was bounced into the air and nearly thrown into the river. The boat heeled over and began to fill with water; and when he finally got it righted, another savage blow tossed him to the other side.

Through all of this there wasn't a sign of his attacker; not a ripple marred the surface. We concluded that it had to be a crocodile lying on the bottom, which André had bumped and aroused. Luckily, it couldn't have been a large one. A fully grown adult, with one blow of its powerful tail, could have blasted André completely out of the water, with possible fatal consequences.

As if to make up for the long time we had been out of their reach, the hippos produced a nightmarish surprise for us just as dusk approached. Paddling together in close formation, following the winding channel past islands and sandbars, we swept around a narrow bend and spotted ten hippos in midstream. Immediately alert, they grunted nervously and faced us. We couldn't stop or change course; the current was too strong. Landing was impossible; the reeds were too thick on the bank, and the island to our left was rank with growth.

One bull added to our mounting tension by an ostentatious territorial display, throwing his massive head around and baring his deadly curving tusks in a great yawn that threatened to split his jaws. It left no doubt as to his intentions if we should intrude on his domain. We backpaddled strongly, but that only delayed the inevitable. We drew closer to the herd with each pounding heartbeat. There was only one possible course of action: to go forward and pray we could run the blockade safely.

I shot forward on the current, steering as closely as possible to the right bank. The hippos became more agitated as I approached, ramming their broad muzzles in and out of the water with stentorian snorts of anger. I maneuvered with slow, gentle strokes of the paddles to keep heading in the right direction with the least movement possible. I had the strongest feeling that a sudden move or loud sound would trigger a mass charge from the herd that would have pulverized me and my kayak on the spot.

The current increased in speed as I drew abreast of the hippos nearest me. This was the break I needed. It allowed me to sit virtually motionless, every nerve tingling, until I was swept beyond the herd, where I came alive and paddled furiously to safe waters. I parked in the reeds to watch my companions' progress.

While my passage was distracting the herd, Jean had seized the chance to advance on the left side, staying close to the island. As the herd turned toward him, his kayak grounded sickeningly on a sand bar less than fifteen yards away from two of the largest hippos. Despite their menacing proximity and intensified gruntings, Jean jumped out, dragged the boat free, clambered back into the cockpit, and then began paddling faster than I had ever seen him, scraping the riverbottom with each frantic stroke.

André, hunched over his paddle, sped close behind in Jean's foaming wake, doing his best to escape without antagonizing the herd any further. He later reported that he was praying to God, the Virgin Mary, and all the saints to protect him as he raced after Jean.

But all of us passed through without being attacked, and it occurred to me that the great animals might have been just as frightened and intimidated by the confrontation as we were.

Finding no landing, we paddled on after dark until drums guided us to a Mondari village near a settlement called Mongalla. Here we camped for the night, utterly spent after our first strenuous paddle in almost a month.

January 31: *Between Juba and Bor*

An overcast sky shielded us from the sun's rays during the morning, but by noon it had dispersed, allowing the sun to beat down on us. It is amazing how well the human body can acclimate to extremes of temperature and weather. We have become so conditioned to heat that the temperature has to hit at least 105 degrees Fahrenheit before we are really distressed. Being very fairskinned from my Anglo-Scandinavian heritage, I used to joke, "I don't tan; I stroke." But three months of exposure to tropical sun have given me a rich mahogany color, deeper than any tan I ever thought possible for me.

Every time we round a bend, the crocodiles on the banks, startled at our sudden appearance, come alive, a great slithering mass plunging into the water. They execute spectacular dives from their sunning positions six or eight feet above the water, and some actually perform a somersault in midair, landing with a mighty splash on their horny backs. It was a thrill to see four crocodiles, each about eight feet in length, launch themselves off a high bank and splash into the water in almost perfect unison, like a superbly trained circus act.

An hour later as I was quietly paddling alone near the west bank, scanning the shores for birds and other wildlife, I heard a commotion in a thicket on a high bank just ahead. Seconds later I was horrified to look up and see a ten-foot crocodile, its fanged jaws slightly open, bursting out of the greenery. Without a moment's hesitation it leaped off the bank toward me—but smashed explosively into the water a scant yard away, drenching me completely. The river was so shallow he barely had room to scrape under the hull, so that in squeezing past he raised the kayak part way out of the water, and I could feel the hard serrations of his back on my bare feet.

After my heartbeat returned to normal, I realized that the crocodile had merely been startled by my coming and, following instinct, had plunged into the river. Luckily he didn't overshoot his target, or I might have had ten feet of frantic crocodile in my lap. Anyway, I have been cured of paddling too near the shore.

We made a lunch stop at a Mondari village, which seemed deserted until we found everyone gathered in a long, open-air council hall, where the chief and his noblemen were holding court. Three young warriors, wearing nothing but head and arm ornaments, were heatedly presenting their cases for judgment but all speaking at the same time. It was a colorful sight—a tightly packed audience of about a hundred Mondaris, squatting shoulder to shoulder as they raptly followed the proceedings between the litigants standing before them and the dignified elder statesmen seated on wood and hide seats. They paid us little attention, and after we had watched for a time, we returned to the river.

We had some fun on the river below the village when we discovered an acoustical phenomenon: any sound was amplified and bounced around in a triple echo. We had a grand time yodeling and warbling operatic arias, our vocalizing sounding as if it were coming from a vast echo chamber. It was infinitely superior to singing in a shower, although we probably scared the wildlife for miles around.

A little later, Jean and I passed two hippos with no trouble from either one, but André, lagging behind, was forced to paddle for his life when they suddenly charged him. When he caught up with us, breathless and sweaty, he laughed it off with a wry, "I didn't think my singing was that bad!"

We saw incredible numbers of hippopotamuses and crocodiles today. It was reminiscent of Murchison Falls, with dozens of crocs of all sizes sunning on the sandy beaches and hippos, almost constantly in view, strung out along the Nile in one herd after another.

We arrived at a Dinka village just before sunset, and there a teenager named Juak welcomed us as we unloaded and set up camp. He had learned some English at a Protestant mission, and he told us that the people were in mourning over a double tragedy. Just a few days apart, a warrior and a young boy had been snatched away by crocodiles while they were bathing in shallow water near the village.

We bought a long, eel-like fish that had been speared with the Dinkas' favorite weapon, a twelve-foot lance. While André cooked dinner, several other fishermen stopped by to offer us their catches, which included a boy-sized Nile perch that must have weighed forty pounds, but we had more than enough with the fish we had already bought. As we ate, a circle of twenty Dinka men, following their tribe's timeworn fashion of strict nudity, gathered around us as we ate before our fire, curiously eyeing our every move. Most of them were plastered from head to foot with fine wood ash as a protection against mosquitoes. They looked like tall grey spectres in the flickering light of the bonfire. But by the time we finished our meal, they had all drifted off without a sound.

Tonight we slept on top of our sleeping bags–the night was too humid to sleep inside them.

February 1: *Between Juba and Bor*

The Dinka men and boys turned out to see us off in the morning, standing entrenched along the bank in a long row of gangly humanity. A headwind hampered our progress most of the day, but it also kept away the usual hordes of mosquitoes and small black flies that had been tormenting us.

We came upon one sand bar, submerged in shallow water, where a dozen or more crocodiles rested quietly, only their eyes, nostrils, and back-plates protruding above the surface. They burst into activity as we neared them, churning the water to froth as they rushed away. One big fellow set our kayaks rocking violently with the waves created by his strenuous efforts to reach deep water, his heavy body ploughing through the shallows in a series of curious lunges. When surprised on land or in shallow water they seem timid enough– but let them catch you swimming or capsizing, and it's an entirely different story!

We camped near another Dinka village tonight, and though the night was alive with a seething fog of tiny humming vampires, we were able to take a leisurely bath in the Nile behind a protective croc-proof log barrier erected by the villagers. As we splashed around, women strolled down the banks to fill their water jars and to observe and comment on the three white strangers. It would have been fascinating to know what they were saying about us!

February 2: *Bor*

We landed at Bor this morning after only a three-hour stint at the paddles. Now that we weren't held back by a dugout, we had covered the hundred-plus miles from Juba in only three full days, the fastest progress we had made to date.

Bor is labeled prominently on maps of Africa, but consists only of a sprawling Dinka village, a steamer dock, and a small administrative headquarters with one British district commissioner, the only white man living between Juba and Bor, and a garrison of Sudanese soldiers. And when we found Major

Cummings, the commissioner, he was seriously ill with a virulent combination of malaria and amoebic dysentery. Judging from his emaciated appearance and fever-bright eyes, his proper place was in a hospital—yet he graciously insisted on getting out of bed to sit with us in his living room and ask about our experiences and plans.

He told us we had been fortunate to have survived the hippo charges during our voyage; Dinka hunters frequently had fatal run-ins with the animals. Just the day before, at a place on the Nile that we had paddled past within the hour a dugout bearing six Dinka hippo hunters had been smashed and sunk by a maddened hippo. Two men had been killed, one of them bitten nearly in half. Three other Dinkas drowned, and just one man survived to reach the riverbank alive. But the Dinkas accept disaster with such fatalistic resignation that the survivor, no doubt, would be off on another hippo hunt at his first opportunity, just as a motorist would return to driving after a major automobile accident.

The District Commissioner had discouraging news—a lengthy telegram from his superior, the governor of the Upper Nile Province, politely forbidding us to travel by kayak through the Sudd, the vast swamp that for 250 miles spreads over a clay plain from Bor to Lake No. Since ancient times the Sudd has obstructed travel and exploration.[26] The Nile in this region has no defined banks, but rather expands into lagoons and marshes clogged with gigantic masses of unstable floating islands of papyrus, reeds, and grass.[27]

The Sudd is the scene of constant change, as the rise or fall of the Nile changes its borders, as the wind and current shift the mass of vegetation from one place to another. Because the elevation drops by only inches every hundred miles, there is no strong force to cut a path through the floating islands, and they often clump together, blocking channels of open water. And if one happens to be caught between two such islands that are floating together, the effect is much the same as polar ice—the hull of any boat, from a kayak to a steamer, can be crushed.

---

26. Two Roman centurions discovered the Sudd nearly 2,000 years ago while on an exploratory mission for the Emperor Nero in search of the Nile's source. They were thwarted in their quest by this great watery wilderness, "of which the inhabitants knew not and despaired knowing the limits . . . marshes so oozy and so choked with grass that it was impossible to cross them, even by boat." Sir Samuel Baker was delayed by the Sudd for months during his expedition to the Sudan in 1869–70 even though he had a work force of as many as 1,600 men assigned to channel cutting.

27. Since 1957 the prolific South American water hyacinth has contributed to this huge glut of aquatic vegetation.

For a long time I had been fretting over the problem of penetrating the Sudd in our kayaks, but I felt we would be able to work it out somehow when we got there. The official refusal decisively settled the issue. And the District Commissioner attempted to console us by reminding us of a famous Sudd catastrophe we had read about in our research: Gessi, the Italian governor of the Bahr el Ghazal province in 1880, had set off by steamboat for Khartoum with three weeks of provisions. But after two weeks of arduous travel, the boat had covered less than sixty miles through the barriers of aquatic vegetation. The soldiers would laboriously hack a passage, enabling the vessel to advance a few miles, then another dense mass would block the way.

"The three Nileteers" (André in middle), about to depart from Juba in the southern Sudan.

Jonglei Canal Scheme

For many years a plan has been developing to
drain the Sudd swamps by diverting the
waters of the Bahr el Jebel through a huge
artificial canal. In 1975 Egypt and Sudan
agreed to jointly finance and construct a 200-
mile channel from Jonglei in the south due
north to the Nile at the mouth of the Sobat
River below Malakal. Called the Jonglei Canal
Scheme, this detour of the Nile's flow would
cut off the river's 300-mile tangent to the
west and thus would completely bypass the
vast sponge of the Sudd. A consortium of
French firms is working out the details of
constructing what would be the world's
largest canal. The dollar cost of the project is
estimated in the hundreds of millions, but the
water saved would provide irrigation to
millions of acres of sterile desert land in Egypt
and Sudan; and with the Sudd drained, the
land would then be available for farming and
pasturage. If the plan is successful, the Sudan
could become a breadbasket for other African
and Arab nations. But no one knows what the
ecological effects might be of so monumental
a project. The building of the canal would
have a catastrophic effect on the lives of the
people who live in and around the Sudd and
on all wild life abounding there. Some
scientists believe that draining the Sudd could

drastically affect the weather over a third of the million square miles of Sudan, Africa's largest country. The winds from the south flow over the Sudd, absorbing massive amounts of moisture, which is then delivered to the extensive farming areas of central Sudan in the form of rain. Draining the Sudd could dry up the wind and end the rains forever.

After losing half its water to seepage and evaporation in passing through the spongy Sudd, the enfeebled Bahr el Jebel is reinforced at Lake No by its largest left bank tributary, the Bahr el Ghazal (River of the Gazelle). This great river, flowing for 500 miles from southwestern Sudan, is also so depleted in its passage through the Sudd that only about a fourth of its volume survives to flow into the Bahr el Jebel. The two rivers merge at the western end of Lake No to become the Bahr el Abyad, or White Nile, which extends for 600 miles northward to the confluence of the Blue Nile at Khartoum.

Lake No is the remnant of an immense inland sea that once covered all the Sudd area but shriveled to its present small dimensions as its waters silted up or filled in with thick vegetation.

The group was faced with starvation and had to supplement rations with waterplants, which often made them violently ill. Then the steamboat ran out of fuel, so that the men had to resort to ropes and improvised paddles to move the heavy vessels through the narrow channels. After eleven endless weeks of nightmarish labor and suffering, they knew the end was near. In his journal for 20 December 1880, Gessi recorded:

"We have reached the worst. I cannot remember anything like it in all my life. Scarcely does someone die than he is devoured during the night by the survivors. It is impossible to describe the horrors of such scenes. One soldier ate his own son.

"Of the 149 Sudanese soldiers, except twelve whom I left in the slep and the nugger, only eight are alive, but they are in a desperate state. As to the women and children, I cannot at this moment give the exact number of dead, but I believe it is more than two hundred and seventy. . . . I am confident that with the new year my fate will change, having taken all possible measures to extricate myself from my present position, the worst I have known since I came into the world."

When the governor-general's rescue party arrived, Gessi and only three others were still alive.

After two years of great effort, workers finally forged through the Sudd in 1900 and used dynamite to break up some of the largest islands. In 1936, a steamer went astray in the Sudd, following a false channel to a dead end twenty miles down. Retracing his path, the captain discovered that the islands had closed behind him, and before rescuers could find them, the captain and twenty-two passengers and crew members had starved to death.

Steamer travel through the Sudd is usually safe enough today, but in kayaks, navigation would be hopeless; we would never be able to find our way through the intricate maze of channels, and we would find no solid ground for camping.[28] But the District Commissioner cheered us considerably when he said, "Don't worry, lads. You won't have to give up your trip through the Sudd. A steamer is due to be stopping here tomorrow afternoon, and you can ride it through the most dangerous areas, then continue from Lake No in your own boats."

---

28. An ambitious scheme to exploit Sudd papyrus for paper and fuel was inaugurated in 1912 by a group of British promoters, who envisioned a fortune in the prolific sedge. Unfortunately, the papyrus of the White Nile was of a different species than the plant of ancient Egypt, which was introduced from Abyssinia and Syria. Its fiber proved too coarse and porous, and finally, after four years of effort with mediocre results, they abandoned the project.

Major Cummings kindly arranged for us to have some lettuce, lemons, and grapefruit from his own garden, then invited us to use his guest house on the riverbank.

February 10: *Bor*

The steamer still didn't appear, and we began to wonder if it had been swallowed up by the Nile. Every afternoon Hussein, the Assistant District Commissioner, an educated Moslem from northern Sudan, cheerfully announced that the paddlewheeler was just about to arrive. Each time we scrambled around, gathering up and packing our equipment for a quick departure, only to stand on the banks straining to see the boat that never came.

Out of exasperation, Jean suggested that we defy officialdom and take off for Lake No on our own; but even if we were to get through successfully, our act of defiance would lead to serious consequences. We had to keep our hopes alive.

The wait proved really worthwhile. I was zonked by malaria again. But between attacks I visited some of the nearby Dinka villages and made copious notes on their activities.[29] Hussein spoke some of the complex Dinka language and was a great help as a translator and a font of information on the tribe.

February 12: *Bor*

Our long-awaited steamer, the *Rejaf,* finally arrived today. It had run aground near Mongalla, and the crew had been able to work it free only yesterday. We happily loaded our gear aboard, then said our farewells to the District Commissioner, Hussein, our Dinka friends, and the Arab merchants we had come to know. The D.C. was still sick in bed but gave us a farewell gift of fresh vegetables from his garden. I feel great sympathy and respect for this good man, who leads such a lonely existence far from his home and loved ones. He is able to visit his family in England only once a year, and his next leave isn't due for several months.

Captain Ahmed Aggad salaamed us aboard his antique steamer, a quaint double-decked, shallow-drafted paddlewheeler, which served as mother ship for four barges clustered around it. One was lashed to the port side and the other three were positioned around the prow, each one crammed with African pas-

---

29. Almost all of the Negroid tribes in the three provinces of the southern Sudan speak Sudanic languages, or dialects called Nilo-Hamitic, which have both Sudanic and Hamitic characteristics. The Dinka speak a language belonging to the Eastern Sudanic branch of the Chari-Nile subfamily of the Nilo-Saharan family.

Men of a Dinka village escort Goddard on a tour of their grazing land.

sengers, cargo, and bags of mail. Our quarters were located in the lead barge, where Jean was assigned a bunk in a single cabin and André and I were given another with two bunk beds—a cubicle so cramped that we couldn't both stand inside at the same time.

One look at the grimy sheets covering the straw mattresses sent us running for our sleeping bags. The Captain apologized for the poor accommodations, but assured us that we were lucky to be able to book passage with him at this time, since he would not be attempting another voyage through the Sudd until the rainy season because of the unusually low water.

So we would have been stranded at Bor for weeks if we hadn't been able to get aboard the *Rejaf.* That grim realization made the thought of the voyage more endurable—also the hordes of large cockroaches and ants that busily prospected over and around me in the cabin as I wrote this in my journal by the flickering light of a candle.

February 13: *In the Sudd (Our fourth month in Africa)*

It took our little flotilla twenty-three difficult hours to travel the first seventy miles through the Sudd to Shambe, where we stopped for a load of logs to fuel our boilers. Sometimes, I could reach out from our top deck and touch the tasselled heads of fifteen foot-tall papyruses. It was hard to tell land from floating island. Nothing seemed solid, and yet in the distance today I saw several elephants on what could only have been a grassy field of solid land.

We were forced to travel down a side channel all afternoon because the river proper was too low for navigation, and the tributary had a deeper bottom.

Stretching endlessly to the horizons around us were vast green forests of densely compacted papyruses rippling in the sunlight, with occasional lagoons of open water. Though papyrus dominated the marshes, there were also thick clusters of tall reeds; groves of ambatch—a shrub that grows up to sixteen feet, with pithy wood as light as cork, favored by Nilotic tribesmen for the building of rafts; and clumps of scraggly grass the Arabs call *um-soof* ("mother of wool"). Water lilies with bright yellow and blue blossoms floated on the surface of the still water, and endless clumps of water lettuce drifted on the sluggish current.

Several times during the day the barges crunched into the mass of vegetation on one side or the other of the narrow passage, stopping us with a sickening jerk that threw everyone off balance. Then the captain would run from one side of the boat to the other, sizing up the situation; he shouted his instructions to the nervous black helmsman. At the order "Full speed astern" the great paddlewheel reversed direction, churning up the stinking black ooze and thrashing papyrus and reeds to pulp as it backed us off into deep water. The little steamer shuddered violently and creaked from prow to stern as we pulled free. Then on we would go, creeping forward, until the next collision. I marveled that the ancient steamer and barges could absorb so many shocks, and I half expected the antiquated boiler to explode from the tremendous strain imposed on it.

February 14: *The Sudd*

Though it pained us to admit it, Jean, André, and I acknowledged that we would have become hopelessly lost had we attempted to kayak through the

Dinka hippo hunters.

134

Sudd on our own. Such a bewildering array of channels intersected with the main river and, at times, were indistinguishable from it, that we were often confused as to which way to proceed even though we had a broad view ahead from our high vantage point on the steamer's upper deck. We began to suspect that the Sudanese pilot, without benefit of a single map (maps here become outdated hourly), guided the ship through the labyrinth by means of ESP.

February 15: *The Sudd*

Finally, after three days of groping through the Sudd, we docked today in the early morning at a small wood stop near the eastern end of Lake No, where we left the *Rejaf* to continue in our kayaks. After a quick tour of the area, we loaded up and launched our boats into the dark green water. It was like being paroled from prison to be back on the water again, free to paddle quietly along at our own pace, away from the monotonous vibrations and noises of the thrashing paddlewheeler. We had an even hundred miles to cover to reach Malakal, the next major settlement. Heading eastward now, we skirted the marshy shoreline in single formation, drenched in sweat from paddling in the hothouse atmosphere.

I was eager to visit a Shilluk village, since Lake No is the southern boundary of the territory inhabited by these proud and handsome people. But there were no settlements near the water. We did come upon one lone fisherman wading in the shallows of a bay, a naked giant black as obsidian with a long fishing spear attached to his wrist by a cord. He silently moved along, hurling his spear at random with expert ease, a featureless shadow against the brilliant glare of the sunlit water. "If at first you don't succeed, try five or six hundred times again," I thought to myself as I watched him tirelessly probing the bay. It must be great to have so little concern about time that you can fish just by throwing a spear into the water hither and thither until you hit one! But I knew his patience would eventually be rewarded; the shallows teemed with bottom-loving catfish and lungfish, and I had seen Dinkas with big specimens they had harpooned using the same haphazard method.

By noon we had emerged from Lake No and were paddling due east on the White Nile. We moved along at a steady five knots, strung out over the water in our usual formation of me in the lead, André about a half-mile behind, and Jean a mile or two behind him. The Nile, exhausted from its passage through the Sudd, flowed sluggishly, its slight current of little help to our paddling.

I had a thrill today when I spotted a whale-headed or shoebill stork, one of the rarest and least known of all African birds. The giant bird, at least three and a half feet tall, was standing motionless on a muddy hummock and looked like a living relic from the ancient world.[30] I coasted to within a few yards before it saw me and showed alarm by loudly clacking its massive bill.

I managed to snap one photograph before it vanished into the reeds.

After the enforced vacation from kayaking, our muscles were sore and twitching with fatigue from the long day of paddling. The discomfort was trivial, however, because of the happiness and renewed sense of freedom that came from being on our own again on the Nile. At dusk the air cooled, and the pungent smell of swamp vegetation was actually pleasant. As the stars appeared, hordes of fireflies materialized—"the lanterns of the mosquitoes," as the Nuers call them. Hippo gruntings, the mournful cries of night birds, and the lapping of the Nile lulled us to sleep.

February 16: *Tonga*

This morning we arrived at Tonga, a government outpost, where we were welcomed by four genial Scottish Catholic priests who maintained a mission and elementary school for the local Shilluks. They let us store our gear in their guest house, and we spent the rest of the day and evening roving through the surrounding Shilluk communities.

At first the bands of children that followed us were shy; but I won them over with the magic Rolliflex, and soon they were posing delightedly and even staging a mock spear battle for the camera. The people wear togas of light brown or rust red cloth tied over the left shoulder. Their main tribal insignia is a neat row of scars shaped like little knobs on their foreheads. Many of the men wore the most elaborate coiffures we had ever seen on Africans, with a favorite headdress being two thick pancake-shaped mats of hair that bracket the head just above the ears; another favorite is a double pompadour pattern that projects stiffly from the crown and the back of the head like a giant coxcomb.

Shilluk men have their hair dressed before important events in their lives, such as courting a girl or presenting the bride-price to her father. The work is

---

30. The whale-head is an amusing caricature of a bird, called by the Arabs *Abu Markub* ("father of a slipper"). It has a grotesquely large head and bill. The head is capped by a rakish tuft of feathers, and the bill, which resembles a Dutch wooden shoe, is tipped with a formidable hook that secures any fish or turtle the bird might capture for food. The other physical features of this improbable creature are novel, too: large, yellow owl-like eyes, a thick neck, plump body, pearl-gray plumage, and unusually long toes, which enable it to tread on floating vegetation. Known to ornithologists as *Balaeniceps rex,* the silent and solitary bird has never been properly classified because of its confusing characteristics. The structure of its skull is similar to that of a pelican; its back feathers are heronlike, and other features of its anatomy resemble those of a stork.

done by the village barber, a highly respected personage whose profession is hereditary and second in importance only to cattle raising and fighting. Therefore he is able to charge the exorbitant price of a sheep or a goat for each barbering. The actual operation begins with the barber shaving half the customer's head, then shampooing the remaining hair with cow's urine, which washes out or kills most of the head lice. While the hair steams in the hot sun for a few minutes, the barber prepares a special pomade in a large clay bowl, pounding and stirring an exotic blend of black mud, gum arabic, cow manure, and wine into a thick paste.

This malodorous mixture is smeared onto the customer's head and kneaded into the warm, moist hair; then the desired coiffure is skillfully molded into shape before the hair dries out and hardens. The final touch is a dusting of cow manure and red ocher.

But the job isn't really complete until the customer attaches a black ostrich feather to the top of his hairdo. And because the headdress is so important and expensive, to keep it from being disarranged at night, the men must sleep in an awkward position, like Japanese Geishas, with their necks and the base of their heads resting on a hard wooden support.

At dusk we attended a lively village dance and had a grand time watching the local dandies—decked out in their best Sunday-go-to-meetin' leopard skins—performing strenuously to the exciting drumming of three talented and durable musicians. The brawny dancers, caked in wood ash and red ocher, looked formidable, and despite frequent refreshments of strong merissa beer, they never lost control. The party was still going full tilt when we left late at night to go to bed.

February 17: *Atar*

A strong headwind hindered us again today. The scenery was flat and Kansas-like, with mostly treeless plains. After we left Lake No, the thick papyrus gradually gave way to grass and reeds and occasional forests of small trees. We passed the Nile's second major tributary and subsidiary channel, the Bahr el Zeraf, or Giraffe River, flowing in from a lagoon on the right, its waters originating from the Bahr el Jebel almost 200 miles to the south. We covered thirty miles today despite the wind, and camped tonight at Atar, a quiet hamlet on the right bank.

February 18: *Atar to Malakal*

More headwinds. An hour after setting out I noticed some strange objects at a clearing on the left bank and stopped to check them out. They were the

The Shilluk King

To the people the king is not only a
ruling monarch but a sacred and
divine priest—the mystical
incarnation of *Nyikang,* the culture
hero and original founder of the
kingdom. The Shilluk do believe in a
Supreme Being, a Creator of all
things they call *Juok,* similar to the
Heavenly Father of Christianity. But
Nyikang is the complex, divine and
immortal, first king of the Shilluk, a
personage who is probably based on a
dimly remembered chief of long ago
who led his people from their original
home in East Africa, established them
in their present land, and ruled over
them as their first monarch.
Because the king personifies the
whole life and soul of the Shilluk, he
must keep himself pure and in good
health, for if he becomes ill or his
people experience adversity, he will be
suspected of losing his divine powers,
creating the danger of Nyikang's
abandoning his people.
If this happened, everything—
crops, cattle, and the people
themselves would sicken and die.
In the past, if a king displayed signs

of serious illness or senility, it was believed that he must be killed to preserve the tribe. Thus Shilluk kings generally died under violent circumstances, probably not by assassination, but more likely during a rebellion of discontented subjects led by a prince—heir to the kingship. In my studies on the Shilluk tribe at U.S.C. I became intrigued by the striking similarities between the characteristics and rule of their king and those of the pharoahs of ancient Egypt. These similarities include belief in the ruler's divinity, reverential awe of him (even intimates and relatives of the Shilluk king never look directly at him when in his presence), regarding a sacred stool as the symbol of office, the practice of marrying a sister or half-sister, and the separation of the kingdom into northern and southern divisions. It seems plausible to me that the Shilluk somehow borrowed many of their ideas about their religious monarchy from Egypt, through cultural dissemination up the Nile.

fresh carcasses of three nine- or ten-foot crocodiles apparently killed by local Shilluks, who speared them and left the bodies after taking the skins. I wanted to cut them open and examine the stomachs and see what they had been feeding on, but the stench and swarms of flies drove me back to the kayak.

Around noon we came to an important landmark on our long journey, the great Sobat River, its mouth forming a gap more than a hundred yards wide in the lush greenery of the right bank, twenty-seven miles downstream from the Bahr el Zeraf. The Sobat is the first of the three rivers from Ethiopia that feed the Nile 85 percent of the water it carries to Egypt. However, since this is the dry season, the Sobat made little difference in the current or color of the river; the waters of the White Nile actually back up the Sobat for several miles. During the rainy season, however, the Sobat swells mightily to a flow of up to 35,000 cubic feet per second, forcing back the White Nile to form a ponding

Two Dinkas ferrying across the Nile in an ambatch raft.

effect. And during the flood, the Sobat discolors the waters of the Nile with a milky-colored sediment that gave the White Nile its name, though geographers have assigned the name to the Nile all the way up to Lake No rather than beginning it at the Sobat confluence.

By sundown we had landed at Malakal, the capital of the Upper Nile Province and the largest town we had seen since leaving Lake Victoria, 1,672 miles upstream. It didn't take long for news of our arrival to spread through the small European community of twenty people, and the governor of the province, Herbert Longe, put us up for the night at the official rest house, an immaculate and large building with a neat thatched roof.

February 19: *Malakal*

A quiet day devoted to personal needs: laundry, letter-writing, and shopping. we cleaned our gear and the cameras and wrote in our journals. As André and I canvassed the open stalls for supplies in Malakal's open market, we saw half-clad Nilotic tribesmen in the midst of crowds of dark-skinned Moslems wearing white turbans and djellabahs—the first mingling of the Sudan's Arabs and Blacks we had seen. At four o'clock we had tea with the governor and his lady. Our khakis were rumpled but clean, and we wore our long pants for the first time in six weeks.

In the evening the District Commissioner's well-meaning wife had prepared what she called an American dinner: french fries (to Jean and André they were "American fries"), hamburgers, and apple pie. At least that's what she told us we were eating—they were unidentifiable to me. But I did appreciate the kind intention behind the meal and pretended a relish I didn't feel as I gulped down everything, much to the satisfaction of our beaming hosts.

February 20: *Malakal to Lul*

Governor Longe and the local Europeans saw us off this morning and Mrs. Longe gave us a real treat for a Bon Voyage present—two dozen oranges.

Throughout the day we fought against a really stiff northeaster, which whipped up the river into choppy and rough waves that bounced our kayaks up and down like rocking horses. For the first time Jean actually became seasick. The wind kept the heat down, but even though February is usually one of the hottest months of the year in this part of Africa, we would have much preferred the usual torrid weather to the tedious labor of stroking against wind and wave on the broad river.

I stopped to visit with four Dinka herdsmen camped at a back water in the flat eastern bank. One of the men could speak a little English and helped me add to my notebook of Dinka words and phrases. André arrived a few minutes later, and we shared two sandwiches he had brought from Malakal. We were preparing to shove off when the Dinkas grabbed hold of our kayaks and demanded we give them sandwiches, too. But we had only the two, and we had eaten them. They were not pacified even when André offered them some of our precious oranges.

We finally lost patience, pulling their hands off our boats and brushing past them so we could continue. Their rude behavior puzzled us. The Nilotic people often regard whites as somewhat inferior to themselves and may even pity us for the unfortunate paleness of our skins and our foolishness in wearing clothing in a land of constant warmth, but we had, until now, found them always civil.

The wind gradually abated during the afternoon. We passed several ambatch rafts near a Dinka village; on one of them a lad was ferrying a pair of calves across the river, their heads lashed to the stern of his ambatch with only their noses and mouths above water. I gave a silent prayer that he would make it across before the crocodiles came; I had noticed several during the day, sunning themselves on the flat banks.

I escorted him toward the west bank for a few minutes, then felt the need for more prayer: a Shilluk fisherman was wading in the water up to his knees, casting a net around him, blithely indifferent to the danger he was exposing himself to from crocodiles. Like most people of the Nile basin, whether black or Arab, the Shilluk are fatalistically resigned to tragedy and sudden death, accepting it as a foreordained destiny over which they have no control. When a Nilote is killed by a hippo during a hunt or snatched away by a crocodile while fishing, his friends and relatives might even joke about the calamity, regarding it as a comical happening, much as a modern might look upon someone slipping on a banana peel and taking a pratfall. Certainly they wouldn't hesitate to return to the scene of the death to continue the same activity.

We paddled on to Lul, which we reached after dark. We were taken in by two Catholic priests, Father Teriele, a merry-eyed Dutchman, and Father Granger, an Englishman. They fed us a dinner of bully beef, rice, and bread, then showed us to three separate cubicles, where we slept on rope beds—thin strands of woven rope stretched across a wooden frame. It was austere, but much better than the hard ground, and I dropped off in less than five minutes.

February 21: *Lul to Kodok*

As Father Granger showed us around the mission this morning, we came to a row of small brick huts behind the chapel. He startled us when, with an impish grin, he announced, "This is where my widows live!" He explained that the Shilluk practice the institution of the levirate, the ancient Jewish custom of giving a widow, upon the death of her husband, to her husband's brother or uncle as part of her husband's estate. Sometimes a widow rebels, and the fathers give such women sanctuary at the mission, at least "until the pressure wears off or until I can find them acceptable husbands, preferably Christian." But when we met some of the aged and toothless rebels, I doubted any of them had much hope of attracting a husband, Christian or pagan.

The river has widened considerably since we left Malakal, in places reaching 1,000 yards from Dinka land on the east bank to Shilluk territory on the west. But the elevation drops only thirty feet in the 500 miles from Malakal to Khartoum, and so the current is little help to us—the headwinds are much stronger, sometimes forcing us into the dense papyrus and um-soof grass bordering the river.

Bird life was abundant and colorful throughout the day and more than compensated for the monotony of the deserted landscape. There were birds of every conceivable color, size, and shape—some flying low with the wind, others perched in acacia trees near the water or congregated in cozy togetherness on sandy banks, mud bars, and at the mouths of dry wadis. Many of them were transients, having made long migrations from far-off homelands in winter-bound Europe or Asia. They varied in appearance from the stilt-legged and gawky storks to the little trim, stubby-legged terns. Some birds had beaks that curved upwards, like the dainty bill of the avocet, others that turned downwards, like that of the hadada ibis. The sight of each new species lifted my spirits and distracted my attention from the aches and pains of hard paddling. Imprisoned as I was on the heaving river in my cramped kayak, fingers fused to the hot aluminum paddle, and thrashing along at a snail's pace, how I envied them their freedom.

Besides the beautiful birds, the only other wildlife I saw today was a puff adder, one of Africa's deadliest snakes. It was late afternoon, and the wind had slackened somewhat when I saw the snake struggling desperately in the choppy waves, trying to reach the far-off western shore. I could see it was exhausted and in danger of drowning, and my lifelong affection for reptiles asserted itself. There were no settlements nearby, and so I decided to lend it a helping hand. I scooped up the heavy-bodied reptile on my paddle and deposited it on the prow of the tossing kayak, then headed for the opposite bank to release it there. What seemed to be an uneventful rescue suddenly turned into a dangerous predicament. As I was working the paddle blade under the adder to ease it into the water next to the rank papyrus bordering the shore, a sudden

A Shilluk village near Kodok. Note the doum palm behind the tukls—the only palm tree in the world that has branches instead of a single trunk.

swell lifted the prow high, throwing me off balance. At the same time a capricious wave slapped into the shell broadside, flipping it completely over—and throwing me into the river with the snake.

Fear lent speed to my reaction. I scrambled out of the water in a flash and clung to the hull of the overturned boat. For a few moments I couldn't see the snake anywhere; then I saw him swimming frantically against the waves but being swept toward the papyrus and safety. I let the billows carry me along until I reached solid footing, where I emptied the water from my kayak, righted it, and continued downstream.

We reached the historic hamlet of Kodok, once known as Fashoda, where Mrs. Blashford, wife of the District Commissioner, greeted us. She explained that her husband had left that morning to investigate a clash between the Shilluks and the Dinkas. Some Shilluk herders had surprised two Dinkas in the act of rustling several head of their cattle. The Shilluks organized a war expedition and marched to the village of the would-be thieves, where they found every able-bodied warrior armed and ready to defend their erring tribesmen. In the battle that followed, some twenty-six people were killed.[31]

As we ate dinner with Mrs. Blashford, she described the loneliness of living in such an isolated place as Kodok, where the nearest white woman lived forty miles away at Malakal, and the only neighbors were tribal villagers who spoke another language. Understandably she longed to return to a more normal life among friends and relatives in England.

We slept fitfully in a Shilluk tukl, a bare mud and grass hut; but not before hiking a mile to watch an ecstatic moon dance staged by the unmarried young adults of a Shilluk village.

February 22: *Kodok*

Kodok is the capital of the Shilluk people, and I spent the day among them. The 150,000 Shilluks live in more than 100 villages strung out through the territory on the left bank of the Nile for 250 miles and extending 60 miles inland. They have been less isolated than the Nuer and Dinka and have had broader contacts with the north; as a result their culture is more highly developed, to the point of becoming the most complex social organization along the Nile, with six social classes headed by a highly revered divine king, called

---

31. Intertribal warfare was once common and widespread in the Sudan. In recent years the government has largely been effective in curbing these conflicts—until the bloody seventeen-year civil war between Arab northerners and southern blacks, in which more than 500,000 Sudanese died either violently or from famine and disease brought on by the fighting. Since 1972, when a peace treaty was signed, any fighting that has broken out has been primarily over cattle raiding and disagreements over pasturage.

Reth. André and Jean were particularly interested in Fashoda because it was here that in 1898 the famous "Fashoda crisis" occurred.

I reached the village at dawn just as the breakfast fires were being lighted and enlisted two teenagers, Atei and Jir, as translators and bearers. Typical of Shilluk villages, this one was composed of a cluster of hamlets, each with a number of individual homesteads. The usual homestead consists of several tukls enclosed within walls of woven grass and occupied by a polygamous family. Each wife has her own tukl; other huts serve as kitchens or housing for children and relatives. Everything was immaculately clean, and some of the tukls were works of art, with decorative ridges in the thatch and fine workmanship throughout.

The ordinary pursuits of Shilluk life flowed around us as we strolled around the community. After eating a light breakfast, some women left the village to fill their water crocks at the river; others went in the opposite direction to cultivate their sorghum, millet, cowpeas, and melons. Some of the men followed them soon, since both sexes work in the fields. Another group of men headed out carrying spears and neat bundles of nets for a day of hunting and fishing, an exclusive male occupation.[32] Other men and boys left to milk and perform other chores with the cattle. In common with all Nilotic peoples, the Shilluk devote much time to their livestock and equate a man's wealth and social status with the size of his herd. Cattle are used in the payment of fines and for bride-price.[33] But the Shilluk do not revere their cattle as the Dinka and Nuer do—nor do they follow the Dinka and Nuer practice of bleeding their cattle in order to drink the blood.

I had the bejabbers scared out of me just after Atei and Jir had departed. A procession of about two dozen warriors came marching by, led by two who pranced and leaped around. Each man carried a long spear in his right hand, and a big hippo-hide shield in his left. I filmed them as they swept past; then they suddenly wheeled around and headed back toward me. When they were a few yards away, they abruptly broke ranks and spread out, crouching down

---

32. With their tall frames, long legs, and muscular physiques, the Shilluk men are ideally equipped for hunting. They fearlessly go after every type of game from hippo (I saw one tree in the village festooned with long strips of drying hippo meat) to elephant. One of their favorite techniques is to surround an animal, then race in and, with powerful launches of their spears, kill it on the run. Most of the men we saw at the dance owned their own leopard-skin costumes from animals they had speared to death.

33. Bride-price is a much misunderstood institution. Widespread through black Africa, it does not imply the purchase of a wife but is a marriage payment or dowry paid by a woman's suitor or his family to her father to compensate him for the loss of a daughter. The payment of bride-price also establishes rights and obligations between the respective families of the man and woman.

Near their tukls (huts), Shilluk men weave storage baskets for grain.

The Fashoda Crisis

The Fashoda Crisis was a critical showdown between Great Britain and France that brought these two rival nations to the verge of war, at a time when the great European powers were scrambling to carve out their imperialistic empires in Africa. The crisis was created when a French Army officer, Captain Jean Baptiste Marchand, made France's first and only claim on the Upper Nile, after a grueling 3,000 mile march across Africa through the Congo basin with an expedition of thirty-three whites and 500 Senegalese. The French government had commissioned Marchand with the difficult assignment of establishing a fortified post on the White Nile to block the British from linking Egypt to Uganda. Fulfilling his mission with conspicuous dedication, Marchand reached Fashoda on July 10, 1898, after a year and a half of arduous travel. He built a defensive stockade, established peaceful relations with the local Shilluk and their king, and settled in for a long stay. In September the announcement of unidentified foreigners at Fashoda sent General Horatio Herbert Kitchener, fresh from his capture of Khartoum from the Mahdi's army, racing upstream with a flotilla flying the Egyptian flag and bearing a well-armed force of 1,000 Sudanese troops and 100 Scottish Highlanders.

In the tense confrontation that followed, Kitchener, in effect, informed Marchand that he was trespassing on Egyptian territory and that his claim was invalid. Kitchener then hoisted the Egyptian flag representing the Khedive of Egypt, who had exerted authority over the Sudan since 1820, and the Turkish flag, representing the Ottoman Sultan, puppet ruler of Egypt under the British. After six weeks of vitriolic negotiations between the Cabinets of Britain and France, which inflamed the citizens of both nations, the issue was settled peaceably with France capitulating to avoid bloodshed. By order of his government, Marchand lowered the tricolor and evacuated Fashoda on December 11, 1898. Too proud to accept Kitchener's gallant offer of safe and comfortable transport aboard his own steamer, the heartbroken Frenchman and his men retreated on foot through the wilds of the eastern Sudan and Abyssinia, arriving, after several months, at Djibouti on the Red Sea. Here he boarded a ship for France and a hero's welcome. The only surviving relic of this momentous international confrontation we could find was a shabby little tablet on the facade of the police post, with the inscription: MARCHAND, 1898.

behind their shields until they were almost hidden. Then, at a command from their leader, they suddenly sprang erect and came rushing at me en masse, in a classical head-on battle charge.

I was so alarmed by this dramatic maneuver that I lowered the camera, half expecting to have my epidermis punctured in a dozen places; but they stopped short just in front of me. Relieved, I started filming again, thinking it best to keep cool rather than reveal any of the nervousness I felt. They retreated a few steps, loudly striking their spears on their shields as they moved back, then hunkered down and made a second sham attack. This time I got it all on film. The fired-up warriors finally backed off and continued on their way, leaving me to speculate on the meaning of the incident. I decided that I had been the target of an outburst of pure esprit de corps from a group of warriors who were aching for a fight.

Jean and André joined me in the late afternoon to watch some of the men get gussied up for the moon dance tonight. As blue is the favorite color of the

One of the Shilluk warriors who charged Goddard (with large hippo-hide shield).

Nuer tribe, so red, in every imaginable shade from faded rust to the brightest vermilion, is the dominant hue used by the Shilluk: red bead necklaces, bracelets, and waist bands; bright red sashes or bandoliers; red ocher smeared liberally in their hair and on their bodies. One man even wore a fine Egyptian tarboosh of red felt on his head.

The rest of the costume varied among the dancers, except for the mandatory leopardskin kilt. And some of the men wore the ivory armbands around their biceps that signified an act of bravery in war or on the hunt, a highly prized award.

The girls were positively dowdy compared to the dandified men; except for a little jewelry, they wore only their usual cloth garments, and their heads were either bald or shaved into modest little doilies.

The dance was held in an open field near the river and fortunately began at the first appearance of the moon, just before dark, so that I was able to film the warmup, a genteel prelude in which the tall and statuesque men stood jigging in place around the drummers, who had elevated their instruments on chest-high pedestals in the center of the dance grounds. A pair of long white sticks were tied around each man's neck and hung down the back, rapping together with every movement.

I noticed that skin color varied markedly among the tribe, from blue-black to yellowish brown, and that facial features varied from pure Negroid to nearly European.

The thundering drums soon worked their intoxicating magic as the girls joined the men, forming a wide circle around them. The two groups faced each other, rotating slowly around the drummers in a slow shuffling dance. As the tempo of the drums sped up, the men edged toward the girls, who coyly retreated in perfect unison, graceful as gazelles. The giant warriors looked masterful in all their finery with the moonlight glinting on a forest of their upright spears. They stomped their bare feet on the hard-packed earth, their feathered plumes tossing in rhythm to the beat and their dancing sticks clapping together like castanets. As the dance progressed, women in the audience of older people uttered shrill cries of excitement, and the men intoned a deep chant.

We left as the dancers paused to refresh themselves from the big pots of merissa, their mildly intoxicating beer made from fermented durra grain. Jean, André, and I had agreed to take advantage of the windless and moonlit night to paddle on to the next settlement, Detwok, the last Catholic mission on the river. We arrived there after a peaceful passage on the moon-dappled river (only one hippo attack!) at 10 p.m. to find the three English priests sociably drinking beer and smoking together, dressed in casual slacks and sportshirts, with no evidence of their station in life. Despite our sudden appearance in the night, they welcomed us; indeed, since they had learned of our expedition from a newscast last September, they had been expecting us and were pleased to see we hadn't given up the expedition as they had begun to suspect.

February 23: *From Kodok to Melut*

The fathers waved us off on the windiest day yet. We bucked wild waves all day, whipped up by gale force winds that several times came close to capsizing us. We had our hands full every minute keeping our boats heading into the

Two of the Shilluk warriors who charged Goddard at a village near Kodok.

152

great undulating swells. If we stopped paddling for a few seconds to rest, our kayaks would begin veering sideways, and it would take all our strength to straighten out and get back on course again. It was like paddling on a stormy sea, complete with whitecaps. I thought of the old sailors' prayer: "Oh God, thy sea is so great and my boat is so small."[34]

Apart from the hard work, however, being tossed about on the rough water was exhilarating. My boat would be lifted high on the crest of a wave; then the bottom would fall out, and I would smash down into the trough with a breathtaking drop and a loud smack, only to be caught up again on the next wave to repeat the process. At times it was such a battle to make any headway at all that we were tempted to call it a day and land. But our goal was Melut, thirty miles away, and we forced ourselves on, paddling twelve long, exhausting hours, finally arriving at the little mud village to find it locked up for the night. We set up our tent immediately on the sandy banks and slept undisturbed until 8:30 a.m.

February 24: *Melut*

The three of us woke so stiff from our marathon paddle yesterday that we could barely get out of our sleeping bags. Part of my soreness came from sleeping on the ground again. Our little collapsible canvas cots fit Jean and André nicely, but I'm too large for mine and am actually more comfortable on the ground. Unfortunately I have another outbreak of boils on my legs; but at least the last two or three malarial fevers that have hit me have been brief and mild.

We came upon our first felucca today. It was bearing a load of cotton to Kaka, the next settlement downstream. It was being pulled along by six husky, sweating Arabs, trudging along the riverbank with a rope slung around their shoulders. Since there was very little current, they were moving at only about two miles per hour.

The captain invited us aboard for tea – the symbol of hospitality throughout the Moslem world. We accepted. To have refused it would have been not only a social blunder, but also an insult. The captain told us the windy season should soon be over, adding the usual *"Al ham'd Allilah"* – if God wills. That was encouraging. I've had enough wind the last few days to last me the rest of my life.

As I stretched my legs on a sandbar during the afternoon, an aged Dinka came poling by in an ambatch raft with a youngster, perhaps his grandson,

---

34. *Brittany Fishermen.*

sitting in the tapered prow. The boat was actually a combination of two rafts with their squared-off sterns tied together. Each raft was capable of carrying two adults, yet the ambatch shrub from which it was made is so light and buoyant that the raft could easily be carried on one man's head, making it an excellent craft for hunters who might have to carry it overland for some distance.

Tonight we called a halt ten miles beyond Kaka, the northernmost boundary of Shilluk territory, and followed a hippo runway through the reeds to pitch the tent in a dry hippo wallow. Apparently it was a favorite spot for one particular river horse, because the old boy lingered in the water just offshore half the night, snorting and bellowing with indignation. We were kept awake for hours, between him and the mosquitoes—not to mention the hippo footprints under us that had been sunbaked to cement hardness.

February 25: *South of Er Renk*

The wind was so bad this morning that the tent was almost swept away before we could get it down. A fire for breakfast was impossible, so we flailed our way downstream a mile to a sheltering grove, where we found, to our delight, the distinctive hoofprints of a giraffe. Around noon, four black hunters appeared, tall and lean and carrying spears, striding along in unashamed nudity. As they approached, I could see the broad horizontal slashes on their foreheads characteristic of the Nuer tribe, and I was reminded again how convenient and practical the scar patterns of Africa can be for quick tribal identification—especially on people who wear no clothes. They were relaxed and friendly, which pleased us, since usually the Nuer are more contemptuous and truculent toward foreigners, white or black, than the Shilluk and the Dinka.

The rugged outdoor life has done wonders for Jean. He is tan and healthy, as he has never been before. He lived in Paris for years as a bachelor, more oriented to the intellectual than the physical, with little regard for exercise or nutrition. Being forced to live together is making better men of each of us, and we have developed greater tolerance and consideration.

Before setting out again in the afternoon, we took a swim in the shallows, daring the crocodiles for a few refreshing minutes. We splashed and dived like kids and said to hell with the dragons of the Nile. Jean even tried to use his kayak as a diving board, performing some hilarious belly flops. It was the most fun we had had in a long time, and it must have been good therapy: we were so invigorated by the dip that we paddled on until midnight.

However, I felt perhaps we had been tempting fate unduly when a few miles downstream I saw an enormous crocodile slither into the water from his sunning spot. He was longer than my sixteen-foot kayak, with a massive body. Most of the many crocs we've seen since leaving Malakal have been relatively small, with few longer than seven or eight feet.

André stopped to investigate a band of disturbed monkeys that were chattering uproariously in a thicket along the east bank—and found a Dinka at the top of a dead tree collecting honeycomb from a wild hive there. André shouted for Jean and me to come see what he had found, but by the time we got there, the alarmed man had fled.

As usual, the wind died at dusk, and the river, which is now a mile wide, became smooth as glass, a vast reflecting mirror molten in the sunset, over which our silhouetted kayaks glided like tiny water creatures.

Using his only weapon, a single-shot .22 rifle, Goddard bagged this plump Egyptian goose.

February 26: *South of Er Renk to Torakit Village*

I got a heat rash today from the sun, despite the high winds and my deep tan.

An hour or so after nightfall we came upon a Shilluk encampment and called out to the men there. At first they snuffed out their campfire, but when we proved to be harmless, they rekindled it and offered us some of their stew of durra and catfish from a large calabash. The Shilluk were on a hunting expedition far from home. They must have been thunderstruck to see white men materialize out of the dark, yet their faces remained impassive as they watched us from the opposite side of the campfire.

André was a talented chef whenever he had the proper foods to work with, and tonight he was in his glory, for during the day I had shot a plump Nile goose with my .22 rifle. André steamed the juicy bird with onions and spices and produced a delectable feast. We would have liked to share the meal with our companions, but there were five of them and they had just eaten their own supper. They did, however, appreciate André's hot tea, which they regarded as a luxury—the best thing we could have offered.

When the moon rose at nine o'clock, we decided to keep going another two hours before we looked for a place to camp. And when we did stop, our first campsite was a poor choice; we were about to disembark when we found ourselves the targets of a foul bombardment from a startled colony of cormorants roosting in the trees overhead. As they flapped around in panic, they pelted us and our kayaks with great stinking gobs of creamy guano. We were forced to undergo a nocturnal cleansing before we turned downstream to find a more suitable spot for bedding down.

We heard dogs barking and knew we must be close to a village; it took us an hour to find it, however, and everyone had retired. An Arab shopkeeper heard us and got up to extend his hospitality; he told us we were in the village of Torakit, and let us sleep in the large thatched hut he used as a storehouse. In spite of cats yowling, jackasses braying, dogs yapping, and mosquitoes biting, we slept like infants.

February 27: *Torakit*

Though Torakit was a Shilluk village, there were about fifteen Arabs, and we bought eggs, onions, sim-sim oil, and some Arabic bread, which looked and tasted like a damp brown dishrag. One bite was enough for André and me, but Jean seemed to enjoy it. So we gave it all to him.

We saw our first camel here since we visited Djibouti on the Red Sea long before starting the expedition; and we realized we were leaving black Africa and entering an entirely different world: Moslem Africa.

156

I performed my good deed for the day by coming to the aid of a herd of distressed cattle. They had become trapped on a narrow sandbar and were milling around there, frightened and confused, as a fast-burning grassfire crackled nearer and nearer to them. I jumped out of the kayak and drove them back through the thick smoke to safe pasturage. Their herdsman was nowhere in sight, nor was anyone else.

February 28: *Er Renk*

We are really entering Arab country now. We didn't see a single hippo and saw only a few crocodiles, but it was great seeing our first herd of camels, even though it consisted of only a few mangy animals grazing near the river. I also saw my first Nile monitor lizard, a brownish five-foot beauty that made me jump a foot when he dived out of a dead tree and struck the water head first.[35]

As night fell, the seemingly uninhabited countryside began sprouting pinpoints of light as herders and fishermen lighted their cooking fires. One fire got out of control, blossoming into a full-blown conflagration as we approached—the leaping flames reflecting on the water as they roared through the dry grass.

We reached Er Renk by 10 p.m. The settlement itself is a mile from the river; we would have missed it completely if we hadn't spotted the little pier beside the river. We camped nearby and were besieged by clouds of man-eating mosquitoes.

March 1: *Er Renk*

Our first contact with a Moslem Sudanese official came this morning when the District Commissioner, Abdullah el Khatim, invited us to breakfast. He wore his uniform of immaculate khaki—and had long tribal slashes on his cheeks. His English was excellent, and he took us on a driving tour of the area; though except for a tiny post office, an army barracks, and a few brick administrative buildings, Er Renk is a dreary collection of mud huts and tin stalls.

Its main distinction is that it is the northernmost frontier of Dinka territory. From here on, beginning at 12° north latitude, we will be in the other Sudan, northern rather than southern. Here the two worlds come together graphically as Arab merchants, many of them with blue-black Dinka wives,

---

35. The Nile Monitor (*Varanus niloticus*) is related to the largest lizard on earth, the nine- or ten-foot Komodo Dragon of Indonesia. It has an unusually long and flexible neck. Its forked tongue is an organ of smell that is used to track down prey through its odor. Though its chief enemy is the crocodile, it is particularly fond of crocodile eggs. The Nile Monitor is largely aquatic and uses its flattened and elongated tail for swimming.

Goddard with the District Commissioner, Abdullah el Khatim, and the Omdah of Renk.

rub shoulders with naked spear-carrying Dinka men. Abdullah helped me start an Arabic vocabulary notebook this morning, and I recorded several words and conversational phrases. I had a chance to try them out on the shopkeepers, who were polite and didn't laugh. Although there are a hundred languages and dialects in the country, Arabic is the official language of the Sudan—and of Egypt, too—and thus the language we will most need from now until the Nile's mouth.

Abdullah saw us off this morning at ten o'clock with gifts of tomatoes, oranges, and eggplant—and a parting warning about the hippos, which had recently attacked four men in a dugout and killed them. He confirmed my guess that they had died while hunting hippos. Though we anxiously scanned the river all day long, we didn't see a single hippo.

Two feluccas passed us with their lateen sails full in the wind. We were virtually on a different river now—the wildlife changing, the population different. The Nilotic villages are now all behind us and entirely different cultures are ahead.

Nubia
and the
Cataracts

March 1: *North of Er Renk*

The Nile flows on, broad and sluggish, following a meandering course that alters the direction from which the wind hits us. We never have the wind at our backs where it would be helpful; it blasts down on us from head-on or at an angle as a constant hindrance. We were so frustrated by the wind today that we paddled on long after dark, taking advantage of the calm that sets in with the cooling of the atmosphere at dusk. We live a day at a time, enjoying each new experience, but there are moments of despair, especially after a rugged session of paddling such as we put in today. We made only twenty miles, and we still have a whopping 2,000 miles ahead of us. At times like this, our expedition seems almost too insurmountable a challenge.

We are overnighting at a pungent but friendly Arab fish camp, with commercial fishermen from Omdurman who sailed up the Nile with the seasonal north wind. They spend four months of the year in the area netting fish for the souks (markets) and now are soon to return home with the holds of their feluccas crammed with salted Nile fish.

March 2: *North of Er Renk*

This has been the calmest day since we left Bor over two weeks ago. It was stimulating to zing along on the still water in the daytime. Papyrus is really becoming scarce—just a few stands of it here and there. I still find it immensely attractive in spite of the claustrophobic green hell it creates in the Sudd. We have now entered Blue Nile province, after passing through Equatoria province (Juba to Bor) and Upper Nile province (Bor to Er Renk).

Most of the land behind us has for centuries been—and in many cases still is—*terra incognita.* Now we are beginning to encounter settlements with written histories.

We have seen no hippos for three days, so it appears that we have been successful in running the dangerous hippo gauntlet, though we did have several heart-stopping escapes. Our days and nights have been haunted by the unpredictable animals for so many weeks that I am afraid we have become a bit paranoid about them. They may be gone—but we will never forget them.

We saw great numbers of birds today, primarily ducks and geese, but early this morning I scared up a flock of magnificent crowned cranes when I got too close. They look as if their backs are broken when they fly, but they are one of the most exotic birds of Africa. This feathered beauty is a long-legged marsh dweller that stands with regal dignity three feet tall; it has a red-and-white face

Nile ferry near El Jebelein, Sudan.

and an extraordinary headcrest of stiff yellow feathers that make it look as if it had stuck its beak into an electric light socket.

We are updating our map as we go: today we added the name of an unrecorded village. The only really detailed map of the Nile we were able to bring with us is a twenty-five-year-old German production that is proving seriously inaccurate. So many of the features and villages depicted on the map have somehow developed different spellings or characteristics or have vanished altogether.

For a long time we have scarcely been aware that we are living in the twentieth century. The people of the Nile and their lifestyles haven't changed much since ancient times. The Nilotes are still in the Iron Age, with no practical knowledge of the wheel. Dugouts and feluccas have remained virtually the same for 2,000 years; the mud villages are based on age-old patterns and construction; and the fashions and decorations are of ancient style. Even the paddlewheel steamers are of nineteenth-century design.

We ran across a mystery tonight: though it is the dry season, we crashed unexpectedly into a forest of flooded trees and bushes. Clearly the water level has risen here, much to our dismay: we keep getting hung up on low branches protruding from the water. It was hard going in the dark; when we came to an Arab fish camp beside a stretch of open water, we gave it up for the night and pitched our tent while the fishermen sat around the fire weaving new nets and chanting for us.

March 3: *El Jebelein*

Shortly after dawn, by studying our charts, we figured out what caused the flooded forest. The White Nile is backing up behind the Jebel Aulia dam. Though the barricade is 200 miles downstream, it still can affect this area because of the shallow slope of the river as it flows over the alluvial clay plain between Malakal and Khartoum. Today, in the light, we were able to maneuver easily among the trees. It was pleasant paddling in the shade for the first time, even though it lasted only ten minutes.

We have an intimate relationship with the Nile in our little boats. A space of only two feet separates the surface of the water from the level of our eyes. But we do suffer from a numb derriere; the thin rubber wafers we sit on have become hard with use and feel like concrete. It's rough having to remain immobile in the confining cockpits of the kayaks day after day, with our legs crowded by baggage and with only our arms active, although our arms and backs are becoming muscular from the daily rugged exercise.

It seems that by tacit agreement I have become pacesetter for the expedition. I always end up leading our procession down the Nile, with André next and Jean last, even though in his kayak Jean is superbly well coordinated.

In the late afternoon, worn out and hungry, we arrived at El Jebelein, a checkerboard of mud houses spread out at the base of two low rugged hills of naked rocks.[36] This was the first all-Arab town we had seen, with not one black African. The local men wore white cotton djellabahs and white skullcaps or twisted turbans. A curious crowd of them followed us all around town.

We were delighted at the availability of fresh fruits. I gorged on about a dozen small tomatoes. Too often we've had to go days without any fresh food at all; to compensate, at our camp three miles downstream from El Jebelein we had tomato soup, tomato salad, and stewed tomatoes for supper.

March 4: *North of El Jebelein*

The Nile's metamorphosis from a stream of the tropical forest, woody savanna, and marshland to a river of the desert is nearing completion. Everything in the way of climate, vegetation, wildlife, and people has been undergoing a slow and subtle but continuous transformation. The countryside is becoming more arid and is covered with thorny scrub, mainly acacias but also mimosa trees and doum, borassus, and wild date palms. The riverbanks are still lush and green with reeds and grasses, and while game has largely disappeared from the banks, the marvelous variety and profusion of waterfowl has more than compensated. Cormorants are everywhere. They pop up for a breath, then dive under again to hunt fish. Kingfishers, giant herons, spoonbills, plump Nile geese, sandpipers, and charming little ruffs are a common sight. Today several African skimmers, with long wings and tern-like bodies flew over me in formation, then zoomed down like hedge-hopping fighters and ploughed the surface of the Nile with their extended lower beaks to scoop up tidbits.

We saw the first beds of waterlilies since leaving the Sudd—a pleasantly incongruous sight against the background of semidesert. We also found the first navigational marker on the river, an eight-foot-high conical buoy with black and white stripes. We camped tonight with five Sudanese fishermen, some of the many fishermen we had seen during the day.

The mosquitoes are outrageous tonight, but much more irritating are sore muscles. I would give anything for a good rubdown. What we need on this expedition is a resident masseur.

---

36. El Jebelein means "The Two Mountains," inspired by the rocky crags above the town, the first elevated topography we have seen in a long time, aside from low hills along the White Nile.

March 5: *Kosti*

I paddled far ahead of Jean and André today, eager to reach Kosti, thirty miles from our camp. On the way I came upon a great caravan of about 200 camels watering at the river. The lead animals were lined up for a couple of hundred yards along the sandy banks, drinking rapturously with loud slurps, while the rest of the herd milled around behind them, impatiently waiting their turn. The nearest animals looked at me in consternation as I landed. They burst forth with raucous bellows of alarm when I walked up to them; then they turned away in haughty disdain at my offense to their dignity.

The herdsmen and their sons plied me with questions, which I couldn't answer very well with my limited Arabic. The men told me they were of the Gule tribe and had trekked far across the desert with their camels from the direction of Ethiopia. One of the older herdsmen presented me with a gourd of fresh, warm camel's milk, which was strong-tasting but a refreshing change from the powdered milk we had been using.

After battling with the wind all day it was a thrill to round a bend and see the ten-section 1,500-foot steel railroad bridge four miles upstream from Kosti. This was the first bridge and railroad we had seen in the 1,400 miles from Jinja, where a bridge crosses the Nile as it flows out of Lake Victoria. The bridge guard casually glanced at me, turned away, and then leaped to the rail to stare. That wasn't a crocodile; it was a boat, driven by a man who dipped long, stiff arms into the water!

I raced on to get to Kosti before the post office closed and arrived at dusk. At the cubbyhole post office I received a great batch of mail from home and again was grateful for a loyal family and for friends who had been faithful in writing to me. My joy was diminished when André and Jean arrived to find no mail for them, no doubt it having been delayed en route from France.

At the kind invitation of the chief engineer, we spent the night aboard a sternwheeler. Some Sudanese kept us awake for a long time with their merry-making. Several were grouped in a circle near the steamer, clapping their hands rhythmically and chanting to the accompaniment of a lute, while two of them danced a sort of buck and wing in the center. Whenever two dancers tired, they were replaced by two others, until finally, well past midnight, they all grew tired and went to bed, leaving us in peace.

March 6: *Kosti*

Before leaving this morning, we stocked up on supplies at Kosti's large and teeming souk, where merchants and buyers of a half dozen different Arab tribes mingled, including the Gimma, Kufaa, Bederia, and Fezara. At the waterfront we watched sweating stevedores load cotton, grain, and gum arabic aboard barges bound for Khartoum.[37]

With 28,000 Sudanese, seventeen British, and the railroad, Kosti is the most important town on the Nile south of Khartoum; yet no sooner had we left Kosti and civilization this morning than I was jolted back into the world of nature by a collision with a crocodile. In paddling over a shallow spot I must have grazed the back of the croc as he rested on the river bottom. He protested violently by giving a powerful spasmodic lurch that threw me off my seat and just about upset my kayak. I prayed he wouldn't take any further action in reprisal for my intrusion. And, thankfully, he didn't.

March 7: *North of Kosti*

This morning we inspected our first sakieh, the ancient waterwheel used by farmers along the Nile since the days of the Pharoahs to irrigate their crops. A docile ox, urged on by a boy with a stick, plodded around and around on a flat place atop the high bank, providing the power to turn a large horizontal cogwheel, which in turn was meshed to a vertical wooden wheel studded with clay pots that scooped up water from a basin at river level. The pots emptied into a trough that channeled water to a shallow canal leading to the produce fields, where women in flowing dark garments were hoeing.

We stopped to visit four fishermen driving large wooden pins into new planking on their felucca, which was shaped like a flatiron. The men laughed at the small size and flimsy construction of our kayaks and marveled that they operated solely on our muscle power. One of them hefted the prow of my beached kayak to gauge its weight, then set it down again, shaking his head in wonderment. The Sudanese fishermen and villagers we meet are always amazed at our presence in their part of the world—and at the way we are traveling. They are intensely curious about us, but the first thing they want to know is where we have come from and where we are going. At first they can't comprehend that we have come from the beginning of the river and are going to its ending at the sea. Finally, when they understand us, they invariably shake their heads, puff out their cheeks, and say, "Oooooh wooooh!"

André shared my experience of yesterday—a submerged croc bounced him half into the air. But aside from minor ailments, the three of us are fit, tan, and generally healthy, with our endurance considerably increased in the past two weeks. Even malaria has largely left us alone.

---

37. The Sudan produces most of the world's supply of gum arabic, a versatile resin derived from acacia trees and used chiefly in medicines, adhesives, ink, and even candy.

The Gule herdsman—helping drive a large caravan of camels to market across a vast desert in the Sudan—who gave the author a gourd of camel's milk.

March 8: *North of Kosti*

We stopped at an important pumping station used to irrigate the vast Gezira cotton fields that begin near Kosti.[38] This is one of the largest and most
important cotton-growing regions of the world. But the wind has hampered
our progress again, blowing us upstream whenever we stop paddling for a moment. It is frustrating to work so hard for so little progress downstream, while
feluccas in full sail going upstream slip quickly and easily by us.

More and more groves of trees flooded by the dam at Jebel Aulia, or Jabal
Al-Awluja, have provided welcome shade—and not just for us. Weaver birds
and shrikes nest in the branches; and on the shoreline stand hundreds of waterfowl, among them some of the biggest pelicans I have ever seen.

Today, while Jean and André started supper, I made an effort to fulfill my
role as expedition breadwinner. I found some fresh tracks along the water's
edge, and on a hunch followed them down until I found what I had been
hoping for—turtle eggs. There were eighteen of them, almost perfect replicas
of little white ping pong balls, and they made a marvelous omelette, though
André's sensitive palate was offended by them. "It would have been better,
John," he said, "if we could have eaten these eggs last month."

"Well, this omelette tastes better than those termites we ate with the Baganda, or those locusts we had with the Bari," I said defensively. André was
right, though; the turtle eggs tasted pretty rank. But they provided valuable
nutrition and added a touch of variety to our bland diet.

For the first time in the five months we have been in Africa, there were no
mosquitoes: we were able to sleep without shelter or netting over us. It was
marvelous to be free of the stifling tent and to feel the evening breeze on our
faces and bare bodies.

I was inspired by an ineffable sensation of spiritual upliftment as I lay studying the twinkling stars. Swallowed up in the middle of the wind-tossed river, I
have felt physically puny; but the immense star-studded night sky is not over-

---

38. The Gezira is a great five-million-acre triangle of flat land, betwen the Blue and White Niles south
of Khartoum. In 1925 government officials inaugurated the Gezira Scheme to develop Nile water for
agriculture in what was then arid wasteland. The Scheme was the biggest and most farsighted project of
colonial Africa. By 1977 nearly 2 million acres of the Gezira were under irrigation through an intricate
network of canals that extends for 10,000 miles. This once desolate plain has now become the Sudan's
granary and its most productive cotton growing area and provides a home and employment for thousands of tenant farmers. The Gezira has become an outstanding model for other African nations.

Gezira cotton is the "white gold" of the Sudan, since it is the nation's principal cash crop, the source
of more than half of its export income, and the backbone of the whole economy.

powering as the river can be. It fills me instead with an infinite sense of peace and of communion with its Creator.

March 9: *North of Kosti*

Our wake-up call came at dawn in the form of the harsh squawking of a hadada ibis, a water fowl that has the most raucous cry of any bird we have heard. However, as a generous compensation of nature, its plumage has a metallic sheen, as if the feathers had been coated with green sequins.

Our nemesis, the Wicked Wind of the North, is as oppressive as ever.

My senses have never been so keen. This life close to nature has really sharpened my faculties, and I hear and see and feel things with sensitive awareness that normally I would be oblivious to in civilized surroundings.

Campsite on the White Nile, with the river backing up and expanding behind the Jebel Aulia dam, even though the dam is 100 miles to the north.

André and I have worn our shirts and shoes only a few times the past three weeks. We go all day in only our khaki shorts and a hat. Jean, more modest and less of a sunworshipper, wears a shirt.

After stopping at the village of Ed Kawa for eggs, oil, and dates, we camped near the larger settlement of Um Garr. A hospitable young Sudanese cotton grower sent us an invitation to have supper with him. By the time we had arrived at his whitewashed home, our host had assembled eight of his friends to meet us—all male, following the Moslem practice of purdah, or seclusion of females. We gladly followed another custom, and removed our shoes. The barefoot company all sat and ate around a large food salver of mutton and rice, with our feet tucked beneath us, eating from the common plate with our right hands.

March 10: *Ed Dueim*

As usual we got underway shortly after dawn. The wind persevered all day long and so did we.

I saw some more lung fish along the way, one of the most ancient and primitive forms of life in existence. They surface to gulp air or to just laze along on their side as if to enjoy a little warm sunshine and then dive back down to the dark river bottom. (Authorities say the Nile has more fish per cubic foot of water than any other river. These fish consist of 360 species).

Our need for fresh food is being well satisfied—today a cotton plantation owner who had heard of our expedition on the news and had been looking for us ever since not only fed us but also insisted that I accept a gift of eggs, bread, jam, two cans of sardines, and two limes as a little contribution to our larder.

The White Nile is really spreading out as we near the Jebel Aulia dam. The river water is a pale milky green color and tastes fine. We are drinking it in increasing quantities as the temperature becomes hotter, scooping it up with our hands in midstream as we have done all along. Despite the river the air is drier here; at Lake Victoria the annual rainfall is around seventy-five inches, while here it is more like fifteen. We are seeing more sand dunes, and the more frequent sandy shores are making landing easier—except tonight when we were hunting for a place to camp. The banks were either barricaded by flooded trees or by a wide border of spongy marsh, making a landing impossible. We were forced to continue even though the wind, failing for the first time to die away at dusk, continued sweeping over the river, keeping the surface heaving restlessly. As we paddled on in the dark, the waves came at us in all directions, making us feel disoriented and on the verge of capsizing. We battled on until we saw pinpoints of light. By the time we reached them, our shouts to Jean to guide him to our landing had aroused the residents of the homes near the shore, and we were greeted by the Clarkes, an English couple living in the town of Ed Dueim, who appeared on the beach with kerosene lanterns. Though it was late, they fed us, put us up for the night, and introduced us to the other members of the British colony there; they had been expecting us to come tomorrow.

March 11: *Past Ed Dueim*

The wind was terrible today. Because of the dam, the Nile ballooned to three miles in width, the widest point of the river, so that we could barely see the flat bank on the opposite side; yet because this is the dry season, the Nile in this area is so shallow that for a stretch of four miles it is actually fordable on foot.

Lunch was on a picturesque little desert island with a white sand beach and dry vegetation. I shot a duck; it was greasy but good.

March 12: *South of Khartoum*

I shook a scorpion out of my shorts this morning. A little one, only five inches long. Scorpions grow to be as long as eight inches in the Sudan.

We fought a hot wind until late afternoon, then stopped at the village of Shabasha. A Sudanese who could speak English invited us to a welcome supper, and we spent the night in a government rest house.

Oh, for a steam bath and a rubdown! We can barely open our hands after eight hours of clasping the paddles.

March 13: *South of Khartoum*

The wind was gentle as a zephyr as we shoved off, but it grew steadily stronger until, by noon, it was of squall intensity. The high rollers blown up by the howling gusts became so rough that I was forced to head for shore. I suddenly realized that I had reached the middle of the river, and the shores were a mile away on either side. I was tossed around like a chip, violently pitching and rolling with the erratic waves and struggling with the paddle to keep from being swept upstream. When the gusts slackened, I paddled furiously to gain a few yards. This exhausting ordeal continued for an hour, but I finally worked my way to the eastern shore, where Jean and André were waiting for me. I was just about to land when I received a one-two knockout punch from a pair of mischievous waves, one setting me up by tossing my prow high in the air, and the other swooping in with perfect timing to smash into the kayak broadside. Over I went. Luckily the water was shallow; I righted the shell and towed it to solid ground.

My first thought was of the cameras and the film. I had snatched the cameras out of the boat quickly – they didn't get a drop of water on them when it capsized. But then I noticed that the cover on the side compartment of the camera bag had sprung open, and the three telephoto lenses had fallen out. There was only one thing to do, and, trusting that the high wind would keep the crocodiles inactive today, I dived for the lenses in my diving mask. After diving repeatedly in the turbulent water without success, I finally found them nestled together as I groveled over the sandy bottom.

At about this time the wind changed from the usual northerly direction to an easterly one, scouring over the dessicated land and enveloping us in a raging sandstorm. The flying sand bit into our bare skin and through our clothes, into our eyes, mouths, ears, and hair. Blinded and stinging from the blast, we rushed downstream a few hundred yards to take refuge in a vacant fisherman's hut, splashing through the shallow water just offshore and towing our kayaks along behind us. The hut reeked of dead fish; but we lay down on the floor,

Ahmed Hamza Bey, Egyptian Minister of Supply, and luncheon party (see following page).

though it was covered with silvery scales and fish bones, and covered our faces with our towels, waiting for the storm to abate.

At dusk the wind finally calmed down, and, after washing the sand from our grimy bodies, we set out to compensate for the afternoon's delay by traveling at night, which now was pleasant, with no hippos around to watch out for. The river was majestic in the hushed blue of the evening, with bats dodging and darting above the swallows swirling over the glassy surface.

We had no lunch or supper because we had no food.

March 14: *South of Khartoum*

At dawn we woke with the wind threatening to blow our tent over. A group of Sudanese were gathered by our boats, examining them with great curiosity, and at a nearby village we bought six eggs, some dates, and dry biscuits, which we had for breakfast. The wind discourages us considerably: we have made only fifty miles in the last three days.

We stopped for supper at a hilltop settlement where an ancient Sudanese gravely presented us with fifteen eggs (ten of them, unfortunately, rotten) and some onions—a touching gesture we appreciated. We traveled until 10:30 p.m., then collapsed for the night on a sand bank.

March 15: *South of Khartoum*

No wind! Splendid progress all day.

March 16: *Jebel Aulia*

We reached the dam by 8 a.m. and spent an hour and a half passing through the lock in company with a small steamer. The dam is 16,400 feet long and fifteen feet high, a storage reservoir built by Egypt in 1937 to help the Egyptian farmers during the low water season.[39] Our kayaks were the smallest craft ever to pass through the lock, according to Ahmed Helmy, the Egyptian resident engineer; he came to the lock to meet us and invite us to lunch. He told us that the officials in Khartoum had phoned him several times during the week to see if we had arrived yet.

We had not planned to visit the town of Jebel Aulia, but we were glad we did, since it provided us a chance to meet the Egyptian minister of supply, Ahmed Hamza Bey, who was in the Sudan on a fact-finding mission. We had

---

39. The dam's 50 sluices are regulated to ration water from the Sobat River during its flooding stage and to take advantage of the ponding effect created by the Blue Nile during its annual flood when it forces back the flow of the White Nile at Khartoum, where the two rivers meet.

a long and animated conversation with this cultured man, who spoke fluent English to me and impeccable French to André and Jean.

The luncheon was a sumptuous banquet—fit for a sultan—served on a fifteen-foot-long flower-bedecked table set with beautiful china and silverware—an extraordinary contrast to our normal pattern of eating. Our only regret was that Moslem etiquette kept the wives of several aides at a separate table, where they did not take part in the conversation. After months without feminine companionship, we would have enjoyed talking with them.

In the midst of our feast, Baron Louis de Cabrol, the French charge d'affaires in the Sudan, telephoned us and informed us that the celebration of our arrival in Khartoum had been set for 4:30 p.m. the next day. We were back on the river in the afternoon, stuffed and contented, loafing along, with only twenty-eight miles of paddling to reach Khartoum.

March 17: *Khartoum*

The Nile was narrower as we set out from our thornbush shelter eighteen miles from the capital city of Khartoum, but it was still more than half a mile in width. The banks were green with truck gardens where many villagers labored. Lovely groves of trees sheltered herds of floppy-eared Nubian goats, several of them standing on low branches nibbling leaves. We rounded a bend just before noon and thrilled at the sight of Khartoum, a shimmering mirage—like a smudge of green on the horizon.

Five miles away from the Omdurman-Khartoum bridge, where we were expected to arrive at 4:30, we stopped to bathe and put on clean clothing. But first we scrubbed down our kayaks; then we decked them out with the small flags representing France, the United States, and the various organizations patronizing our expedition.

We were met by several launches bearing Baron de Cabrol and a score of high-ranking officials, including the governor of Khartoum and the president of the Sudanese parliament. In their wake came three boatloads of journalists and well-wishers, everyone waving and snapping pictures.

Just past the bridge is the confluence of two of the world's greatest rivers, the White Nile ("our" Nile) and the Blue Nile, which flows for 1,000 miles from the mountains of Ethiopia. We met some turbulence in the water there, but proceeded for two miles up the Blue Nile with the flotilla following close behind or alongside us.

The waters of the two rivers are sharply defined, with that of the Bahr el Abyad, the White Nile, a milky green, and that of the Bahr el Azrek, the Blue Nile, a clear, dark jade green. I was struck by the verdancy of the boulevard bordering the Blue Nile, called Kitchener Avenue [now called En Nil Avenue]. It was lined with huge, leafy lebbek trees and gnarled but lush banyans.

We disembarked at the antique steamer that served as overflow quarters for the venerable Grand Hotel, Khartoum's most comfortable hotel. We were immediately surrounded by a multitude of well-dressed people who thumped us on our backs and shouted congratulations in our ears. They led us to the top deck of the quaint old steamer, where our already churning emotions were stirred even more by a four-piece band of specially hired Swiss musicians playing the nostalgic Marseillaise and the Star-Spangled Banner. Our hosts had thought of everything! We met the prominent people of Khartoum's Sudanese and international community.[40] Mary Coughlin, the Baron's vivacious American secretary, produced a minor miracle by tracking down three white dress suits for us to wear. So for the first time since leaving Paris six months before, we were dressed in the fanciest finery, complete with cufflinks, black bowtie, and cummerbund. Mary, an attractive Boston girl the same age as I, accepted my invitation to be my date for the evening, making everything even more pleasurable. After our months of arduous living in the primitive world of Africa, the bright lights, modern music, abundant food, and elegantly dressed men and women had the fabric of a sharply focused dream.

The baron had reserved rooms for us in the hotel at his expense; so after the festivities, we retired to soft beds, grateful for the bounteous hospitality. We also felt great satisfaction in the knowledge that after 4½ months and many hardships, obstacles, and setbacks, we had traveled 2,265 miles from the Burundi source and were now more than halfway down the river.

March 23: *Khartoum*

Khartoum has been treating us like royalty, and we have been kept on the go to make all of our appointments for dinners, teas, interviews, and excursions. All twenty of the Sudanese newspapers in Khartoum and Omdurman have carried stories about the expedition; and Hamish Davidson, the local representative for *Time* and *Life* magazines, had me give an exclusive phone interview to the Associated Press correspondent in Cairo. I answered his questions for almost half an hour. He told me his feature story of our expedition would update the numerous reports that had been appearing on radio and in the press throughout the world. Maybe people are beginning to believe that we really *do* have a chance to make it to the Mediterranean.

---

40. Incredibly, at the time of our visit there was no American ambassador or consul in Khartoum because the United States had been denied diplomatic representation in the Sudan.

Khartoum

Khartoum was originally a quiet fishing
village until an invading army from
Turkish Egypt occupied it in 1821. In
1886 it was largely demolished by the
Mahdi's fanatical dervishes, who then
established their capital at Omdurman
on the nearby west bank of the main
Nile. In the Battle of Omdurman in
1898 General Kitchener's army defeated
the Mahdi's forces, and, at Kitchener's
order, Khartoum was rebuilt by 5,000
workmen in the shape of a Union Jack
(not from chauvinism but so that
machine guns could have a clear
command of the streets in the event of
another revolt). Even though it is the
hottest capital in Africa (108° in the
shade was the average high each day of
our visit), Khartoum has developed over
the years into a thriving, international
metropolis (with a population of
400,000 [1978]) with a European flavor
in its governmental and business
buildings, university, School of
Medicine, and hospitals; its Protestant,
Catholic, Greek, and Coptic churches;
and its tree-lined avenues (Kitchener
had 7,000 trees planted to provide shade
for the citizens).

We have also enjoyed touring around Khartoum, one of the finest cities the British have built in Africa. The name of the city means "elephant trunk," because the confluence of the Blue and White Niles outlines the shape of the trunk of an elephant.

One of the first things we visited was the Gordon monument, situated in the middle of one of Khartoum's main intersections, a bronze statue of the valiant British general astride an elaborately caparisoned camel. Charles George Gordon was the legendary British general who, on January 26, 1885, became a martyr when he was speared to death at Khartoum by troops of the Mahdi just two days before a British relief expedition arrived. Gordon's brilliant and heroic defense of Khartoum enabled his overwhelmingly outnumbered force to hold at bay an army of fanatical Mahdists for ten harrowing months before the city was conquered and Gordon and his small garrison massacred. (Charlton Heston, the movie actor, portrayed Gordon in the film, *Khartoum,* and Sir Lawrence Olivier, the great English actor, took the part of the Mahdi).

March 24: *Khartoum*

This morning I took Mary Coughlin and Baron de Cabrol's seven-year-old son Jean Louis to the Khartoum Zoo at the river's edge. He especially liked the chimpanzee that played with my beard as if it fascinated him. The zoo is well stocked with all the major kinds of African wildlife, but it was depressing to see them imprisoned in cages and stockades rather than running free, as we have become accustomed to seeing them.

When Jean Louis asked if it wasn't cruel to cage up wild things, I explained that if it were not for zoos, most people would never have a chance to develop an appreciation of wildlife; and if they didn't learn to value them, there was a far greater chance that someday those creatures would become extinct.

In the afternoon I enjoyed an old-fashioned picnic on a grassy island in the Nile with the Baron, Mary, and Jean Louis. After eating, the baron stationed himself along the riverbank and potted away at several flights of ducks winging north. He hit two, and both fell into the Nile. I dived in and retrieved one of them, but the current was too swift for me to reach the other.

We had planned to leave Khartoum today, but the governor has invited us to be his guests for the big War Memorial unveiling ceremony; so we're staying on.

March 25: *Khartoum*

I have been the houseguest of Mohammed Ahmed Omar, a gifted and dynamic civil leader, who has had me accompany him on several of his business

The Mahdi

The Mahdi was a politico-religious ascetic by the name of Mohammed Ahmed, who claimed descent from Mohammed the Prophet and, in 1881 proclaimed himself the long-awaited Messiah of Islam. (Two weeks earlier we had paddled past Aba Island just north of Kosti, where he had his original headquarters.) In 1882 the Mahdi called for a *jihad* or holy war against the Turco-Egyptian government, which became for the Sudanese a war of liberation from the corruption, exploitation, and colonialism of the Egyptians occupying the Sudan. He built up a great army of dervishes and in the name of Allah fought an effectively aggressive rebellion against British and Egyptians alike. The Mahdi died in 1885, five months after his armies had overrun and liberated the entire Sudan. When Anglo-Egyptian troops captured Omdurman in 1898, they destroyed the Mahdi's tomb, burned the corpse, and strewed the ashes in the Nile, lest the spot become a symbol of fanatacism and rebellion. But in 1947 one of the Mahdi's sons built the present shrine, a virtual reproduction of the original tomb, which attracts pilgrims from all parts of the country.

One of Mohammed Omar's own grandfathers had fought in and survived the great Battle of Omdurman. On September 2, 1898, General Kitchener's 8,000 British troops, including one young officer by the name of Winston Churchill, and 18,000 Egyptians, engaged the 52,000 dervishes of the Mahdi in what has been described as the last romantic battle of history. There were bold cavalry charges, hand-to-hand duels with swords and spears, and incredible displays of individual heroism on both sides. But Kitchener's more disciplined and better equipped army was victorious, and the Anglo-Egyptian condominium of the Sudan was the result. (Although Egypt theoretically was an equal partner, Britain actually ran the country until independence came in 1956.)

and political appointments around town. Today he took me to Khartoum's totally different sister city, Omdurman, just across the Nile from Khartoum. This is the primary center of Sudanese cultural and religious life and is the third largest city on the Nile (Cairo is first and Khartoum second). Sprawling for six miles along the west bank, Omdurman is a typical big Arab town (1977 population 200,000) of neat, square buildings of unfired mud brick, white-robed citizens, and donkey and camel traffic along dusty, narrow, treeless streets.

Our first stop was at the most famous historical landmark in the Sudan, the Mahdi's tomb. It was an impressive structure with a large silver-plated dome, shaped like an inverted goblet gleaming brightly in the early morning sun,

The Gordon monument at Khartoum.

180

surrounded by four miniature bell-shaped cupolas, with an emblem combining the spear of the Sudan and the crescent of Islam topping each of the five domes.

We drove out to the rocky, wind-swept plains of Kerreri, the battleground where Kitchener defeated the Mahdi in 1898. I could picture the dramatic spectacle of the Mahdi's huge army of ferocious dervish warriors, spread out on a battle line four miles wide, fearlessly charging en masse upon the waiting Anglo-Egyptian troops, only to be massacred by a holocaust of British artillery on land and the cannon fire from the armed steamers on the Nile. The battle began at dawn and was all over by 11:30, with 9,700 dervishes killed and 400 casualties among Kitchener's men.

When we returned in the evening, I was given a message from our good friend Jim Dodson, who had done more for us in Juba than we can ever repay. He had arrived yesterday at Central Prison in Khartoum North, convicted of smuggling and sentenced to twelve months' imprisonment. I was shocked and saddened—and remembered with a start that I had helped him unload the smuggled radiators from his pickup. I made arrangements to be driven out to the prison tomorrow afternoon to see him.

March 26: *Khartoum*

This morning André, Jean, and I paddled across to the sand island of Tuti in the Blue Nile to clean and repair the kayaks and to film the assembling process. First we sewed a patch over the hole in the canvas top of my kayak, put there last month by a curious Dinka when he probed the thin sheath with his spear a little too vigorously. We had picked the island because of its isolation in hopes of some privacy, but within ten minutes we were surrounded by curious Sudanese who live on Tuti.[41]

At the prison this afternoon I pounded on a huge steel door for several minutes before a khaki-clad Sudanese guard let me in. "Stanis shwyer," he said, Arabic for wait a minute. I sat for over half an hour in the stifling courtyard of the prison waiting for some official who was home taking a siesta. The prison was stark, dreary, depressing, especially so when I discovered that Jim was the only Englishman in the place, all the other prisoners being Sudanese except for three Greeks.

I was about to give up and return to Khartoum when a burly Sudanese in street clothes came through the entrance and rather truculently informed me

---

41. In 1885 a British fort on Tuti Island was attacked and captured by Moslem dervishes of the Mahdi.

A kayak on the Island of Tuti, with its rubber and canvas envelope removed.

that "the prisoners are allowed one visitor a month and Mr. Dodson had one yesterday; so it will be quite impossible for you to see him."

There was nothing I could do. I settled for writing a note to him. My heart aches when I realize that Jim will be confined to this hellhole for nine long months at least, assuming he gets three months off for good behavior.

March 27: *Khartoum*

The official photographer for the War Memorial unveiling was ill today, and so the director, Major Oldham, asked me to take his place and make a detailed film record of Khartoum's biggest event of the year. I was given a press pass that allowed me to rove about at will.

The ceremony was colorful and impressive as 400 elite troops of the Sudan Defense Force, in tan uniforms and turbans, promenaded on foot and camelback before the large audience and then came to a halt before the reviewing stand, where their Kaid (commander), Major-General Scoones, and his officers and guests stood at attention. At an order from the General they marched over

A World War II War Memorial unveiling at Khartoum.

and formed ranks around the large shrouded monument. The muslin sheet was pulled away, revealing a grey marble pyramid erected as a tribute to the Sudanese soldiers and their British officers who had died in World War II. I was intently filming all this from the stands when there was a loud crash and a commotion from the crowds: one of the temporary bleachers set up for the occasion had just collapsed with more than a hundred Sudanese spectators. Led by their officers, many of the soldiers rushed over to render aid; fortunately, no one seemed injured seriously enough to require medical attention. The ceremony was resumed, with a moving eulogy delivered by the governor-general of the Sudan, Sir Robert Howe.

The baron held a farewell party for us tonight, since we are leaving tomorrow. We danced, sang, and in general had a smashing good time. I was amazed at how vigorously Baron de Cabrol danced. During World War II he had been a tank commander and a highly decorated hero in France. He lost both legs when his tank received a direct hit from a German shell, and he has walked on artificial limbs ever since.

Mohammed O., our host and guide for many days, also came to the party, with his girlfriend Zahouri, a gorgeous Sudanese girl with large black eyes, long raven hair, and a full-bodied figure clothed in a deep blue sari. The dinner was also exquisite, and I imagine we'll remember it with nostalgia in the very near future.

March 28: *North of Khartoum*

I wrote a farewell message addressed to the many people in Khartoum who had been helpful to us, expressing our deep gratitude for their friendliness and hospitality. Mohammed said he would publish it right away. We were on the Blue Nile ready to leave by noon. All our friends and a number of other well-wishers saw us off with cheers and confetti, although we all were choked with emotion, and there were even a few tears shed, especially by Mary.

And now the wind was not too strong, and we actually had a current to help us make good progress. As we swept along the confluence of the rivers, we noticed that the Blue Nile retained its deep emerald color and identity for several hundred yards before finally blending with the pale green White Nile.[42]

---

42. The Blue Nile originates from a spring 6,000 feet high in the rugged mountains of northwestern Ethiopia. The spring, considered holy by the Coptic Church of Ethiopia, develops into a stream called the Abbai, which flows for seventy miles before emptying into Lake Tana, then continues as the Blue Nile in the lake's overflow just eight miles away. The Blue Nile contributes more water to the main Nile than any other tributary, providing more than half the water carried from Khartoum to Egypt over the course of a year.

(During the flood stage from June to October the Blue Nile is rust brown.) And once the waters of the two rivers have joined, the river is simply the Nile, having no other name from here to the mouth; until now it has been called the Victoria, Somerset, Albert, and White Nile, as well as the Arabic name Bahr el Jebel.

It was good to be underway again after eleven days of rest. André and I sped on as quickly as possible, not even pausing to eat the big box lunch that had been given us by Mary Coughlin. Before we realized it, we had left Jean far behind. Though we waited for him to catch up, he never appeared, and for the first time we camped without him, sleeping in the open again without the tent.

We are now well into the southern bounds of the ancient country known as Nubia, and won't leave it until we reach Aswan more than a thousand miles to the north. The ancient Egyptians called the northern Sudan the land of Kush—Cush, in the Bible—and the Greeks knew it as Ethiopia.[43]

March 29: *North of Khartoum*

Jean came paddling up to our campsite this morning as if nothing had happened, explaining that after our short vacation he was out of condition and had tired quickly. When he couldn't catch up, he had stopped for the night at a little village where he had been warmly received.

We stopped to inspect the tallest sakieh we had seen, this one located on the top of a forty-foot-high bank with a vertical wooden wheel continuously spinning two parallel loops of rope studded with evenly spaced pottery jars that scooped up the river water. The big wheel was operated by a team of oxen driven by a little boy who scampered off as we landed. He must have run ahead to report our arrival because at the village a short distance downstream, the omdah (headman) was waiting on the bank to meet us with several men and boys. They were captivated with our kayaks, particularly the young omdah, who asked if he might try my boat. After he had climbed into the cockpit, I handed him the paddle and gave him some basic instructions. He seemed to understand, so I launched him into the river. But he became panicky trying to maneuver the delicately balanced little shell and began flailing so wildly with the long paddle he almost tipped over. Finally calming down, he began paddling with steadier, more coordinated strokes, a proud smile breaking out on his handsome black face as he rowed around in a perfect circle—backward! He was

---

43. As far back as 4,500 years ago Nubia was an important crossroads for cultural and material exchanges between the Egyptians and the peoples to the south and west of Egypt.

The tall sakieh waterwheel along the banks of the Nile north of Khartoum.

so delighted with the kayak that he offered me one of his three wives in exchange for it! Needless to say, we departed rather hastily with a "thanks but no thanks" (freely translated).

We slept outside again without erecting the tent, but for the first time since coming to Africa we were kept awake by the cold—the temperature drops drastically at night because in desert air there is little or no moisture to retain heat, and after dark there is a rapid loss of heat from the ground.

March 30: *Near the Sixth Cataract*

We discovered that Jean, who had been entrusted to buy food in Khartoum to last us until we reached Atbara, about a ten-day paddle downstream, had only a stock of bread, tea, powdered milk, cereal, catsup, and macaroni. We needed much more, but the village we stopped at had no souk or even a store, and we came away empty-handed except for dry dates. We couldn't even scrounge up any of our old standby—eggs.

Sudanese women spread laundry to dry on rocks near Sablukah Gorge, north of Khartoum.

For the first time in three weeks we saw crocodiles, small ones, and though we seem to have left the mosquitoes behind, we are now plagued with tiny flies the Sudanese call "nimits," which swarmed around us at dusk, crawling into our ears and eyes. Their bite draws blood and produces an itchy welt.

A cake-shaped mountain loomed above us as we entered the fabulous Sablu-kah Gorge fifty miles from Khartoum. For ten miles the Nile flows with a strong current through this great chasm in the Jebel Rauwaya Range, bordered on both banks by steep, sun-scorched hills of granite, gneiss, and basalt.

We camped early on a flat shelf of rock next to a large boulder in the heart of the canyon. I climbed to the top of a jumbled mass of granite high above camp, where I beheld a magnificent panorama of the Nile far below, peaceful and golden in the fiery sunset. It occurred to me that this scene had remained unchanged since prehistoric times. The rugged landscape and the drifting river seemed so infinitely enduring that for a moment I became conscious of how brief and fragile the span of my own life must be.

As we headed into a little back bay to camp, we flushed a magnificent ten-foot crocodile. He was really a whopper—his body unusually massive. Jean and André slept in the tent because of the chilly night, but the stars were so beautiful I decided to sleep in the open, choosing the base of a big thorny acacia. Venus, the evening star, was so bright it cast a shimmering wake on the water.

March 31: *The Sixth Cataract.*

Before we left this morning, the three of us scrambled up the steep and unstable rock debris to the top of the cliffs, where a pair of eagles were flying. From there we viewed the river gorge in the early morning sunlight, and then I waited until Jean and André had returned to the kayaks and filmed them as they paddled off downriver, two tiny white specks bobbing on the pale green water.

Sometimes in the gorge the river narrowed to less than 200 feet, crowded by vertical cliffs of dark, water-polished basalt marked by various streaks of silt marking previous highwater levels.

With the memory of the Kagera River disaster still fresh on our minds, we were anxious about running the whitewater of the Sixth Cataract, just beyond the mouth of the canyon.[44] Our maps indicated thirty-one individual rapids

---

44. In reality this is the *first* of the six cataracts that have been a barrier to river navigation since ancient times, but it is called the Sixth Cataract because ancient Egyptian geographers counted upstream, from north to south, following the direction in which civilization developed.

188

between the Sixth Cataract and the First Cataract at Aswan 1,200 miles down-stream, but gave no details as to their size or violence.

Preparing for our run through the cataract, we had carefully packed everything away in our equipment bags and lashed them securely in place. Then Jean had installed his spray cover that fitted over the cockpit and around his waist (André's and mine had been swept away on the Kagera) to keep the kayak as watertight as possible. As we emerged from the gorge, the Nile, freed now from the constricting chasm, broadened and split into several narrow channels flowing with increasing speed and turbulence over and around granite reefs and green islets.

The river was at a low level and had only a mild slope; we swept through the Sixth Cataract with no difficulty, easily dodging around the rocks and boulders in our way, and barely getting splashed in the few rough places. A

Goddard makes friends with a camel and her offspring at the village of Wadi Hamid.

sharp submerged rock gouged a hole in the bottom of Jean's boat, but he stopped and quickly patched it. If we had come through in high water, with a flooding current sweeping over the jagged reefs, we would have had a much more hazardous experience.

We relaxed when we reached calm water and felt euphoric with relief as we dawdled along downstream. During the day we enjoyed some of the most beautiful scenery of the trip: fertile green banks covered with morning glory, ivy climbing to irrigated gardens, and groves of tall date palms where doves fluttered and cooed. There were dozens of little granite islands covered with luxuriant grass and shrubs and fringed with beaches of gleaming white sand where ducks and geese rested. We saw several flattish, soft-shelled turtles with long necks and pointed heads sunning themselves on the rocks and two species of monitor lizards along the banks.

April 1: *Desert country*

We have really entered desert country now, with the Nile flowing placidly in the midst of endless undulating sand dunes. It has been a calm, hot day and the current has been a great help to us. We were delayed by a succession of sandbars that forced us, several times, to get out and tow our kayaks through the shallow water.

As we were setting up an early camp, two Sudanese soldiers came riding in on camels. They were on a three-day patrol of the area and stopped to check us out. After a chat and some tea, they continued to their bivouac farther downstream.

April 2: *Shendi*

Another windless day—a real break for us. We can average four miles an hour when there is a fair current and no wind, although the crushing heat saps our strength and slows us down. We reached Shendi, the first town since we left Khartoum a hundred miles back, and were welcomed by Siddik Nadim, Assistant District Commissioner, who spoke no English. In the nondescript market town with its monotonous cubical dwellings and shops of greyish mud, we bought bananas, oranges, small melons, tomatoes, and onions.[45] Shendi and El Metomna, across the river, are the main towns of the Gaaliin

---

45. During the early nineteenth century, Shendi was one of the most important market towns and slave centers in Africa, positioned at the crossroads of three busy caravan routes. In 1823 invading soldiers from Turco-Egypt burned the town to the ground. It gradually recovered as a commercial center, but on a much smaller scale.

people, the descendants of Arab immigrants into the Sudan who, from the fourteenth century on, settled along the Nile from Abu Hamed to Khartoum and intermarried among the Nubian tribes.

We had arrived on a Monday, a market day, so the souk was bustling with activity. The wide main street was lined with shops and open-air stalls, where merchants sat beside large baskets filled with durra, lentils, dates, salt, and fruit. On the livestock market, nomadic herdsmen haggled emotionally with villagers over the price of their camels and goats. We learned from Nadim that we could buy a good camel here for 1,500 piasters—$45.00 U.S.

April 3: *Naga*

We had a fine breakfast with Mr. Nadim, and got along surprisingly well with our meager but expanding Arabic. We had a full and fascinating day devoted to exploring the first major antiquities of the Upper Nile Valley—the 2,000-year-old ruins of Naga, thirty-five miles away in the vast desert surrounding Shendi. Nadim provided us with a government lorry, and as protection against nomad bandits, a military escort of two Sudanese soldiers with rifles.

We soon discovered why these important ruins are so rarely visited. Half the time we made our own road or followed a crusty old caravan trail. Three times we bogged down in the sand and had to work our way free with shovels and planks—with the sun beating down on us in 125 degrees of heat. Three hours later we reached the richly carved stone relics of what had once been the capital of the ancient independent kingdom of Kush.[46] Strewn over the gravelly landscape were the walls of three temples, a palace, granite rams, pylons, and columns—evidence of Kush's sophisticated architecture.

One of the temples, known as the Kiosk, was unusually attractive and well preserved. It had a mixture of styles: Roman in its Corinthian capitals and rounded arches, and Egyptian in its stone friezes carved with cobras and wing sun disks—an incredible structure to find in Africa so far south. Dominating the ruins was the impressive Lion Temple, with a curious relief on its rear wall of the lion-god, with multi-faces and arms that hint of an influence from India.

Near the ruins we watched nomad herders draw water from the deepest well I had ever seen—150 feet, judging from the length of the rope. To make the

---

46. Some archaeologists believe the Kushitic civilization was the most African of the continent's ancient societies, and, beginning as far back as the eighth century B.C., had a greater influence over the cultures of black Africa in the fields of agriculture, social organization, and metallurgy than any other. The Kushites were, in turn, greatly influenced by Egyptian culture, religion, and techniques, but were able to retain their own identity throughout their long history.

drawing easier, they had fastened the ropes to bantam donkeys that they drove back and forth, alternately raising and lowering the goatskin waterbags.

Young girls, black-skinned and barebreasted with prominent tribal slashes on their cheeks, emptied the buckets into the ground basin until it was full, then began filling goatskin waterbags with the brackish liquid while their little brothers handled the animals.

They had never seen an "Americani" before—not surprising, since they spent their lives wandering from one oasis to another through some of the world's most uninhabited and out-of-the-way wildernesses, enduring continual heat, dust, and hardship. Yet they are robust and handsome, despite austere lives that are an unending round of torrid days, chilling nights, suffocating sandstorms, and perpetual thirst.

I wish it had been possible for me to travel with them a few days to get to know them better. I visited with them as long as possible, but finally had to tear myself away so that we could return to Shendi before dark. As we drove off, a few of my new friends raced along beside the truck on their fine white camels as a farewell gesture.

On the return to Shendi we passed another Kushitic ruin at Musawwarat, site of one of the largest Kushite buildings, believed to be a mammoth stable built for the royal elephants. (The Kushites used elephants in warfare and as symbols of royal prestige.) Back in Shendi, we spent some time at the local social club—a small building with a courtyard—and then slept in the open.

April 4: *North of Shendi*

The wind was not bothersome today, and the scenery was beautiful. One strand was like a south sea island setting, with gracefully curving palms and flowering shrubs above a broad slope of sandy beach.

We also saw several brass-green crocodiles. They seemed to melt soundlessly from the bank into the water as we neared them, although one nine-footer I surprised some distance from the river amazed me with its speed. It reared up and ran along with its body off the ground in a mad dash back to the water.

April 5: *Meroë*

This morning we hiked a quarter of a mile inland to explore the ruins of Meroë in the Bayuda Desert, where an elderly Sudanese caretaker with rheumy but kindly eyes welcomed us, seemingly befuddled at the appearance of foreign visitors. Considered one of the most important archaeological sites in Africa, the ruined palaces and temples before us and the fragmentary walls, columns, and stone rams (symbols of Amon-Re, god of the sun) with curlicued hair etched in their sides gave scant evidence of the glory and tremendous influence of the Meroitic culture that once flourished here.

When we returned to our kayaks we were so enervated by the heat that we didn't bother removing our clothes before plunging into the river for a cooling respite. Swimming on a day like today, with the temperature hovering around 120 degrees in the shade, is sheer bliss. The sun has dried our lips into cracks, and our noses go through a continual round of peeling, then sunburning. André and I have become "evenly toasted" in following the Nile's twists and turns, and are now so tan that we can paddle all day in the hottest weather without wearing a stitch except our hats. Jean seems to accept the Arab belief that clothing insulates the body against heat and prefers to stay bundled up, wearing his shoes, khaki pants, shirt, and hat. It seems to work for him, but he has no tan except on his face and arms.

We camped tonight in a stand of luxuriant alfalfalike weed, and instead of the grunting of hippos, we went to sleep to the comical noise of donkeys hee-hawing, a sound that is a perfect imitation of a rusty pump.

April 6: *El Damer*

We almost passed El Damer, until a boatman told us it was half a mile inland. Since it is Friday, the Moslem holy day, the British were gathered at the British Club in Atbara—they don't work on the Moslem sabbath. So we accompanied the District Commissioner, Mr. Buchanan, to the club, where we passed an enjoyable evening and dispelled the rumor that seemed to have started weeks ago that one of us had been eaten by a crocodile. They seemed relieved to find it wasn't true.

We were driven back to El Damer to spend the night at our camp, with invitations for breakfast and lunch tomorrow.

April 7: *El Damer*

We woke this morning to find André's kayak gone. The wind had blown it into the water, and it had floated downstream about 200 yards, then come to rest on a spur of land. After retrieving the boat, we paddled the eight miles to Atbara, a tidy town of tree-lined streets, flower gardens, and attractive homes, where we beached in front of the residence of Mr. and Mrs. Maxwell-Mackey, located on the banks of the Atbara River near the point where it joins the Nile.

We had met our hostess at the party the night before and breakfasted with her this morning. She is Swiss and speaks French, much to Jean's joy (though his English is picking up, under tutelage by André and me).

We visited a cement factory, the only one in Sudan, and walked along the high, gravelly banks of the Atbara River, the Nile's last tributary, 200 miles from Khartoum. From here to the sea, almost 1700 miles, the Nile flows through some of the most sun-scorched territory on earth without receiving another contribution of water, either from rain or from another stream. Like the Blue Nile, the Atbara rises in the mountains of Ethiopia near Lake Tana. In flood, beginning in August, the river roars along for 500 miles up to a thousand feet wide; in the dry season, it shrivels to a series of deep muddy pools where hippos, crocodiles, and fish take refuge for more than half the year.

We had thought to leave after lunch, but were pressed into attending a party in our honor. Our periodic contacts with Europeans along the Nile have been enjoyable but really make us aware of the dramatic contrast between what our lives had been in the modern world and our now primitive and sometimes lonely life on the river. Tonight we sleep on cots in the Fordhams' back yard.

April 8: *Berber*

As we left, we were told that the temperature had gone up to 130 degrees on April 5. No wonder we were so fagged out from the heat. Shakespeare wrote, "All the world is cheered by the sun." Obviously he had never been to the Anglo-Egyptian Sudan.

We reached Berber at 3 p.m. A hundred years ago it had been the most flourishing and important town on the upper Nile—a slave, ivory, and gold market. Now it is nothing more than a typical Sudanese settlement, somewhat larger than most, with many crumbling ruins, relics of its one-time glory.[47]

April 9: *Berber*

We went to sleep out-of-doors last night, with no hint of the ordeal we were to go through before morning. Around midnight the fitful wind suddenly went beserk. We woke from deep sleep coughing and choking; the clear sky was blotted out, and everything was enveloped in a shrieking explosion of sand-filled wind. It was the violent sandstorm the Sudanese call a *haboob,* the terror of the desert that unpredictably sweeps over the northern Sudan during the months of March and April. A haboob is intimidating enough in the daytime, but in the dead of night it is terrifying.

The grit-laden gale swept over us in such a strangling blast that to keep from being suffocated we were forced to curl ourselves into a fetal position

---

47. Berber had been completely destroyed by the followers of the Mahdi in 1885 but was rebuilt by his order. This second town was in turn leveled by the shells from General Gordon's steamers, resulting in the construction of the third and present settlement.

inside our sleeping bags with just a crack open for air. As the howling tempest reached its peak, it seemed to us that, even with our low silhouette on the sloping beach, we were going to be blown away into the river. We had to kick and squirm throughout a sleepless and miserable night to keep from being buried alive by the sand building up around us. The fine particles penetrated into every part of our bodies, from our eyes and hair to between our toes.

We were held captive until dawn, when the storm lessened enough for us to escape our nylon cocoons. With great relief we got up, shook the sand from our bodies and our sleeping bags, and groped around in the sand for our buried clothes, preparing to move downstream to the shelter of some trees. It was

El Khandaq in northern Sudan, formerly an important market for slaves, ivory, and gold (see page 215).

A typical Sudanese sand storm about to envelope a riverside village.

only then that we noticed with horror that two of the kayaks were missing—André's and mine! They had been swept away on the heaving river when the sandy shore upon which they rested was undermined by the pounding waves. In another few minutes Jean's boat would have been swallowed up and lost, too.

We looked frantically upstream and down to catch sight of them, but the atmosphere was so thick we could barely see across the river. We set out upstream to search for the boats, the wind cannonading sand and grit at us in stinging blasts. Jean paddled close to the bank; André and I groped over the dunes along the shore, heads bent and eyes squinting against the hot blizzard. We had gone half a mile when I spotted one kayak safely at rest in a cove on the opposite side of the river. I scrambled down the bank, dived into the water, and swam with all my strength through the tossing waves to retrieve the half-awash but undamaged shell. It was André's.

Mine was nowhere in sight. I felt sick at the thought that the boat was capsized and lost for good, with more than 1,600 miles still to cover. Everything I owned, except the shorts I wore, including my irreplaceable movie camera, was in my kayak. While my friends continued the search downstream in their kayaks, I swam across to an island in the middle of the river a mile from camp to see if the capricious wind could have blown the boat there, but with no success.

I returned to shore and headed back to join the men, walking along barefoot over the hot ground. The sky finally began to clear as the wind velocity slackened, and the sun, blotted out until now, beat down on my bandannaed head as if it would shrivel me up.

After five exhausting hours of searching, it was Jean who found *Cleo,* my kayak, her prow nosed into a sandbar a mile downstream. The three of us were baffled by the mystery of finding André's craft a half mile *upstream,* resting on the western bank, and mine beached a mile *downstream* on the eastern shore. How could two boats beached side by side be blown by the same wind in two opposite directions? The villagers would probably have explained it as the prank of a mischievous djinn or spirit.

Once bitten, twice shy. We promised ourselves that henceforth each night we would take the kayaks completely out of the water.

We reached Gadawag late in the afternoon, exhausted after our sleepless night and the frantic search for the kayaks. The omdah, a rotund middle-aged Sudanese, rode up on a donkey so small that he had to spread his legs to keep his pointed slippers from dragging in the dust. "There's more omdah than donkey," I said to my friends. The headman cordially invited us to be his guests for the night and led us across a durra field to his large mud dwelling in a shady palm grove. Nailed over the doorway like a grotesque coat of arms were the grinning heads of three freshly killed crocodiles.

April 9: *North of Berber*

Our host ushered us into the main room, where we sat on dusty divans. The four walls were bare but had been coated with amber wash. Within a few minutes a servant appeared with a tray of jelly glasses filled with hot sugary tea, which we sipped gratefully. As usual the womenfolk were discreetly secluded in the family living quarters to the rear of the dwelling, but after a time some of the omdah's male friends joined us, shaking our hands and salaaming with

Ancient method of threshing grain, in which donkeys are driven over piles of wheat; their hooves kick the kernels loose from the straw.

polite bows, then sitting in a group around us. Our limited Arabic caused the conversation to be labored, but we kept it going for a while by showing the men pictures of our families and some of the expedition photos we had had developed at Khartoum. No one seemed to mind when we lapsed into silence. For a long time we all sat still in the gathering dusk in comfortable companionship, the Sudanese lost in their own thoughts and we in ours. The three of us, exhausted from our sleepless ordeal in the sandstorm, had dozed off by nightfall, when we were awakened for a bounteous Sudanese supper. After the servant had poured water from a ewer over our hands, he served a delicious meal consisting of a spicy mutton stew, a fried fish omelette, a vegetable called molakhia, yoghurt, thin disks of fine kisra (unleavened flat bread made from wheat), and fresh dates. The dark green molakhia was like jellified spinach, somewhat slimy in texture but with a pleasant taste. After this feast, we retired to the courtyard, where we spent a peaceful night on beds of leather thongs.

April 10: *North of Berber*

Before leaving Gadawab, we watched wheat being threshed in the age-old way: six donkeys, tethered together and goaded by two little boys, tramped in a circle around a post over piles of wheat, their hooves kicking the kernels loose from the stalks. The boys' father stood nearby, winnowing the threshed grain by slowly dropping handfuls of it into the wind, which blew the chaff away while the heavier kernels piled up in a mound at his feet.

After a hard day on the wind-agitated river, we camped at El Bauga, sleeping at the local rest house.

April 11: *The Fifth Cataract*

This morning, paddling alone, I came upon a group of fierce-looking Beja nomads resting in the shade of a grove of stunted thorn trees, while their large herd of white camels watered along the Nile. They were Hadendowas, small wiry men with fine facial features and muscular physiques, members of the largest tribe of the Beja people, whose history as independent pastoral nomads can be traced back to 4,000 B.C., longer than any other African society.

The Hadendowas have long been renowned for their fearlessness and fighting abilities. The British called them the "fuzzy wuzzies" because of their "afro" type hair style, but considered them the most formidable of the Mahdi's forces. Kipling referred to them as "the brave warriors with hayrack heads of hair," an effect achieved by shampooing in camel's urine and teasing the hair for hours with a special comb to achieve a cloudlike effect. And though dark-skinned, they are caucasoid in race and speak a Hamitic language called To

Bedawi, though these herdsmen spoke fluent Arabic, too. Three of the younger men let me film them, though the others, perhaps fearing the "evil eye," refused.

By the time I returned to my kayak, Jean and André had caught up, and we continued together for a time. Paddling is such an individual effort, conditioned by personal metabolism and interest, that it is impossible to keep together. Traveling as we do, strung out over the Nile as much as three or four miles apart, we often have entirely different experiences. We stop to visit different sights, villages, and people. For one the day may be eventful and filled with interest; for another dull and tedious. We are three separate travelers down the Nile on different trips.

Late in the afternoon we passed a granite island marking the beginning of the Fifth Cataract, which consists of about seven miles of intermittent whitewater, where the Nile is enclosed by rugged outcroppings of granite and black basalt.

A mile or two farther along, the Nile widened and we came to the first series of rapids, with the current accelerating, then boiling over the rocks and boulders. We shot through swiftly, zigzagging down the narrow twisting channels with thrills and a few moments of fear. It is five months to the day since our disastrous crackup in the Kagera rapids. This time I had prepared for the worst, tying everything securely in the kayak and removing all my clothing in anticipation of an unexpected dunking which, happy to say, never came.

We kept close together to be able to render aid to one another if necessary and were swept along over one wild chute after another. It took all our skill to thread our way through some of the trickier runs in the roaring cataract, especially with the sun in our eyes and swarms of flies and gnats pelting us in the face.

Because we couldn't find a campsite until sundown, we had to shoot one of the wildest rapids in the evening. We finally stopped on a rocky shelf where we cooked and ate supper and then slept behind a sheltering altar of stone, wondering if pagans had ever held rites here. We were disturbed during the night by a pair of curious jerboas. They are a rodent much like the kangaroo rat of the American Southwest, with outsized hind legs that enable them to jump fifteen feet when hard pressed. One bit me on the finger as I slept.

April 12: *North of the Fifth Cataract*

We negotiated the rest of the Fifth Cataract this morning, the first men to do so in small craft, bouncing along through the rapids in a shower of spray, our kayaks pitching and rolling like toy boats. It did nothing to ease our minds that a flock of vultures followed us for a few minutes, wheeling low overhead to match our speed—an omen of imminent death, according to Arab superstition. But we emerged safely with only minor gashes in the rubberized canvas hulls of the kayaks, which we promptly patched.

To get an idea of what we experience when we run a rapid by kayak, imagine yourself sitting on a big board and trying to stay upright in a giant, churning washing machine. We sit below the water-level which gives us a flat view of the river but also a feeling of intimacy with its every mood. Our legs, stretched out and resting on the kayak's frame or skin, can feel the water sliding by and are sometimes bruised when we collide with submerged rocks.

After the whitewater we visited a trio of goatherds, then stopped to investigate a ruined stone fortress of the Mahdi era, perched atop a cliff on the east bank. A little jackal dashed away over the rubble as we climbed to the top of the highest parapet, where we had a splendid view of the Nile, speckled with green and black islets, flowing through an infinitude of amber desert. Later on, André struck another crocodile with his kayak in shallow water—his third collision with the creatures. "André," I told him, "you've got to stop teasing the crocodiles."

We camped on a grass knoll tonight, and two charitable men from a nearby village brought us gifts of food for our supper. One gave us fourteen eggs, of which three had been boiled and five were spoiled. The other gave us a pan of warm goat's milk, which helped put us to sleep—in spite of the cold night.

April 13: *Friday. Abu Hashir—North of the Fifth Cataract*

Just six months ago today we landed in Africa. It is Friday the thirteenth, supposedly an unlucky combination, but it proved to be a good day for us. We made thirty-five miles because there was no wind and the current was strong.

We haven't seen any fishermen on the Nile since Ed Dueim, but the fish must still be plentiful—one jumped into Jean's kayak this morning. One jumped into my lap a few weeks ago, too, but both of us threw the fish back in. The weather is too hot to keep them through the day until supper.

We shot more rapids today, but they were more fun than dangerous; we had no close calls. We have passed some islands completely overgrown with foliage, others fringed with low palm and thorn trees—a welcome sight in this land of true desert. From a distance they look like mirages shimmering in the heat haze. The Nile is the only sustainer of life in this area; wherever it flows, life springs up.

We ate and slept in the home of the omdah of Abu Hashir. We must have looked famished to the chubby headman, because he kept urging us to eat

A stone fortress of the Mahdi era.

more long after we were stuffed. But we could appreciate his attitude. The Nubians consider plumpness desirable—an indication of affluence and therefore a source of prestige. The combination of hard work in oppressive heat on a sparse diet has brought me from 180 pounds at the start of the expedition to 165 at Khartoum, and my companions have lost similarly.

April 14: *South of Abu Hamed*

Another thirty-five-mile day on the tannish-green river, about the maximum distance we can paddle in one day without total exhaustion. We saw no humans today, but we did see many sunning crocodiles, a few soft-shelled turtles and monitors, and, in the air, ducks and fish eagles. It is remarkable that the banks continue lovely and fertile, yet a totally dead landscape exists just beyond the river. Dust devils, the dusty whirlwinds Sudanese Moslems believe are *djinns,* or spirits, are becoming a common sight.

After Abu Hamed, the river takes a great curve to the west and south, almost doubling back on itself before returning northward toward the Mediterranean.

We slept in the open without clothing through a hot, windless night.

April 15: *Abu Hamed*

Five hours of sweaty paddling brought us to the small town of Abu Hamed by noon today. We settled in at the government rest house to literally sweat out the long afternoon, with the temperature soaring to a high of 122 degrees. We enjoyed the rare luxury of a nap, then spent time writing letters and updating our journals. It has taken us almost three weeks to paddle the 350 miles from Khartoum, but we have traveled 2,000 miles from the head of the Nile at Lake Victoria.

April 16: *The Fourth Cataract*

We ransacked torpid little Abu Hamed all morning in search of food supplies without much success. Fortunately, we all still like dates and, if necessary, can subsist all day on a handful. Mostly the dates we have been able to buy since leaving Khartoum are the dried (i.e., petrified) kind, which start out with the consistency of a dumdum bullet. Each date requires lengthy chewing with faith and determination before the taste buds detect anything.

But the palms hereabouts produce the finest dates in the Sudan, and we purchased a supply of two varieties at the otherwise poorly stocked local shops. One of the merchants supplemented this with a donation of two big cauliflowers freshly picked from his garden—a princely gift in this parched land.

For the next month we will be traveling through one of the hottest, most isolated and little-known areas of the world—the vast Nubian Desert.

We would give the Nile mapmakers a real argument as to the location of the Fourth Cataract. They indicate that it is situated about 100 miles downstream, but in our experienced opinion it begins near Abu Hamed. We hadn't been on the river ten minutes this afternoon when we shot the first stretch of rapids, swooping along toward the west on a dazzling glacier of radiant sunlit water, with glare and spray veiling our vision and scores of blood-sucking seroot flies feasting on our bare bodies.

We also began following the great detour today, in which the Nile, beginning at Abu Hamed, is forced to shunt around a colossal barrier of rock for 175 miles, first flowing westward and then southwest, before finally returning to its regular northerly direction at Dongola.

At one place we were alerted by the booming thunder of falls ahead and landed for a reconnaissance. I started out barefoot to climb a cliff for a better view, but the rock was sizzling and scorched my feet. I fancy-stepped back to the kayak to put on my shoes. When the three of us stood on a promontory overlooking the river, it was so choked by a forest of boulders that we couldn't see the best channels to follow. We had no choice but to push off and do our best to get through.

Jean took the lead because of his greater experience with rapids-running. As we drifted toward the leaping water, he stood in his seat to scan the possibilities ahead, an action requiring perfect control and balance. He waited until the last moment, then quickly sat down as his kayak reached the first riffles. In seconds it was my turn, followed by André.

My pulse shook my whole body as I lined up on Jean's course and let the swift current have its way. For the next few minutes I was too busy dodging rocks and falls to feel much fear—my kayak danced along at breakneck speed through a long series of steep, narrow channels seething with violence, seeming more fragile than ever as the wooden frame creaked and shifted with each toss of the angry waves.

After a nerve-wracking passage through the rocky obstacle course, I found Jean safely waiting in calm water. I joined him, and André appeared a minute or two later.

After catching our breath and comparing experiences, we continued and shot several more dangerous stretches of river that challenged our skill. We camped at the base of a big sand dune near a clamorous rapid.

I went for a hike on the silent desert looking for some kind of fuel for our campfire and quite unexpectedly came upon a large fortress consisting of a wide rectangular courtyard enclosed by the high walls and two towers. As I climbed one of the towers to watch the sunset, I flushed a jackal that had been hiding in the rubble. In the twilight it looked like the coyotes I used to see when I worked on my Uncle Royal's cattle ranch near Rexburg, Idaho. The sun sank behind a range of bare granite mountains in a haze of fiery rose and pink, leaving me sitting on the old battlement dreaming of the men and events connected with the fortress.

April 17: *The Fourth Cataract*

Being so low on the water, we have a strange distortion of perspective sometimes. In running some of the broader rapids, we have the illusion that the river is tilting at a slant from the horizontal; so we lean to one side of our kayaks or the other to compensate.

André and I are enjoying rapids running more with each successful passage. Until the Nile expedition we had never been near a kayak, let alone whitewater. Jean has the skill and knowledge to cope with the hazards of the river, gained from long experience in kayaking on European rivers; but André and I have learned by trial and error, and the rapids have been a particularly harsh taskmaster, often forcing us to make split-second decisions as to which of several channels to take, with the threat hanging over us of destruction on the jagged reefs or of drowning in the boils and whirlpools. And our usually high optimism has sometimes been eroded at the sight of crocodiles resting on the sandy borders of rock islands in the midst of the rapids, but what an inspiration they are for efficient paddling!

The stars and constellations have become like old friends after studying them night after night. The frosty crystal of light that forms the top of the Southern Cross I have picked as my own special favorite. I call it *Jamil,* which means beautiful in Arabic.

April 18: *The Fourth Cataract*

We spent hours today exploring more old ruins, sometimes a frustrating experience because we have so little information about them. The palaces, forts, and mosques we have been seeing the past two weeks are a mixture of Meroitic, early Christian,[48] and Mahdist construction.

---

48. There were three Christian kingdoms in ancient Nubia, largely due to the proselyting efforts of monks from Constantinople. One of the earliest and most influential missionaries was a monk named Julian, who began his ministry in 543 but had a difficult time enduring the notorious Nubian heat. According to his biographer, Julian was obliged to take refuge in caves full of water, where he sat undressed from nine o'clock until four in the afternoon. Christianity endured in Nubia for nine hundred years; then in the 16th century the last trace of it was engulfed by Islam.

Though Sudan is Africa's largest country, less than half of it is inhabited by a settled population. The Nubian desert is one of the least populated areas; but I marvel to find *any* people in this arid region. They are totally cut off from the outside world, yet subsist contentedly on a patch of cultivated ground and their goat herds.

Even though we are surrounded by a dead sea of rock and sand, bird life is still prolific. Shore birds, waterfowl, and raptors abound, but we have also seen flocks of speckled pigeons, little long-tailed namaqua doves, gorgeous metallic green cuckoos, and many strange and beautiful birds that are unfamiliar to us. Today I saw an African hoopoe, a medium-sized bird with a rakish crest of pinkish feathers that could have been the inspiration for Woody Woodpecker.

We passed through another series of rapids in the late afternoon, with the sun in our eyes again and sunglasses useless because of the spray. Our kayaks were designed for two paddlers; so they handle awkwardly with just one, and especially in white water we have to paddle hard and fast to keep heading straight and to dodge boulders. I raced through first without trouble, but Jean and André both struck rocks and tore rents in their hulls, which Jean repaired as they camped.

The black river boulders have been polished by the rushing torrent until they are shiny and satin smooth, and have been worn into all kinds of grotesque forms, some as shapely as modern sculpture.

We chose a grassy spot for the night and were surprised, upon climbing the high bank, to find a cluster of huts nestled at the base of the rocky crags. We saw two women in black gowns churning butter by swinging a suspended goatskin bag back and forth. When they saw us, they darted inside a hut. The only other person around was a crippled man who sold us a large bunch of onions, which we ate with a goose I had shot earlier. It was a tough old bird, and I have a feeling it would have died soon from senility if I hadn't bagged it.

April 19: *The Fourth Cataract*

The colorful, rugged scenery we are passing through looks more like what you would expect in a Utah national park. The river winds through narrow gorges hemmed in by great knobby masses of porphyry, gneiss, and basalt. Sometimes I get the feeling we are exploring the Colorado River rather than the Nile. We are descending continuously, but the river has a particularly steep slope in the rapids. It seems we must run out of altitude soon.

At noon we heard human voices calling out, a rare sound in this virtually uninhabited region. We soon spotted two young men swimming along, hugging inflated goatskin bags and kicking vigorously toward the opposite shore.

One of the lads seemed to be having a tough time of it in the swift current, so I paddled over and gave him a tow to a safe landing. His bright grin of appreciation was worth the effort.

April 20: *The Fourth Cataract*

A scorchingly hot day. The sun's rays seem to double in intensity as they reflect off the rock, sand, and water, and the heat envelopes us like a heavy blanket. It would be interesting to know how many BTUs our bodies have absorbed.

We shot a succession of rapids this morning and at midday successfully negotiated the biggest one we have encountered to date. Here the river was jammed through a narrow craggy gorge that dropped steeply through its whole length. We came upon it so unexpectedly that we barely had time to size it up before the current sucked us through. Then the fun began—a real roller coaster with our kayaks bucking and plunging down the foamy chute of rushing water and nearly swamped by the tempestuous waves and wild current. For the second time Jean took the lead, and as he was swept around the corner of the canyon wall where the river turned, he appeared to be enveloped in jagged, foam-topped waves. His kayak was tossed about as though it were in the grip of an angry giant.

André, trailing a hundred yards behind, had the same view of me and thought for a moment that I had been completely engulfed and had gone under. Miraculously we came through unscathed, although we did have a few scary moments and shipped a barrel of water apiece.

Later in the afternoon we reached the four-mile stretch officially known as the Fourth Cataract. It had only one really exciting section in it—a narrow descending alleyway of rock-fanged rapids, which we swept over safely.

We camped on a sand dune below the last riffle, happy over having come through the first half of the six cataracts so well and a little proud of the fact that we were the first to actually paddle through them, especially since no one had been able to really tell us what to expect, except General Scoones in Khartoum, who said, "I congratulate you on reaching Khartoum, but I strongly urge you to end your voyage here and now. You will never survive the great cataracts in your small boats. Believe me, I know what I'm talking about; some of them are extremely violent and if you get into trouble, help just won't be available."

Unfortunately, from the time we first arrived in Africa until the present nearly all the information we have received about the Nile from supposedly well-informed officials has been inaccurate and unreliable. Consequently we

Meroë

Meroë was founded as the second capital of Kush in 591 B.C. and developed the largest iron-working industry of its time in Negro Africa. The iron tools and weapons it produced were disseminated and used throughout central and east Africa, profoundly affecting the lives of the people there. The independent Nubian kingdom of Kush was formed in the 8th century B.C. and existed for a span of 1,000 years as one of the most important of all African civilizations—unfortunately one of the least known because of its inaccessibility and the inability of scholars to decipher its language. By the middle of the 8th century B.C. Kush was powerful enough to conquer Egypt, and its King Kashta became the first pharoah of the 25th dynasty. After a rule of about seventy years the Kushites were driven out by Assyrian invaders. They retreated to their first capital, Napata, and then, attacked again by the Assyrians, moved their capital to Meroë, where the kingdom survived for a thousand years, finally being destroyed by a conquering army from Aksum (Ethiopia) in A.D. 350. Meroë was at one time the home of the proud queens called Candace, one of whom fought the Romans valorously until overwhelmed by their armies under Petronius in 23 B.C. She fled to Meroë and eventually died there. Her sarcophagus is covered by one of the forty-one ruined pyramids in the North Cemetery of Meroë, where thirty-four kings, two crowned princes, and four other queens are buried.

have come to distrust the well-meaning advice offered to us about the river, though General Scoones was justified in his negative opinions about the cataracts. Our research indicated they included several really hazardous rapids that we might have to portage around. But as we have preferred to do from the beginning, we'll learn for ourselves through firsthand experience.

April 21: *Merowe*

The high rocky banks have ended; now the river is wide, the current smooth, and our view of the broad sandy desert virtually unobstructed. The dominating feature of this plain is a high angular hill standing in majestic loneliness out on the desert. This is Jebel Barkal, one of the famed historic landmarks of the Sudan, which we will visit tomorrow.

We paused for lunch at the community of Kareima and saw two small paddle steamers, the first since Khartoum. We reached the town of Merowe at 4 p.m., where we bathed, changed our clothes, and spent the night in the rest house near the river.

April 22: *Napata*

A typical government truck—ready to blow up or disintegrate at every major dip in the road—took us to the ruins of Napata near the base of the 1,200-foot hill of Barkal. Here we explored remnants of several temples and a dozen pylon-shaped pyramids twelve to sixty-five feet in height, built from sandstone quarried at Barkal.

Then we hiked up the steep slopes to the top of Jebel Barkal, regarded by the ancient Egyptians and Kushites as the throne of Amon-re, god of the Sun, and therefore a holy mountain. A temple to Amon was built by the Egyptians at the base of Barkal in the time of Tutankhamen, more than 3,000 years ago, and restored by Piankhi and his successors.

After months of travel just above the surface of the river, often with tall reeds, steep cliffs, or endless sand dunes crowding in upon us, it was a tonic to have a bird's-eye view of miles and miles of landscape and river. And after I had shot several scenes of the broad vista with the movie camera, the three of us glissaded in great, sliding leaps down Barkal's steep, sandy slopes to the base of the hill.

The rest of the day we devoted to exploring the ancient Kushite cemetery of Kurru, nine miles downstream. Here all the early kings of Kush had been buried with the exception of Taharqa, the most noted and dynamic monarch of the 25th dynasty.

The Ruins at Napata

Like their enormous Egyptian counterparts,
the pyramids at Napata were used for royal
burials, each one serving as an impressive
grave marker over a mortuary chamber.
Spanning 1,000 years, the kingdom of Kush
was founded just prior to 750 B.C., with
Napata (an area rather than a town) as the
religious and first political capital. In 750 B.C.
Kashta became the first king of Kush. He
launched forth from Napata to conquer
Upper Egypt and founded the 25th Kushite
Egyptian (Ethiopian) dynasty. His son
Piankhi completed his conquest by subduing
Lower Egypt around 725 B.C. and thereafter
ruled over both kingdoms. He and his four
successors ruled all of Egypt and what is now
the Sudan until 660 B.C., at which time the
Assyrians broke Napatan power, and the last
Kushite king retreated. Except for a period of
about seventy years, Napata was the capital of
the ancient world. It was sacked and destroyed
by an expedition of Greek mercenaries from
Egypt in 590 B.C., forcing the Kushites to
move their capital to Meroë. Napata
continued to be the religious capital until
about 315 B.C., the kings still continuing to
be buried there beneath pyramids until that
time.

It was almost dark by the time we got back to Merowe where, after a cleansing swim in the river, we were guests of honor at a dinner-reception held for us by Sudanese government officials.

April 23: *Nuri*

We spent the day at the large pyramid field of Nuri, nine miles north of Merowe on the east bank, where the Kushites established their second royal cemetery. Most of the knowledge about the Kushite civilization has come from the study of the sixty-odd pyramids here and at Napata and Merowe, even though most of them had been violated by robbers. Many of the features of Kushite burials were direct imitations of Egyptian practices.

April 24: *Tangasi*

We left Merowe this morning and paddled to Tangasi, where we visited one of the most colorful souks we have seen to date, a tremendous market held only twice a week. Every commodity had its own specially reserved section in the sprawling marketplace, and goods ranged from saddles to bed frames, baskets to melons, jewelry to goats, camels, and donkeys. After the humble little stalls we have seen so often in the Sudan, the abundance here was overwhelming.

But far more interesting than the goods for sale were the people selling. Several Bedouin nomad traders had brought their sheep and camels to the market for sale or barter. What a breed of men! Lean, strong types with a ramrod erectness, black curly beards, and a certain swashbuckling air that distinguished them from their more sedate town-dwelling cousins.

The three of us were obviously a novelty to the people, for as we threaded our way between the goods and wares spread out on the ground, we were followed closely by no less than fifty individuals of all ages, all eager to get a close look at the trio of strangers. It wasn't easy to get good pictures with hordes of excited kids impishly trying to crowd into every scene and getting underfoot every way we turned.

We stocked up on fruits and vegetables, had a light lunch, and continued on our way. The people living along the banks between the Third and Fourth cataracts are of the Danagla tribe, survivors and direct descendants of the pre-Islamic Nubians.

A half hour before dusk we stopped at a cluster of mud huts high on the left bank to stay the night—but were surprised to find them completely deserted, with only mongrel dogs yapping away to greet us. We went on, and at sunset we saw a young lad washing in the river. We stopped to talk to him, and he assured us that to have a place to stay the night all we had to do was park our boats and follow him—he'd take us to the omdah of his village, who lived only a short distance away.

After stumbling around in the dark for half an hour, we were about to call it quits when the youngster announced that Eznir Ibrahim's *menzil* (house) was just over the next dune. Upon topping the sand hill, we saw below us a big courtyard and a fine mud house. We had to sit on the warm sand for another half hour while our little guide ran to fetch the omdah, who was visiting a neighbor. He finally came and was immediately the perfect host, throwing open his guest house, which all omdahs have for visitors, and telling us, "*mafeash takleef!*"—Make yourself at home.

Within fifteen minutes the little guest house was bursting at the seams with ten gowned and turbaned men—curious neighbors who just happened to be passing by and thought they would drop in. We spent the evening answering the stock questions: Who are you? (*Meen enta?*) Where have you come from? (*Enta git menain?*) Where are you going? (*Enta raiya fin?*) Why are you here? (*Enta henna leh?*) Have your boats got motors or sails? (*Andak motor walla shoraa?*) At ten o'clock our company finally masalaamed us and headed for their beds, allowing us to do the same.

April 25: *Ganetti Village*

This morning we had a repeat performance of an omdah trying to paddle a kayak. Eznir attempted a ride in mine. Like his predecessor, he couldn't quite get the hang of it, but he didn't panic; he simply paddled, with great dignity, in a big circle—backward. He was not so impressed with the boat, however, and didn't offer anything for it, not even a camel, let alone a wife.

After weeks of paddling in Cleo I have become deeply attached to my kayak. The thought of losing her to thieves is painful. I think W. S. Gilbert, of Gilbert and Sullivan fame, must have been inspired by a boat something like Cleo when he wrote:

> *For she is such a smart little craft,*
> *Such a neat little, sweet little craft—*
> *Such a bright little,*
> *Tight little*
> *Slight little,*
> *Light little,*
> *Trim little, slim little craft.*

Despite the crushing heat, I really enjoy paddling through this part of the Sudan. The wide, shimmering river flows along through a tan desert dominated by mammoth dunes, bordered by green banks where grow fluffy tamarisk, meem and thorn trees, and, occasionally, date and doum palms. The sky is blue and vivid. Every few miles we pass a village where a cluster of grey mud cubicles bake in the fierce sun, and sakiehs endlessly grind away at their task of drawing water. Birds of every description are in the air and on the sandbars, often standing next to a sleeping crocodile.

We made thirty-five miles today—no wind and a good current. We stopped at Ganetti Village, and though the omdah was not in, his fifteen-year-old son filled his shoes admirably, feeding us and putting us through the standard interrogation along with his friends. We had comfortable beds for a change, with no bedbugs. My bed was longer than usual so that I could sleep stretched out instead of curling up or dangling my feet over the end.

April 26: *South of the Third Cataract*

All the men and boys of Ganetti accompanied us to our kayaks to see us off this morning. The rich dark complexions of the Sudanese provide an attractive contrast to the whites of their eyes, teeth, and clothing.

We tried to take pictures of the village women filling water jars at the river this morning, but they consider it shameful to be confronted by strange men, and either they ran off or crouched down and covered their faces with their shawls.

The desert approaches the water's edge on the right bank, but the left bank continues to be pleasantly green with palms, occasional huts, and sakiehs. This is the bottom of the great Nile loop, so we will be paddling on a westerly course for about thirty-five miles.

At noon I stopped at the village of El Debba, where another souk was in progress—almost as colorful and bountiful as the one at Tangasi. A shopkeeper invited me into his home to rest, but the trailing crowd pressed me on until a schoolmaster who spoke good English came to my rescue and took me home. Later in the afternoon Jean and André arrived, and we ate a very spicy lunch with the teacher. My companions can wolf down the most highly seasoned Sudanese food, but I can eat only a little before it becomes too much for me.

We are now in the middle of the Dongola Reach, that calm stretch of the Nile unbroken by any rapids, extending for 250 miles between the Third and Fourth cataracts. We spent the night at the home of an omdah who owned a short-wave radio—a rare luxury in a Sudanese village. We tried to tune in the BBC or Voice of America, hoping for a news broadcast, but there was too much static, and we ended up hearing a concert of Sudanese music and chants being broadcast from Omdurman. With a kerosene lamp I managed to write a few letters. We had fried sheep brains for supper, and really enjoyed this exotic dish.

April 27: *South of the Third Cataract*

We had dates for breakfast, eaten as we moved along. Our host wanted to provide food for us, but we have learned by experience that it takes from one to three hours for a meal to be prepared in a Sudanese home. The bread-making process alone is a lengthy one.

The wind was bad again.

We stopped briefly at Old Dongola, virtually deserted, where a fourteenth-century Christian church has sometime during the past years been converted into a mosque.[49] It sits high on a rocky hill and can be seen for miles. It was interesting to stand and watch the river eating away at a high sand bank, eventually to form a new channel. At intervals big clumps of sand were undermined and tumbled into the water with a loud splash.

Half an hour before sunset I stopped near the village of El Goled Bahri. Like most villages and homes of Nubia, this town was set back from the river in the desert so that the fertile strip along the shore could be used for farming.

As I tramped through the desert, I came upon a multitude of people clustered together. The crowd was composed of young men and girls of the Danagla tribe, enjoying some sort of ceremony, complete with beating drums and much shouting and laughing. I managed to push my way to the edge of the circle, noticed only by those nearest me. Everyone else was too engrossed by the activity in the center of the circle.

There stood five young men at attention, arms akimbo, staring straight ahead with a smile on their dark faces. They were naked to the waist, a fact that astonished me because the northern Sudanese are an extremely modest people and as a rule never expose themselves. But I soon understood the reason for this radical behavior. As the youths stood erect and defiant, another group of

---

49. Old Dongola was a Christian city for more than 800 years. It was once the capital of Mukurra, the central of the three Christian kingdoms of Nubia. In A.D. 569 Mukurra, which included the area between the Third and Fourth Cataracts, was converted to Orthodox Christianity. By 652 it had combined with Nobatia, the northern kingdom, and had become the kingdom of Dongola when it was captured briefly by Moslems from Egypt. In medieval times Old Dongola was a large city enclosed by a wall, with a number of churches, large homes, broad streets, and a red brick palace. In the fourteenth century the Christian kingdom of Dongola collapsed under Arab pressure, and Old Dongola became a Moslem town.

about the same age began circling them, brandishing leather whips, canes, and scabbarded swords. Without warning, one of them cracked out his long whip, lashing the bare chest of one of the stationary ones, who took it unflinchingly, only smiling more broadly.[50] He remained impassive as the others took turns flogging his bare torso, producing a livid welt every time they struck him. In turn each of the other boys received eight or ten severe blows and lashes from their tormentors, and not one of them uttered a cry of pain or in any way indicated fear or discomfort.

In a few minutes these five young stoics were replaced by five more, snatched from the watching crowd by the whippers, who administered the same treatment and got the same controlled reaction from the punished.

Sometimes one of the torturers would rush around the ring of onlookers, rapping their bare feet with his sword handle to keep them back. He gave me quite a clout without even noticing my ragged tennis shoes. And at each blow upon the back or chest of one of the victims, the crowd would give a big shout and raise their arms.

After the young men had proved their courage and manliness, the girls took over the show, entering the arena to dance in rhythm to the drums. I have never seen women dance with such beauty and grace, yet with such economy of movement. They wore jewelry of beaten gold around their necks, in their noses, and in the upper and lower earlobes and were clothed in colorful saris of blue, white, purple, and green. They danced with little mincing steps, their arms at their sides with hands poised outward. Their heads bobbed and nodded rhythmically in a Balinese manner—eyes closed, faces an expressionless mask.

I watched until after dark, fascinated by the unprecedented show. Then I found where the omdah lived, and there Jean and André found me a little later. The omdah provided us with a good dinner of eggs, raub (like cottage cheese), sardines, and molakhia, the green vegetable that tastes like glutinous spinach. We slept outside.

April 28: *South of the Third Cataract*

We visited the hilltop village of El Kahndaq today, a town that is only a shrunken remnant of the great slavery, ivory, and gold center of the past.

---

50. This ritual is generally practiced by tribes of the northern Sudan as part of a wedding ceremony, with the groom whipping young relatives and friends during the preliminary activities. In most cases the flogging is mild and mainly symbolic, but it can be severe, such as the one I witnessed—a harsh ordeal regarded as a real test of endurance and self-control. Often the men have dreadful scars from beatings they received when they were young, and they display them to their sons when they lecture them on the weaknesses of modern youth.

Much of Khandaq was in ruins, but there was a charm of another century about the old town in its whitewashed and ochered houses, neat squares, and mudbrick mosques. The young omdah, Hassan Mahamond, allowed us to view the town from the muezzin's tower above the mosque—we were the first non-Moslems to do so. We also inspected a twelfth-century Christian church standing in ruins overlooking the town.

After taking us on a tour of the town, Hassan, a husky thirty-year-old with the handsome features of a movie star, took us to his home for lunch. This was a large two-story building furnished with gilded armchairs, canopied beds, and carved mahogany chests, and with steel swords and large round shields of maroon leather from the Mahdist era hanging on the walls. Two servants brought the steaming food on large brass trays, but Hassan displayed consummate hospitality by serving us personally. After this generous luncheon we went outside to relax in the shade of a grape arbor. Suddenly we heard a muzzin calling out from the minaret of Khandaq's central mosque. He was chanting the azan, the same ancient call to worship given in every Moslem country throughout the world: "*La ilah illa Allah, Muhammed rasul Allah!*"—There is no God but Allah, Mohammed is the prophet of God. After washing himself thoroughly from a ewer held by a servant, Hassan shook out a mat, faced toward the holy Kaaba in Mecca, and prostrated himself for the third of the five daily prayers, silently reciting passages from the Koran with no trace of self-consciousness.

Since arriving in Moslem Sudan, we have frequently seen men praying like this wherever they happened to be—going through the ritual of bowing, touching the forehead to the ground, and standing, whether aboard a felucca, along the banks, in the fields, or in front of their dwellings. I have always been moved by this fervent expression of devotion to their faith.

After the meal Hassan escorted us back to our kayaks. He was the kind of man one would want to have as a friend for life, and we were reluctant to leave. But we paddled on to the village of Urbi and spent the night in the guest room of the headman.

April 29: *South of the Third Cataract*

We didn't wait for breakfast at Urbi because we hoped to reach Dongola by night; so we ate only dates all day. I passed the first fisherman I have seen since leaving Khartoum—a surprising fact, since the river is full of fish which could be a good addition to the Nubian people's diet.

This afternoon I explored the tombs of some important Moslem saints. There were three big tombs about twenty feet high, in the shape of a narrow beehive. Even though they are 200 years old, they are still perfectly preserved as a result of the hot, dry air and almost complete absence of rain. Each one had a small oval opening through which I entered; the interior was suffocatingly heavy and musty from the hundreds of bats who make their gloomy home there. The only thing to be seen inside the tombs except the bats were two narrow troughs on the floors outlined in stone. Hundreds of graves surround each of the tombs, some of recent date, each one marked by a rock and oriented toward Mecca. Elsewhere in the area I photographed fifteen religious monuments dotting the landscape and a sixteenth-century Arab fortress.

Youngsters on the banks usually run away when they see us coming, but as we passed a group of thirty sakiehs the great waterwheels suddenly stopped working, and the children who prodded the oxen to keep the wheels turning deserted their posts to splash out into the river to welcome me and investigate my kayak. Their friendly interest was a delightful change from the usual pattern of fright and flight. A donkey did a perfect double take of me when I paddled past him. He was watering beside the river as I approached. He looked up at me for an instant, then lowered his head to drink again, only to jerk erect and stare at me wide-eyed as if he were trying to figure out what sort of a critter it could be that was half-man, half-boat!

The three of us straggled into the town of Dongola and were welcomed heartily by the *mamur* of the city, Mohammed Baghir, who said he had been expecting us. We slept indoors on nice, long beds.

April 30: *South of the Third Cataract*

While shopping in the souk, we met Joseph Rashid, a Lebanese gentleman farmer, the only European living between Dongola and Atbara, a distance of 500 miles. He delighted Jean and André by conversing with them in excellent French.

During the day we paddled along the western shore of eighteen-mile-long Argo, the longest island in the Nile. We saw a band of Kerarish nomads driving a herd of camels en route to Cairo on what they call the "forty-day trail."

May 1: *South of the Third Cataract*

We left Dongola in a high wind. It was a tough day with much sand in the wind that blinded us half the time. We had only dates to eat all day. We are now passing through the heart of Nubia.[51] A very hospitable omdah at the village of Gharb Benna invited us to spend the night.

---

51. This region has no present-day political status; so its boundaries are only vaguely defined. In ancient times Nubia encompassed an area approximately 550 miles long, from the Sixth Cataract in the south to

May 2: *Beginning of the Third Cataract*

The buildings are getting more elaborate now in the villages we pass, with ventilation provided by a foot-high gap between the top of the walls and the roof, and more decoration appearing in the architecture. Most homes have a design of old dishes and crockery set in the adobe wall over the doorway. Rains are rare but disastrous when they occur in this region, since mud is the major building material. Last year there was a freakish deluge that destroyed or badly damaged many of these earthy edifices, their surfaces melting away like sugar under the downpour.

After shooting several small rapids, we spent the night at the hut of the captain of a large felucca. He told us that boats could pass through the Second and Third Cataracts only during high water, and it would be very dangerous for us to attempt them at this time of the year, when the main channels near the banks are cut off and so many rocks are exposed. He strongly advised us to carry our boats around all the bad spots and not take a chance on being smashed up. We told him, "We'll see."

May 3: *Geddi*

The wind was terrible until afternoon. We finished passing over the Third Cataract safely with just one or two close calls. When we flushed a big croc at the head of one of the rapids, he dashed into the water from the ledge where he had been sunning, like a long, slender chunk of granite magically detached from the mass of rock and hurled into the river. No villages are along the banks now, just a dwelling now and then or at most two or three clustered side by side. The topsoil here is only a thin deposit from the Nile, yet people cling tenaciously to their parched land and refuse to leave for more fertile areas.

The sight of geese and plovers standing in the midst of three basking crocodiles made me think of the millennium, "when the lion shall lie down with the lamb." Later, I saw several ragged feathered ravens looking like poor relations as they stood beside a pair of immaculate white ibis.

Aswan in upper Egypt, and 800 miles wide, from the Libyan Desert to the Red Sea. Linguistically Nubia begins around Meroë and extends to Aswan, with the inhabitants, whose ancestors have occupied this territory since before the rise of ancient Egypt, speaking four dialects of Nubian as their daily language rather than Arabic. Actually there is no Nubian race any more. The people of the Sudan and Egypt who speak Nubian dialects are an Arabicized hybrid race, Negroid in origin, but who have a strong Caucasoid mixture as a result of ancestral inbreeding with ancient Egyptian, Libyan, Arab, Bosnian, Hungarian, Kurdish, and Turkish invaders. They vary in color from fair to very dark, but generally are brown-skinned, have regular features, and are slender in build.

We spent the night at the village of Geddi, where the omdah's brother put us up. All the village headmen of Halfa province were attending a council at Wadi Halfa. Spending our nights with the omdahs we encounter along the way certainly beats sleeping in our tent or on the ground, and it is infinitely more interesting. Omdahs usually seem pleased to have us call on them, and several times we have been told that as far as any of them can remember we are the first Europeans to visit their villages. People we meet are delighted when we speak to them in Arabic.

May 4: *North of Geddi*

Our host took us on a hike out in the desert this morning to some rocky hills, where I photographed a bonanza of well-preserved ancient graffiti, representing a potpourri of travelers who have passed this way. The petroglyphs included primitive etching of lions, giraffes, ostriches, buffalo, and antelope, carved by Stone-Age hunters at a time when Nubia, which is part of the Eastern Sahara, was forested and inhabited by animals now found only hundreds of miles farther south.[52] There were also ancient Egyptian hieroglyphics, signatures in Greek, Meroetic inscriptions, and Christian Jerusalem crosses. The most recent graffiti were in Arabic.

Just outside Geddi the Nile turned from its easterly heading to the north again. We had been cautioned many times by boatmen to look out for a bad rapids just near the turning of the river not far from Geddi, so we were not taken by surprise, as we had been several times before, when we heard the muffled roar of a large cascade in front of us.

However, we had been warned on many other occasions that a rapids was so bad we would have to portage around it only to find that it was relatively easy to handle in our kayaks. So approaching these falls now we decided to take a chance and shoot them. Jean took the lead again, with André bringing up the rear.

The appearance of the Kagbar Falls is certainly deceiving. The throbbing roar, muffled though it was, should have given us a clue to the magnitude and violence of the waterfall, but our low perspective from the kayaks deceived us. At the last moment when the current was too powerful for us to escape its

---

52. The Sahara is the largest desert in the world, but 8,000 years ago it had a much wetter climate and was a fertile region of fish-filled rivers, grassy valleys, some forests, and abundant wildlife. As time went on, some of the bands of nomadic hunters roaming the land settled into permanent communities and developed increasingly advanced towns. Climate changes around 2,000 B.C. caused the Sahara to begin drying up, and the vegetation gradually disappeared as the soil dried out and was blown away.

pull, we saw it for what it really was—a dangerous cascade boiling over a natural dam formed by a line of jagged granite stretching across the river. From our low vantage point on the water it was impossible to see how sharply the river dropped or to realize that there was not one clear channel for us to pass through.

A rocky island in the middle of the river divided the water into two main falls. Jean took the righthand one, sweeping over in an erratic, jerky dive that capsized him, spilling him out into an explosion of rough waves and spray, where he disappeared from sight.

Rather than suffer the same fate, I slowed down as much as possible, then crashed into the little island and pulled my boat up on the rocks. As soon as I had beached the kayak, I jumped out to see how Jean had fared. At first I couldn't see him anywhere and feared that he had been knocked unconscious by the violent buffeting he had undergone. Then, to my relief, I caught sight of him far downstream, clinging to his battered kayak and working his way to shore.

After warning André off as he neared the falls, I surveyed my predicament. I was trapped on the island, and my kayak could not take me anywhere except over the falls. I would have to shoot the cascade and pray for the best. First, though, I decided to take advantage of my unusual position and take some movies of the awesome cataract roaring past me on both sides.

While clambering over the rocks during the filming operation, I thought of a solution. I would drag my kayak overland to the northernmost tip of the little island and take off from there, where the rapids would be somewhat less turbulent. It would be literally a "single-handed" operation—I had a badly infected carbuncle the size of a pigeon's egg on the middle-finger knuckle of my right hand, rendering it almost useless. I had to use the hand frequently as I dragged and carried the kayak, yet I didn't suffer much pain or discomfort from what normally would have been an agonizing ordeal.

It was a hot, sweaty job, and several times I slipped on the slimy rocks and went sprawling, gashing my feet and legs. But at last I arrived at the point of embarkation, and with a prayerful but pounding heart I slid the kayak into the surging water, jumped in, and pushed off. Almost immediately I was swept into the main current and borne along at a pace too fast for comfort.

Aside from the danger of being swamped by the rough water and choppy waves, my main worry was to dodge a pile of rocks directly in my path a short distance downstream. The current was so powerful that I had to use every ounce of strength I had to paddle a diagonal course that carried me past the jagged mass and out of danger. I was bounced around in passing through, but aside from my kayak filling half full with water, thoroughly soaking me, I soon found myself unharmed and in quiet water.

For a few minutes I paddled along, anxiously scanning the rocky shoreline to locate Jean. I finally caught sight of him far downstream where he had been carried. André, who, being forewarned, had been able to find a shallow channel around the falls close to shore, was with him. The two of them were opening up watersoaked bags and spreading the dripping contents out to dry. They were as happy to see me safe and intact as I was them, and we compared notes on each of our experiences in passing the falls.

Jean told André and me that he would have drowned in the capsizing if he had become separated from his kayak. He was able to save his own life by keeping a tight grip on the edge of the cockpit as he was carried along underwater through the powerful boils below the falls. Even with the buoyancy of the kayak supporting his body, Jean still had great difficulty struggling to the surface, swallowing more water than air the first time up, then being sucked under again. He was pulled under a second time before reaching calm water from where he swam to shore with his overturned boat. Apart from bruised ribs and a stomachful of water, Jean came through the accident in good shape.

The only thing lost from Jean's kayak was a pair of tennis shoes, but the boat was broken in three places. We were all grateful that for once I had the 16mm movie camera with me—usually we tie it into Jean's boat before shooting rapids because, with all his experience, he is the least likely to capsize. Both of Jean's cameras got soaked this time, but he was able to dry one, the Rectaflex, and get it back in working order.

Jean and André took shelter from the broiling sun in the shade of an old Arab fortress nearby and cooked a lunch of rice and onions. I wasn't hungry, so I went ahead to Delgo, twelve miles away, to arrange a place for us to spend the night. Delgo was a good-sized town for this impoverished area, and though the omdah was at the Wadi Halfa council, we slept in the menzil at the invitation of his brother. We hardly slept during the night, however, because of the stinging bites of nimits, minute gnatlike flies that are so tiny they can penetrate even the mosquito netting of our tent.

May 5: *North of Delgo*

A local carpenter helped us repair Jean's kayak today. Then we left Delgo and paddled to Abu Sari to look for a gold mine near there. An Irishman aboard the steamer we had taken through the Sudd told us that his brother owned the mine and suggested that we visit him along the way. At dusk we inquired about the mine at the village and were told it was "just over the hill." This proved accurate for a change, and we were pleasantly surprised to find a cluster of five small buildings only half a mile beyond the rocky hill we climbed. We headed directly for one of the shacks illuminated by a kerosene lamp and were met at the door by a tall, bearded gentleman who, if he had been clothed in a frontiersman outfit instead of a beach towel, could have passed for Buffalo Bill. This was Oscar Durham, the assistant mine operator, who welcomed us heartily into his cluttered two-room home. We enjoyed getting acquainted with this personable seventy-year-old Englishman, who told us he had spent the past thirty years of his life prospecting and mining all over Africa and the Middle East. Then we were joined by his partner, Paddy Bishop, a fast-talking, twenty-eight-year-old Irishman from Dublin, who was the son of the mine's owner. His father had "exiled" him to the hottest spot in the Sudan to operate the mine; his shorts, shirt, and peaked cap were stiff with dirt and grease, a six-month growth of beard covered his lean face, and a mane of lank brown hair flowed down to his shoulders. The two men seemed content with their lonely life in the immense desert wilderness, though the nearest town, Wadi Halfa, was 150 miles to the north.

We had supper with them, entirely out of cans, but much more varied than what we had been living on. Paddy told us we were their first visitors in six months and that he was really glad to have someone new to talk to because he and Oscar were "all talked out." After supper I soaked my hand in hot water, and we went to bed outside.

May 6: *Abu Sari, south of the Second Cataract*

The Nile was violently stirred up by a strong wind this morning, so we decided to spend the day inspecting the mine, hoping for better weather later. Most of the mine operations are centered around extracting gold from the quartz tailings of an ancient Egyptian mine. Pharaonic Era mining was quite crude, leaving a good deal of gold still in the ore.

We rode on one of the rickety old trucks, going out five miles into the desert for a load of tailings and had a chance to see the ancient Egyptian mine-shafts. The terrain around Abu Sari reminded me of the badlands of South Dakota, with great black masses of jagged shale and rock standing on end as a result of faulting, giving the appearance of weird forms of vegetation sprouting from the desert—a nightmarish landscape conjuring up expressions like *Devil's Playground* and *Hell's Backyard.*

We found three deep shafts with high mounds of quartz that had been extracted from them nearby. Once he's through with the tailings, Paddy will then go to work on the shafts to mine the main vein of gold-bearing quartz—if anything remains.

May 7: *South of the Second Cataract*

It is another windy day, but we decided to leave anyway. Paddy and Oscar saw us off; we ate dates for lunch with a felucca sailor.

My infected right hand really hampers my paddling. It has become so swollen from the carbuncle that I can't clench the paddle properly but have to pad the handle with my bandanna and take most of the weight on my thumb. But on we go, mile after mile—down and pull with the left hand—up and push with the right—paddling, paddling, day after day, following the endless yet ever-changing waterway that balloons and contracts, twists and winds, rushes and calms; still a mighty river in spite of the perpetual onslaught from the insatiable sakias and irrigation pumps, the thirsty people and animals, and the withering sun.

May 8: *South of the Second Cataract*

Today we spent several hours at Sulb on the east bank, exploring the ruins of the greatest of all Egyptian temples of Nubia. This temple was built by

Amenhotep III, Pharoah of the eighteenth dynasty (1417–1379 B.C.), who spent much of his vast wealth building splendid temples like this one, dedicated to Amon the sun god. Originally the approach to the temple was flanked by granite rams and lions, but these were transferred to the temples at Barkal by the Kushite pharoahs of the twenty-fifth dynasty. Thereafter the ram, which symbolized Amon, became the most important divine symbol of the ancient kingdom of Kush.

We stayed the night with the omdah of Koyekka. He provided us with a meal and a room, but bats fluttered around us as we tried to sleep, and we were needled throughout the night by mosquitoes and the invisible nimits.

May 9: *South of the Second Cataract*

A fair current and no wind. We saw beautiful custard-yellow sand dunes out on the Libyan Desert to the west.

At noon I stopped at Abri and had my hand dressed by the local medic. I didn't recognize my face in the medic's mirror when I borrowed it to trim my beard. I looked as if I had aged ten years since leaving Khartoum.

We noticed that women's costumes have become more colorful lately. The women are still shy, but less so than before. Some work barebreasted in the gardens unashamedly.

I still marvel at the ease with which the people wear their voluminous clothing, often including huge turbans. But the djellabahs do shield their bodies from the torrid sun and the chill of night, and they keep out insects and wind-driven sand. The immas, or turbans, protect against sunstroke, although I have often seen Sudanese and other Africans going about bareheaded under a blistering sun, apparently without ill effects. Scientists have never discovered any major physiological adaptation among the people of the desert-dwelling races, yet they seem unaffected by bareheaded exposure to intense sunlight, while I, despite my heavy felt sloucher, frequently feel giddy, suffer from a befogged brain, and have distorted vision from the concentrated blast of Old Sol.

Today I received a vivid reminder of how overpowering and dangerous the desert is just a few yards from the edge of the Nile. I stopped on the west bank and hiked to some sandstone ridges less than a mile from the river, in hopes of finding and photographing some petroglyphs that were supposed to be in the area. By the time I had trudged across the scorching sand to the outcroppings I felt dizzy from the heat, but soon revived after resting in the shade. I searched the rock walls without finding anything and started back. The river wasn't visible because it was deep in its channel, but I headed eastward knowing I would hit it eventually.

But within a few minutes I began feeling weak and nauseous from heat exhaustion. I rested for a few moments, bent over with my hands on my knees, hoping the feeling would pass. When I stood up and opened my eyes nothing looked the same. I could still see the sandstone formations but they seemed to be in the wrong place. I suddenly felt disoriented in this stark simmering wilderness of sand and rock that stretched to the horizon. Unsure now of which way to head, I set off again and hiked for what seemed more than a mile without coming to the river, feeling more feeble by the minute.

It seemed incredible that the Nile could be so close and yet be so well concealed that I couldn't find it. Obviously the situation was getting critical. I was madly thirsty and suffering from extreme dehydration in the sizzling sun. My head throbbed and my vision blurred, but as I stood trying to get my bearings, I heard the plaintive cry of a bird—to my ears the most glorious sound imaginable. It was a little plover that appeared for an instant above a sand dune only a hundred yards away on my left, then dipped behind it and was gone.

In a burst of new-found energy I rushed toward the dune, struggled to the top, and felt like shouting with happiness at the sight of the pale green Nile flowing peacefully along below me. I tumbled nonstop down the steep sand bank right into the cool water, where I joyfully drank and splashed around until I felt strong enough to continue, silently blessing one small bird that had guided me to safety.[53]

We overnighted at the village of Kosha.

May 10: *South of the Second Cataract*

At Akasha this afternoon a Nubian medical assistant assured me that he could lance my carbuncle for me, and I decided to trust him. After scalding a scalpel he made several clumsy attempts at an incision, shaking even more than I, but the blade was dull, and all he managed to do was gouge a hole in the knuckle large enough to drain only some of the infectious material. So I flamed a razor blade and made an incision that was excruciating but which really drained the large boil properly.

We shot the large cataract at Akasha, then paddled through seven miles of mild rapids to a small settlement called Ukma. We stayed with the omdah's brother again, since the chiefs were all still at Wadi Halfa.

For the next hundred miles, from Ukma to the end of the Second Cataract, we will be paddling through a particularly rocky and desolate valley known as

---

53. In 1805, a caravan of 2,000 men and 1,800 camels died of thirst in the Sahara because the wells along their line of march had dried up.

Batn el Hagar, a descriptive Arabic name which has the appropriate meaning "Belly of Stones."

May 11: *South of the Second Cataract*

We passed safely over the wild Tangour rapids this morning, but a big whirlpool spun me around just as I reached one waterfall, so I was forced to go over the falls backwards. Some thrill!

We really whizz along while shooting rapids—I hate to think what would happen if we ever missed a channel traveling at fifteen or twenty miles an hour and crashed into one of the numerous rock walls we are constantly dodging in whitewater runs.

My throat tightens and becomes dry whenever we are about to pass over rough water, and my hands perspire and tremble. But I don't actually experience a sense of fear, only of excitement and alertness. Rapids-running on the Nile is one of the most thrilling adventures of my life, but I am always relieved when we have safely passed them.

We shot the notorious Dal rapids around noon, the largest cataract we've seen. Many little rock islands, fuzzy with grass, made the run hazardous and obscured our view. Nubians on the bank had been expecting to help us portage around the rapids, and they shouted warnings at us when we decided the bank was too steep and shoved ahead through the water. We kept to the left because all the other channels were dangerously rocky. We had an accident toward the last when we had to walk our kayaks down a narrow rocky channel. We were carefully wading along, feeling our way over the jagged bottom while gradually easing our boats along by means of the tow ropes. André's kayak tilted on a rock, and the rushing current filled and swamped it immediately. Luckily we were next to the bank and were able to tow the boat to still water. I had to swim after the paddle, which had fallen into the water and had been carried downstream. Later we saw a little Dorcas gazelle drinking at the river—the first antelope we had seen in weeks. Besides the abundant birds, the only wild life we have seen in the northern Sudan have been jackals, rats, jerboas, hyraxes, and a wild camel or two.

May 12: *South of the Second Cataract*

At Semna, twenty-five miles from the Second Cataract, we paused to look around at the newly excavated ruins of a huge Egyptian fortress on top of a 125-foot cliff on the west bank. Four thousand years ago there were two of these forts, Semna and Kumma, facing each other from opposite banks in this narrow rocky gorge, to guard Egypt's southern frontier.

Below the ruins we noticed several parallel slashes cut into the wall of the gorge—the first Nilometer we had seen. These cuts were used in ancient times as lines of reference for determining the variation of the Nile's flow from normal levels at the various seasons of the year.

The current was helpful, and today we covered thirty miles.

May 13: *The Second Cataract*

At the village of Gemai, just three miles before the Second Cataract, we were welcomed by the young omdah, who solemnly warned us that at this time of the year the cataract was extremely dangerous and completely impassable. We told him we'd at least have to give it a try.

This was the hottest day of the expedition. In all my travels I have never known such suffocating heat. I'm sure we would have died in the brain-curdling sun except for two factors: we had gradually become acclimated to heat during the seven months we have been in Africa, and we could drink as much as we needed from the Nile to make up for the tremendous water loss through perspiration. We could also jump into the tepid river or fill our hats and pour water over our heads and bodies whenever we felt sunstroke creeping over us. When Jean fished out his thermometer from an equipment bag to check the temperature, he found it had burst, even though it had been scaled to 125 degrees and had been insulated inside the bag and kayak.

The six-mile-long cataract was an intricate maze of narrow channels meandering through a grotesque lunar landscape of black rock islands (350 have been counted at this low-water level). We followed the unanimous advice of the felucca sailors and kept to the left side of the river. I took the lead, clenching my teeth and sitting at attention with only my arms moving to keep the kayak straight and headed slowly towards the thundering white water. It was incredibly tense—there was nothing to guide me, and when I was caught by the current there was no stopping or turning back. I hurtled along at top speed through a tortuous labyrinth of channels, never sure what danger lurked around the next bend, with André and Jean bobbing along close behind me. We successfully ran the first stretch, dodging the rocks and eluding the whirlpools, until the passage we were following became so shallow and clogged with boulders that we had to jump out and carry the kayaks fifty feet to a deeper channel.

We we waded through the warm water, first André and then I was startled out of our heat-induced torpor by a powerful jolt of electricity shooting up our legs when we stepped on what must have been electric catfish, called *raad* by the Sudanese. They are capable of emitting a discharge of up to 400 volts, so we were grateful we hadn't been electrocuted, although our legs were numb and tingly for several minutes.

Lugging the boats and baggage across the burning sand bordering the river with the sun roasting us was one of the toughest jobs of my life. When I began panting from the exertion, it felt as if I were barbecuing my lungs with each breath. It would be interesting to know just how much water we drank today. It must have been an enormous amount. We have been averaging twelve quarts of Nile water daily per man, but we far exceeded that today. We would drink our fill every few minutes, then sweat it out immediately. The bags were too hot to handle until we splashed water over them. I am really worried that all the valuable movie film I have shot at such great effort during the past six weeks will be ruined.

The six-mile-long Second Cataract located near the Egyptian border in northern Sudan.

A family river boat with tattered sail ("the patches have been patched").

230

It took two and a half sweltering hours to portage the three kayaks and twelve equipment bags, our first real portage of the expedition. Then we proceeded to the worst waterfall of all—Abku. The people living in the small village are reputed to make a good living retrieving and salvaging feluccas and their cargoes that crash while traversing this hazardous stretch. A fast but uneventful run and a portage of fifty feet around the far western edge of the falls put Abku behind us and dispatched one of our big worries.

Four miles downstream, after passing over mild rapids, we encountered a tough problem: The channel made a sharp turn at the end of a turbulent chute, and beyond the bend the river bubbled and foamed around large black boulders. It looked deadly, yet we couldn't portage because of the steepness of the bank.

As we were trying to decide what to do, a strapping Nubian with a barrel chest and a voice like a bullfrog came riding up to us on a donkey. We chatted for a few minutes until he understood who we were and what we were trying

A Sudanese village.

to do. Then he said, "Ana hasaadak. Shufo ana rayeh fin, emsho waraia be markebetkum."–"I will help you. Just watch where I go, then follow in your boats." Before we really understood the meaning of his words, this remarkable giant of a man had stripped off his djellabah and turban, blown up a goatskin bag with air, and plunged into the swift current, one arm grasping the bag and the other powerfully stroking in the direction he wanted to take.

He neatly dodged every rock that menaced him and soon had passed through the entire rapids and into quiet water, unharmed.

We quickly rushed to our kayaks and followed the same course he had taken–but not so nonchalantly, I'm afraid. We received a royal tossing by the tumbling water and narrowly missed slamming into some rocks in the center of the rapids, but we passed safely. When we paddled over to the bank to express our appreciation to our fearless guide, who had come out of nowhere to show us the way, we found he had mysteriously disappeared.

We shot the last rapids of the Second Cataract–the final major hazard (we thought) of our expedition, then hurried to Wadi Halfa, the gateway between Sudan and Egypt, and reached the little east-bank frontier town just after sunset.[54] The river broadened after the second cataract until at Wadi Halfa it was a mile and a half wide–a result of the impounding of the Nile by the Aswan Dam, 220 miles farther north.

Joseph Rashid, our Lebanese friend in Dongola, had told us to go directly to his brother Charles's house when we reached Wadi Halfa, and true to his brother's word, Charles put us up at his home. Jean and André took the back porch and I slept under the palm trees in the backyard, with Ahmed, Charles's cook, sleeping on a mat a few feet away. Ahmed woke me up during the night in his attempts to kill a poisonous snake that had come slithering around his feet, but I was too exhausted to get up to identify it.

May 18: *Wadi Halfa*

This is our last day in Wadi Halfa, a little commercial city of 10,000 people where the Sudan Railway terminates and navigation on the Nile into Egypt begins. Yesterday an English Army officer told me the temperature registered a torrid 138 degrees in the shade at the airport. We will leave tomorrow morning after being delayed for the past five days while two of our kayaks, André's and Jean's, were being repaired. They had survived all the natural hazards of the river, including the dangerous white water of the five great cataracts, but it

---

54. Once the only sizable town of the northern Sudan, Wadi Halfa was drowned into oblivion in 1966 by the rising waters of Lake Nasser. A new community has sprung up on higher ground since then.

took two local thieves to put them out of commission. On May 14, the day after our arrival, the boats were stolen, according to eyewitnesses, by two men who took them from the banks where we had beached them.

Paddling a delicately balanced kayak successfully is an acquired skill developed through calm practice, as the nervous thieves soon discovered. Once they had pushed off into the river, they became panic stricken at their inability to control the tippy boats. In their frantic efforts to return, they upset both kayaks and abandoned them to the current as they floundered back to shore and disappeared.

We finally located the boats far downstream upside down and in a deplorable state, with broken sections and slashes in their skins. They looked as if they had been struck by a felucca. The damage repaired, we were eager to move on.

May 19: *Egypt (Lower Nubia)*

This morning we paddled across the border into Egypt, the sixth country of the Nile basin, after nearly five months of memorable adventures in the Sudan. As of this date we have traveled 3,200 miles from the Kagera source in 6½ months, and have another 950 miles to go before reaching the Mediterranean.

We will be traveling through desolate Egyptian Nubia for the next 220 miles on the world's longest man-made lake, created by the impounded waters of the Nile as they back up behind the Aswan Dam. This infertile region is framed by the gleaming yellow sand of the Libyan desert to the west and the greyish brown wastes of the Eastern or Arabian Desert to the east and is still occupied by indomitable Nubians despite their original riverfront villages' being flooded and destroyed after the dam was finished in 1902.⁵⁵

In this whole vast wilderness there isn't a road or railway, hotel or hospital, or even an airstrip. It is accessible only by means of a camel, a four wheel drive vehicle, or, occasionally, a riverboat.

As we stroked along in the radiant morning sunshine, I was impressed by the rich contrasts of color around us—our white kayaks skimming over the dark blue water under a brilliant blue sky, with golden glaciers of sand streaking the western shores and chocolate brown hills and various shades of green

---

55. The Aswan High Dam, completed in 1971, four miles upstream from the earlier dam, has swelled the lake (now known as Lake Nasser) until it extends 100 miles farther south, flooding much of Nubia in Egypt and the Sudan and necessitating the resettlement of approximately 100,000 people in Egyptian Nubia and 50,000 in southern or Sudanese Nubia. Lake Nasser was named in honor of Gamal Abdul Nasser, Egypt's popular president from 1956 to 1970, and one of the most respected and influential Arab leaders of the 20th century.

The great temple of Ramses II at Abu Simbel in Upper Egypt.

in the elegant palms, the tamarisks, mimosas, and reeds fringing the eastern shores. One lovely bucolic scene held my gaze long after I had glided past it: green meadows with plump cows and a herd of shaggy goats grazing. A hundred yards away burned the lifeless desert.

We stopped on the east bank to visit the ruins of a tenth- century fortress and an ancient Egyptian rock temple whose walls were painted over with Christian paintings. After a paddle of twenty-five miles from Wadi Halfa, I reached the village of Faras[56] near dusk; and by chance I hit the one evening of the year when the Nubians from neighboring communities join together in Faras to hold a big feast and bazaar. I mingled with the crowds, and after the initial curiosity about my arrival died down, I was free to join in, including a chance to indulge in a watermelon bust. The melons were the size of cannonballs and were less flavorful than the large variety—but they tasted marvelous to me. A fierce looking Nubian with a handlebar mustache stirred three huge cauldrons of mutton stew, each containing a whole sheep cut into sections. Jean and André showed up in time to join me in eating a bowl of the flavorful stew. We slept on a patch of sand next to the lake.

May 20: *Abu Simbel*

Today we arrived at Abu Simbel (Ipsambul), forty miles downstream from Wadi Halfa, and spent most of the day examining in detail one of the greatest of all ancient architectural wonders, the colossal cliff temple of Ramses II, carved from the tawny rock 1,300 years before Christ. The great temple's recessed facade is dominated by four gigantic statues sixty-six feet tall, seated in pairs on either side of the entrance, representing Ramses, fourth king of the 19th dynasty, who is presumed to be the pharoah from whom Moses freed the Hebrews, and the second of the twelve kings of Egypt to bear the name.

The upper half of the second statue's body has been shattered, possibly by an earthquake shortly after the temple was built; its immense head lies face down in the sand at its feet.

Though Ramses ordered the temple built to honor the sun god, it became a monument to glorify him and to show his wealth and power to his own and future generations. He was one of the most egocentric and boastful of the 300 or more kings of ancient Egypt, the main reason he is best remembered. During his interminable reign of sixty-seven years (1304 B.C. to 1237 B.C.), the

---

56. Faras was an important market town 3,000 years ago, and in later times was the center of Christianity in Sudanese Nubia. In 1961 archaeologists uncovered a 1,200-year-old cathedral here, the largest church ever discovered in Nubia, with well-preserved paintings depicting Biblical scenes. They were able to rescue 100 of these invaluable frescoes before the area was flooded.

Abu Simbel

In 1964 the waters of Lake Nasser, rising
behind the new Aswan High Dam,
threatened to submerge Abu Simbel's
priceless temples. To rescue them, an
international group of German, French,
Swedish, Italian, and Egyptian engineers and
skilled marble cutters from Italy's famed
quarries performed history's most spectacular
moving job. They dismantled the two temples
by cutting them up into 1,060 numbered
blocks, some weighing as much as thirty-three
tons, then lifted them 213 feet above their
original site and reassembled the jigsaw
hodgepodge of stone 690 feet inland from the
former shoreline into an exact reproduction
of the temples' original appearances. The
herculean project, completed in 1968,
required 4,000 man-years of labor to complete,
at a cost of $39,000,000. The money was
contributed primarily by Egypt and the
United States but included donations from
fifty- two countries, raised by UNESCO (the
United Nations Educational Scientific and
Cultural Organization). Lake Nasser has
flooded innumerable antiquities, several
dating from the Stone Age. Abu Simbel was
the largest and most valuable of the nineteen
monuments dismantled and rescued from the
lake.

second longest of Egyptian history, he conducted a prolific building program to immortalize his memory. Consequently half the relics in Egypt are attributed to Ramses, though many were actually built by earlier kings, and shamelessly expropriated to glorify Ramses' name.

We clambered to the top of the ten-foot pedestal supporting the colossal statues and photographed the three serene faces, each thirteen feet wide from ear to ear. From this position we began to appreciate the magnitude of the temple and its massive statues—everything carved out of a solid sandstone cliff, with nothing brought in or added from an outside source. An awestruck French scholar once wrote, "Try to imagine the cathedral of Notre Dame carved out of a single block of stone!" The monument was considered ancient by Greek and Roman tourists 2,000 years ago. Inscriptions on the two southern statues by Greek and Phoenician mercenaries dating from around 590 B.C. have proven invaluable in the early history of the alphabet—graffiti converted to scholarship!

We gained an even greater respect for the genius of the Egyptians who had designed and built the temple when we entered the cavernous underground hypostyle, or pillared hall. Before us stood eight pillarlike statues, each thirty feet tall and representing Osiris, god of the underworld and lord of the dead, but with the face of Ramses. As we penetrated the total darkness, we lit flares for illumination. The reddish glare reflected eerily off the weathered walls and cast gigantic shadows as we walked past the statues, creating an aura of mystery. One huge complicated wall mural, a veritable picture gallery containing 1,100 figures, depicted Ramses's most outstanding military exploit, the victory over the Hittites at the famous battle of Kadesh in 1300 B.C., in which Ramses's personal heroism saved the Egyptian army from annihilation. Another wall mural achieved some kind of historic record for self-adoration, showing Ramses making offerings to himself as a god—literally worshipping himself.

As we sat in the shade of the temple entrance, snacking on dates and cheese, I noticed that the stone murals around us, showing prisoners of war linked together by a rope around their necks, looked strikingly like the Nilotic Africans we had visited in the Sudd country, a thousand miles to the south.

After our rest we trudged 200 yards downstream along the sandy lakeshore and came to the smaller queen's temple, a jewel of a shrine that Ramses built in honor of Nefertari ("Beautiful Companion"), his favorite wife, though officially the temple is devoted to the worship of Hathor, goddess of love and joy. It is small only by contrast with the great temple, for it has an impressive forty-by-ninety-foot facade carved with six giant statues thirty-three feet tall. Typi-

Goddard at the base of the sixty-six-foot high statues at the rock-cut temple of Ramses.

cally, only two of the statues are of Nefertari—the other four are of her vain and self-absorbed husband, Ramses.[57]

As we emerged from the hypostyle hall inside, we saw a Nubian lad driving a small herd of goats along the water's edge in front of the temple. At my

---

57. By 1,000 B.C. these masterworks of pharaonic art had been abandoned to the drifting desert sands. For 2,800 years they remained unknown and unappreciated by the outside world. In 1813 a twenty-nine-year-old Swiss traveler, John Lewis Burckhardt, rediscovered them, though the Great Temple was almost totally buried under a mountain of sand. In 1817 Giovanni Battista Belzoni, an Italian engineer-explorer succeeded in reaching the entrance and entering the interior after he and his five companions labored for twenty-two grueling days to clear away 31 feet of obstructing sand. It was not until 1910 that all the sand entombing the colossi, terrace, forecourt, and temple approaches was completely removed.

request he cheerfully sold us some milk, which he squirted directly from a nanny into an empty water bottle. It was very warm but still refreshed our parched throats.

We left late in the day, anxious to make camp farther on. But I couldn't help looking back to fix in my memory the miraculous cliff-side wonder, a monument built in honor of one man by 20,000 men working twenty years.

May 21: *Tushka*

We kept close to the bank for twenty-five miles today, following a rugged shoreline that featured rock-niche shrines and temples carved into the cliffs. Usually they were high above us, accessible only by rappelling down from the top. However, we visited one grotto-temple close to the water, where a swarm of large bats fluttered around our heads as we entered the dimly lit interior. The stench of bat guano was overpowering, but we lingered long enough to study the 3,000-year-old wall carvings that included scenes of daily life in ancient villages—scenes strikingly similar to the daily activities we had been observing in the present-day Nubian communities.

The afternoon sun beat down on us with pitiless force, and not a breath of wind offered us relief. I couldn't satisfy my thirst no matter how much I drank, and visions of gluttonous drinking obsessed me. I imagined the bliss of guzzling down a punch bowl of cold, fresh orange juice with gobs of sherbet floating on top. We have learned to live with constant thirst, but it is one of the worst hardships of the journey, and today it was especially difficult to endure.

We worked like galley slaves to reach Tushka before dark, but we were so bushed from the effort we didn't bother to contact anyone—just camped on a soft sandbank near the outskirts of town.

May 22: *Ibrim*

We climbed an imposing 300-foot bluff today to see the Roman fortress that had marked the southernmost border of the Roman Empire in the days when Egypt was a province of Rome. Near the fort was the ruin of an Egyptian temple, and beyond that an early Christian church—what a slice of history in this one small area!

The omdah of Ibrim was our host for the night—a haughty man who spent much time trying to convince us he wasn't a lowly Nubian but rather a direct descendant of a sixteenth-century Turkish officer assigned to occupy the Ibrim fortress after Turkey had conquered Egypt in 1517. We were too tired to doubt him.

May 23: *Korosko (Kurusku)*

Today we followed the Nile in a radical deviation from its usual course, meandering first to the southeast, then to the east on a thirteen-mile detour caused by crowding hills of stratified sandstone on both sides of the river. Near the end of the curve was Korosko, where the Aswan dam had made the river flood the old city limits. A forest of palm trees that had once stood on the water's edge now miraculously survived despite the fact that the water came halfway up the trees' trunks.

Since ancient times Korosko has been the embarkation base for caravans bound for Abu Hamed and Khartoum across the Nubian Desert. We paused for a look around, escorted by the usual band of excited children, and happened to meet the local postmaster, the only post office official in all of Egyptian Nubia. He was a plump, affable gentleman who fed us a bowl of lubia beans at his home and told us he was distressed that we wanted to continue paddling down the river in the dangerous afternoon sun when all sensible people and animals stayed under cover and slept. (I restrained an impulse to tell him "only mad dogs, Englishmen, and the three Nileteers go out in the noonday sun.") It is true that as we paddle through the afternoon of each day, the river banks and villages are virtually lifeless. But just a short distance downstream from Korosko we came upon a lively wedding celebration with drumming and chanting among a group of men on the eastern bank. In typical Nubian fashion we were made welcome as soon as we landed. The young groom, acting as head greeter, was decked out in a symphony of colors in his wedding ensemble: an elaborate yellow jacket with large brass buttons, a pair of white billowy pants, fine red leather slippers with pointed toes, and a pale blue silk turban.

After an enthusiastic round of hand-shaking, we were made guests of honor, seated next to the groom, and served bowls of mutton and rice. Shivers went down my spine when the women, in glittering gold jewelry, festive gowns, and red shawls, trilled the high-pitched *zaghareet,* the joy-cry of Moslem women. By the time we left the celebration it was too late to travel much farther, so we treated ourselves to an early bedtime on the west bank.

May 24: *Mahdiq*

This afternoon we arrived at another impressive work of Ramses II, the 3,200-year-old temple of El Sibu, or the lions.[58] The name comes from a sacred

---

58. Now relocated on the shores of Lake Nasser with two other salvaged temples.

avenue of ten man-headed sphinxes leading to the rock-hewn temple. One of the most interesting features of the structure was a list of more than 100 of Ramses' children carved on the walls—he had at least 138.

Because of the ponding of the Nile behind the Aswan Dam, the stone figures are flooded up to their crowns nine months of the year. But now, as the sluice gates were open to provide irrigation water for Lower Egypt, the water only wetted the statues' bases.

Four miles downstream on the opposite shore we came to Mahdiq, our overnight stop, one of Nubia's most isolated communities. It was just a cluster of mud houses, each enclosed by a walled courtyard, nestled in the midst of a

André lands at the temple of El Sibu.

Nubian Archaeological Project

A scientific project of unprecedented magnitude was conducted from 1960 to 1972 by archaeologists and scholars from all over the world in a monumental effort to discover and reclaim as many of the known and unknown historic treasures of the Nubian Valley as possible before they were forever entombed by 300-mile-long Lake Nasser. Previously no large area had been so painstakingly investigated archaeologically. A total of twenty-two expeditions discovered 2,000 new sites throughout Nubia, one of the most priceless storehouses of the ancient world. The scientists excavated, studied, and recorded each site and salvaged any transportable object worth saving to a safe location. Egypt relaxed its usual strict policy regarding the excavation of its ruins and permitted foreign teams to keep 50 percent of their finds and allowed five ancient temples to be dismantled and shipped to other countries. (The Metropolitan Museum of Art in New York City was the recipient of the temple of Dandur.)

rocky hillock. Two adolescent girls filling large clay jugs at the water's edge fled in alarm as we landed at dusk, and there was a flock of black flop-eared goats scavenging around the village for whatever vegetation they could nibble.

A villager presented us to the elderly omdah, who had just completed his prayers on the roof of his house. Following the usual pattern of Nubian dwellings, the omdah's one-story residence consisted of four rooms opening on a rectangular courtyard and enclosed by an eight-foot-high wall. He allowed us to sleep on adobe troughs next to the wall where the family would ordinarily sleep on hot nights.

Shortly after dark, the peace of the village was shattered by a sudden bedlam of shrieks and wails that sounded like somebody being murdered. We quickly

John Goddard visits a pyramid and sphinx in lower Egypt.

243

found out that a young girl in the neighboring dwelling had just been stung by a scorpion and was in agony. The other women of the household, horrified over the calamity, had cried out in sympathy.

Impetuously I ran to the house to offer first aid, but a woman, answering my knock, nervously shut the door again when she saw me standing there; the strict code of purdah wouldn't permit her to accept any help from a male stranger. So I went to sleep wondering how the victim was faring, since a scorpion sting is not only exceedingly painful, but can be fatal to children.

We had often seen crude paintings of scorpions on the walls of Nubian homes, a practice stemming from the ancient belief that the pictures would somehow protect the occupants of the house from the live creatures.

May 25: *Garf Hussein*

Before leaving Mahdiq we looked around the village to study one of the most colorful galleries of wall paintings we had seen in Nubia. Painted in whitewash on the clay exteriors of houses and courtyard walls was a marvelous assortment of what looked like whimsical doodles—fancy steamers, mosques, lions, camels, hearts, suns, moons, stars, and elaborate floral and abstract designs.

One wall looked like a huge page from a children's illustrated storybook: the owner had made the *hadj,* the pilgrimage to Mecca required of every Moslem at least once before dying, and the charming paintings depicted the highlights of what he had seen during the trip.

We crossed the Tropic of Cancer this morning, 23 ½ degrees north of the equator, the northernmost point ever to have the sun directly overhead. The Nile lake grew broader as we traveled downstream and was still bordered by rugged bare hills of rock and sand. Occasionally we paddled over drowned villages, their burials marked by clusters of date palms that looked like giant featherdusters sticking out of the water.

In spite of the punishing sun and constant hunger and thirst, we have come to love the solitude and purity of Nubia's virgin deserts. It has been a joy living in a pristine world peaceful beyond description and unmarred by concrete, noise, or pollution. It is going to be difficult returning to the modern age and an existence bounded by roads, walls, and clocks.

Our days flow along with no boundaries in time or space, filled with vast open vistas of sky and land that expand our minds and enlarge our souls. Though it can be forbidding and harsh, the desert rewards us at times with special beauty, especially during the fresh morning hours and in the cool dusk. The star-spangled nights are an inspiration too. I have never seen the night sky so radiant as in our clear desert air, far from the smog and glow of cities. I can understand now how it was that so many great prophets of old came out of the desert or developed their spirituality there. Like the Nubians, we are poor materially and cut off from the modern world, but we enjoy a great sense of contentment and freedom. We have no real home, not much food, no modern luxuries, sand for a bed, the sky for a roof; but we are blessed with youth, health, friendship, adventure, new experiences daily, beauty in nature, and an unprecedented feeling of closeness to God. I personally could ask for nothing more of life.

We were disappointed that the classic temple of Dakka, which we reached this afternoon, was submerged except for the upper few feet of the twin pylons protruding above the water. We're hoping for better luck with some of the

Nubian women winnowing wheat, as in ancient days.

other important ruins farther downstream. Dakka marked the southern border of the Ptolemaic Empire established by the Greeks in Lower Nubia.

We spent the night with a wizened old gentleman who lived with his eight-year-old granddaughter in a small but immaculate mud house that was white-washed and decorated with cheery blue and orange abstracts. Later a young neighbor came over for a visit, and since he spoke a little English he helped the conversation a great deal. He told us that our host had served as a guide in Lord Kitchener's army during the campaign against the Mahdi's dervishes in 1898, and remembered many details about the great English commander from seeing him in person. Oh, for a tape recorder!

May 26: *North of Garf Hussein*

We were surprised to see several young men in a passing felucca staring at us curiously. We were almost as curious. It has been a long time since we've seen so many young men together at the same time. Most of the villages we have visited since leaving Wadi Halfa have been occupied mostly by women, children, and the elderly. Most of the able-bodied men are forced to emigrate to the cities of Egypt and the Levant to earn a living. They are unable to provide enough food for their families from their narrow plots of arable soil along the Nile.[59]

Because of their honesty, dependability, and cleanliness, they are much in demand as house servants, male nurses, cooks, waiters, and even as crew members aboard ocean liners. They send home as much of their income as possible, and usually visit their families once or twice a year, although it isn't unusual for them to go several years without a reunion. Yet bachelors always seem to return to Nubia for a wife when they have saved enough money to get married.

Around noon we almost paddled right past Kalabsha, one of the largest Roman temples in Nubia. Only the upper portion of its facade broke the surface, so I had to miss out on filming the most important and well-preserved monument in Nubia after Abu Simbel and Philae. With the sun's rays shining

---

59. Since ancient times the inhabitants of Upper Nubia have had a desperate time surviving in this driest and most sterile region of the Nile basin. The construction of the old Aswan Dam and its two increases in height, in 1912 and 1933, made conditions even more difficult for them to produce sufficient food from the scarce land. But Nubians had such a deep-rooted love of their barren homeland, they refused to abandon it even when the Egyptian government offered to resettle them in a more favorable location. The Aswan High Dam now raises the water level an additional 185 feet, making it impossible for them to remain. By 1965 Egypt had relocated 25,000 families on unoccupied land in the Kom Ombo area, thirty-five miles north of Aswan.

down into the clear green water from overhead we could at least get some idea of its design and dimensions.[60]

We traveled a record forty-two miles from Garf Hussein today, the greatest distance we have paddled in one day. Our bodies paid a price for the effort. Our legs were so stiff and rubbery we could barely stand as we landed for the night on a dark sandy beach on the west bank. Our hands were fused into claws from grasping the paddles for ten endless hours, and we were so numb with fatigue we fell asleep immediately, without even a thought of food, although we hadn't eaten all day.

May 27: *Philae and the Aswan Dam*

Philae is the most celebrated island in the Nile, now mostly submerged by the backwater of the Aswan Dam a mile or so away. In Ptolemaic and Roman times, Philae was known as the Pearl of Egypt, one of the loveliest and most sacred places of the country, boasting five splendid temples mainly dedicated to the worship of Isis, the great Divine Mother.

We reached it in the morning, and it was a strange feeling to paddle through the flooded columns of the stately colonnade and then over the courtyard, whose pavements were many feet underwater, to the great temple of Isis.[61] Here I dug through an equipment bag and put on face mask and swim fins and proceeded to enjoy a swimming and diving tour of the sunken shrine. Crocodiles were rare this far north (I had seen only two since arriving in Lower Nubia), so I had a grand time plunging down through the sparkling green water to examine moss-coated columns and inscriptions of this superb temple built thirty lifetimes ago.

For a little recreation I climbed several times to the top of one temple pylon and dived headfirst into the lake, with a silent apology to Isis for the sacrilege. But in all my diving I failed to find Philae's famous symbol, the Kiosk built by

---

60. Kalabsha was constructed during the reign of Augustus Caesar (278 B.C. to A.D. 14), the adopted son of Julius Caesar, who became the first Roman Emperor in 27 B.C. In 31 B.C., when he was known as Octavian, his soldiers defeated the combined forces of Mark Anthony and Cleopatra at the battle of Actium. He indirectly caused the death of Cleopatra, who committed suicide rather than face being taken to Rome as his prisoner. To save it from being lost forever in the waters of Lake Nasser, West German specialists in 1962 dismantled Kalabsha's 13,000 stone blocks, averaging one ton each, and reconstructed them with remarkable precision on a promontory overlooking the High Dam.

61. Built by one of the last native Egyptian Pharaohs, Nectanebo II, final king of the 30th dynasty (359–341 B.C.), the temples of Philae were thought to have special powers for healing and, from Ptolemaic times until the late sixth century, attracted thousands of sick pilgrims of all levels of society, from peasants to emperors.

An immense pillar at Karnak.

the Roman Emperor Trajan called "Pharoah's Bed" because of its resemblance to a giant fourposter.

As we paddled away from Philae we left Nubia and entered Egypt proper, since the sunken island marked the boundary between the two. Our next stop was the little town of Shellal, for us the gateway into Egypt, situated in a back bay of the eastern shore. We passed customs easily—we had been dreading a problem over our heavy supply of cameras, film, and African souvenirs—since the officials had read of the expedition and were expecting us and didn't open one of our twelve bags!

Happily we headed for Egypt's greatest wonder of the twentieth century, the Aswan Dam. [Since then a far higher dam, the Aswan High Dam, has

On a swimming tour of submerged Philae Island, Goddard explores a shrine.

Aswan High Dam

Five miles upstream from the old Aswan Dam is the billion
dollar Aswan High Dam, *Sadd el Aali,* constructed from
1960 to 1971 by a work force of 30,000, consisting mostly
of Egyptians but also of specialists of a dozen other
nationalities, including Americans. A total of 2,000 Russian
engineers and other experts directed the mammoth project,
designed to expand Egypt's farmland an additional
2,000,000 acres and to produce ten billion kilowatt hours of
electricity annually for fueling new industry. The Soviet
government stepped in to build the dam and to contribute
a quarter of its cost when the United States, at the urging
of Secretary of State John Foster Dulles, turned down the
request to participate in 1956, after Egypt purchased Soviet
weaponry and extended recognition to Communist China.
The Pyramidal-shaped dam is 365 feet in height and has a
length of 12,565 feet and a crest width of 132 feet. It is
3,250 feet thick at the base and contains more than
50,000,000 cubic yards of stone, sufficient to build
seventeen Great Pyramids. Its twelve giant turboelectric
generators began producing power in 1967 when the dam
was officially opened and were fully operational by 1970. In
1964 the High Dam began forming Lake Nasser, which, at
its highest level, extends 310 miles and is six to fourteen
miles in width—a reservoir covering 2,000 square miles with
a gross capacity of 130,000,000 acre feet. With the
additional supply of water, Egypt has been able to reclaim
hundreds of thousands of acres of desert and to vastly
increase crop production through perennial irrigation. Lake
Nasser enabled the country to avoid a serious drought in
1972 when the Nile's flow was at its lowest in 50 years.

dwarfed its small predecessor, which so impressed me during the expedition.] Designed by the British, the dam is 7,000 feet long, built from 1898 to 1902 of 1,000,000 tons of Aswan granite by 11,000 Egyptian laborers at the spot where the treacherous First Cataract used to begin. With the dam's construction, year-round irrigation became possible in Egypt for the first time, and the nation's periodic droughts had been brought to an end. From here on the Nile's flow is under complete control by means of the 180 sluice gates. Now, at the time when the Nile used to be in its dry stage, the silt-bearing water floods out of the gates to inundate the agricultural plains of Egypt.

The four locks in the dam's west end are opened only once or twice a week to let river traffic through; we hit an off day and so had to portage kayaks and bags down the staircases to the river below. The air was filled with a pleasant mist, but the thundering roar of the water foaming through the sluices was deafening as we loaded up and pushed off into the savage grandeur of the First Cataract. We swept along over the racing current, dodging the heaped-up masses of lustrous black granite choking the river below the dam, and soon had passed over the last stretch of rapids on the Nile.

We moved along through the beautiful lower gorge on the blue-green Nile, which had now regained its identity as a river, passing many rocky islands whose dark surfaces were coated with a glossy patina of iron oxide, making them appear freshly lacquered. Opposite the town of Aswan we stopped at the mile-long Elephantine Island and found it a jumble of shattered ancient ruins and gaping archaeological excavations.[62] There were the remnants of Egyptian and Roman temples and a Ptolemaic shrine dedicated to Khnum, the ram-headed God of the Cataract. We photographed the best preserved relic, the Nilometer, a steep staircase of cut stones descending into the river.[63]

Before landing for the night at Aswan, we visited Kitchener Island, between Elephantine and the western bank. It was wonderful strolling around this lush oasis where tall palms and sycamores shaded fragrant roses and bou-

---

62. In ancient times Egypt's most important frontier town was on the southern tip of the island. It was known as the "gateway to the south" and the launching point for trade and conquest in Nubia. The Egyptian name, *Yeb,* meaning Elephant Island, was probably inspired by the Nubian ivory market that flourished there. The Greeks translated *Yeb* to Elephantine, the name by which it has been known ever since. The ancient Egyptians believed Elephantine was the source of the Nile, with the river originating from bottomless springs between two rocks.

63. This was one of twenty similar devices used in pharaonic times to measure the height of the Nile flood, thus enabling farmers to estimate the amount of water they would have for their crops and the government to establish the tax rate it would impose on the people. A high reading was cause for rejoicing by everyone, as it meant abundant food for the masses and larger tax revenues for the rulers.

gainvillea. There were even butterflies and birds flitting around us. The garden had been built by Lord Kitchener, the great British soldier who had hoped to retire to this idyllic spot after a career of soldiering. But his dream was tragically destroyed when during World War I his ship struck a German mine and he was drowned.

May 28–29: *Aswan*

Our two days at Aswan were filled with exciting sights and activities, thanks to the hospitality of new Egyptian friends.[64] One of the head engineers gave us a complete tour of the dam. As a special treat he drove us across the top of the huge barrage from bank to bank, informing us that for several years it was the world's largest dam. A vacationing Egyptian archaeologist from the Cairo Museum took us to an ancient quarry where stone had been cut for many ancient temples, tombs, statues, and obelisks by the clever method of driving rows of wooden wedges into depressions and then wetting them down until the wood expanded and split the stone. We were able to stand on one monster 1,000-ton obelisk since it was lying on its side. It had been abandoned in an almost complete state after becoming flawed by long cracks that developed while it was being cut from its bed. It measures 137 feet in length and has a base almost fourteen feet square. Our friend then took us across the river to an ancient cemetery and introduced us to some of his fellow archaeologists working on the delicate task of excavating the newly discovered tomb of a great Egyptian general of the Old Kingdom. They allowed us to take the first photographs at the site, and we watched in fascination as they carefully exhumed the general's mummified wife, adorned with a beaded breastcloth, from a crypt in the side of the mausoleum. It was hard to comprehend that before us was the desiccated body of a fellow human being who had lived 4,600 years ago.

But I was curious about her—what she had been like, what kind of life she had led, what kind of wife, mother, and ruler she had been. As a parting gift, one of the scientists presented me with a perfect skull he had uncovered of one of the servants buried with the general.

A short distance upstream we visited the tomb of Prince Har-Khuf, "Governor of the South and Lord of Elephantine," who had led an expedition so far south that he had found a dancing pygmy to give to the young Pharoah; there

---

64. From ancient times to the present, Aswan (known as *Syene* to the Greeks) has been Egypt's southernmost frontier town and an important marketing center for merchandise from Ethiopia and the Sudan.

252

Portaging around old Aswan Dam.

was also a copy of a touchingly human letter to the prince from the eight-year-old Pepi II, the fifth king of the sixth dynasty (2345–2181 B.C.).[65] The ivory and gold that Har-khuf was bringing were not half so fascinating to the boy as the pygmy: "When he goes down with thee into the vessel," wrote Pepi, "appoint excellent people who shall be beside him on each side of the vessel . . . lest he fall into the water. When he sleeps at night, appoint excellent people who shall sleep beside him in his tent; inspect ten times a night. Your sovereign wishes to see this dwarf more than all the tribute from Sinai and Punt." The presence of the letter inscribed on the tomb is a good indication that the pygmy arrived in good condition.

May 30: *Kom Ombo*

We left Aswan early this morning and entered the land of the fellahin, the peasant farmers of Egypt. From here to the delta we will be paddling through the "Narrow Kingdom," as Upper Egypt has been called, where primarily only the area seven miles from the Nile on either side is settled and cultivated. The people here are lighter-skinned and slightly shorter than the Nubians to the south, and here only Arabic is spoken.

We passed many small mud villages, and while sakiehs were most commonly used to raise water from the river to the fields, those too poor to afford an ox, buffalo, or camel used shadoofs or Archimedes' screws.[66] Herodotus called Egypt "the gift of the Nile," and I understand now as never before that without the mud and water of the Nile, Egypt could never have developed into a nation in this immense burnt-out land; and without Egypt the course of western history would have been drastically changed.

Though from Aswan to Cairo the Nile has a slope of only six inches per mile, today we had a current helping us, to our surprise. We were exhausted from the heat and the exertion of paddling when we stopped to rest at the

---

65. Egyptian civilization, in its familiar form, began about 3,100 B.C. and survived with its most prominent characteristics until the conquest of Egypt by Alexander the Great in 332 B.C. Its 300-plus Pharaohs are grouped into thirty-one dynasties that existed during that period.

66. The shadoof is a simple hand-operated well sweep device, consisting of a long pole mounted on a crossbeam like a seesaw, with a goatskin bag, bucket, or other receptacle suspended from the long end and a counterweight on the short end. The *fellah* (farmer) pulls down the pole, scoops up water in the bag, and lifts it to the basin above. The shadoof can irrigate only about one acre of farmland in the dry season, but the sakieh can take care of eight or nine acres. The archimedes' screw, or "water-snake," is a corkscrew-shaped wooden cylinder invented around 200 B.C. by the brilliant Greek mathematician, Archimedes. The tube rests at a diagonal angle on the bank, one end in the water and the opposite end above an irrigation channel. Hand cranking rotates the cylinder, lifting the water by spirals seven feet, from the stream to the ditch. (See photo, page 260.)

Ptolemaic temple of Ombos, twenty-five miles downstream, set on a promontory of the east bank overlooking the Nile. For centuries it was buried under desert sands and had to be excavated by a large team of workers. It was a double temple, devoted not only to the sun god but also to Suchos, the crocodile god. The local guard brought out some of the mummified crocodiles for us to photograph. In life, the animals had been kept in a pool near the temple by priests who adorned them with jeweled necklaces.

Beyond the temple was the town of Kom Ombo, an important sugar cane and cotton center. Here the traditional methods of siphoning water from the

A young Egyptian casts his net into the midst of the First Cataract below the old Aswan Dam.

The obelisk at Aswan that would have been Egypt's largest if it hadn't developed flaws.

Goddard holds 4,600-year-old skulls from the tomb of a general of the Old Kingdom.

Nile were replaced by four mammoth underwater conduits pumping out prodigious amounts of water to irrigate the largest expanse of agricultural land on the east bank of Upper Egypt, the Kom Ombo Valley.[67]

We camped near Gebel el Silsila, near some large sandstone quarries, now abandoned, where Egyptians excavated enormous amounts of stone over a period of thousands of years for royal and religious monuments.

---

67. When the Aswan High Dam flooded their traditional homeland, 62,000 Nubian Egyptians were resettled in model villages around the valley. This was once a flat desert plain, but has been transformed by abundant Nile water into a twenty-mile-long and ten-mile-wide oasis of farm land and sugar cane.

The Ptolemaic Temple of Ombos.

May 31: *Edfu (Idfu)*

Shortly after launching, we passed through a granite gorge that shrank the river to only 250 yards in width, the narrowest the Nile becomes in Egypt. And during the day I had a strange encounter with minor officialdom. I stopped near a small village to stretch my legs and wait for Jean and André to catch up. Within a few minutes I was surrounded by men and boys, including a khaffir with a rifle on his shoulders. While I talked to the others, the guard inspected my kayak and suddenly began shouting for everyone to come see what he had found. It was the ancient skull—I hadn't been able to cram it into any of my full equipment bags, and so had stowed it in the stern of my boat.

The excited khaffir was positive he had caught a murderer red-handed, with the grim evidence of the crime there for everyone to see. I had no idea how to convince him that the skull was from a person who had died 4,000 years ago—and he wasn't about to let me try. He grabbed my arm and tried to drag me along toward the village; I had no alternative but to escape immediately before things became even more complicated. I shoved him away with all my strength, leaving him in a heap on the ground, dashed to the kayak, and raced off downstream. When I was beyond rifleshot, I looked back to see him and the others running toward the village, evidently to round up help.

I didn't stop again for several miles, this time at a totally deserted stretch where I waited until Jean appeared an hour later, and the two of us continued together.

Edfu appeared on the west bank around 4 p.m. We were met by four engineers on duty at the large pump there, and they escorted us to the town's crowning glory, the huge temple of Horus, most complete and perfectly preserved of all Egyptian temples. It was built over a period of 180 years by several pharaohs of the Ptolemy line, beginning with Ptolemy III in 237 B.C. and completed in 57 B.C. during the reign of Ptolemy XII.[68]

We reached the interior through a forty-foot-high entrance in the center gateway guarded by two large granite hawks representing the sun god Horus. Inside the massive, dimly-lighted structure, we found thirty-two large decorated columns standing in the forecourt, eighteen supporting the ponderous roof of the vestibule, and twelve giant pillars arranged in four rows of three in the hypostyle. The shadowy gloom added to the mystical atmosphere of the

---

68. The Ptolemies were Pharaohs of Egypt of Greek descent who ruled from 323 B.C. to 30 B.C., beginning with Ptolemy I, one of the generals who helped Alexander the Great conquer Egypt in 332 B.C. Cleopatra was the last ruler of the Ptolemaic dynasty.

roofless sanctuary hidden in the deepest recesses of the temple, and I conjured up a mental picture of the richly costumed pharaoh and the senior priests, wreathed in clouds of incense, performing elaborate rituals in this holy of holies, the shrine of Horus. One inscription even suggests that the temple was built on the very site where creation first took place.

André finally caught up with us at dusk, and we spent the night in a fragrant lemon grove near the pumping station.

The archimedes' screw, used for pumping water from the Nile. (See footnote 66, p. 254.)

June 1: *North of Edfu*

André stayed to visit the temple, and Jean and I paddled downstream to visit Saad el Din Sayed Ahmed, chief engineer of Atwani (the big electric plant there) whom we had met in Aswan. The plant was being expanded and heavy machinery and boilers were being installed by a crew of Italians. Then we started for Isna, thirty-four miles north.

But the contrary wind became so violent and hindered us so badly that Jean stopped at a mid-river barge. I continued a few miles farther but was nearly capsized several times by the rough, yeasty waves. So I called it a day at a small pumping station.

June 2: *Isna*

It was hot and misty but perfectly calm as I set off in the light of an opalescent dawn. I watched fishermen in a felucca gracefully cast their nets out into the water, then asked if I could try casting the net and was welcomed aboard and given careful instruction. My first attempt was a fiasco: I threw the heavy cotton net so awkwardly that it landed in a tangled mess. My next few attempts improved a bit, but I finally gave the net back to the men and left with increased respect for their skill.

I reached Isna by noon—a big town bustling with activity. Kids of all ages splashed in the river alongside wallowing buffalo (*gamoosas*). Women garbed in black nunlike gowns waded out to fill big earthenware crocks, then marched away with the heavy vessels balanced at a rakish angle on their heads. Along the bank I was greeted enthusiastically by rivermen as they worked at building new feluccas or repairing old ones. The main street bordering the riverfront was clogged by a herd of black sheep being marched down the center, followed by several heavily loaded camels jogging along, voicing their complaints with a cry of irritation that sounded like a long sustained belch. Pedestrians wisely moved aside to let the petulant animals pass.

I had to pass through a lock on the west side of the barrage at Isna, but it took only a few minutes. (Unlike the two big dams at Aswan, which were built to form storage reservoirs, Egypt's six barrages are low stone dams designed to maintain the height of the Nile so that water can flow into irrigation canals above the barriers throughout the year.) The water was siltier and a duller green than before. The wind blew from noon on—under the first cloudy skies I had seen in months, for which I was grateful, since for once the sun didn't beat down on me as I paddled.

Dinner and bed were given me by a bachelor engineer at a pump station, who insisted against my protests that I sleep in his bed, while he took the couch. It was wonderful to sleep in a good bed with springs—my first in more than eight months.

June 3: *Luxor*

A short distance before reaching Luxor, André and Jean passed me on a barge, having picked up a ride from Armant, where they had spent the night with another Frenchman living there. The barge captain offered to stop for me, but I preferred to reach Luxor under my own power and waved him on.

Not finding Jean and André when I reached Luxor, I looked up the Presbyterian mission which I had been told was stationed in town. Only one person was there, Miss Martha Roy, a tall American from Ohio who has lived in Egypt most of her life. After lunch with her, I found Jean and André at Karnak, a mile away, with a French archaeologist, Dr. Robichon, who is working

Jean Laporte and 2,000-year-old mummified crocodiles at the temple of Ombos.

The beautiful temple of Luxor with the striking papyrus-bud columns.

on some new excavations there and had found a place for them to stay. I devoted the afternoon to studying and filming the magnificent temple of Luxor that stands on the riverbank near the town.[69]

I slept on an army cot in a boys' school.

June 4: *Karnak*

At Karnak, just a mile and a half north of Luxor, I watched a golden dawn illuminate the most colossal temple complex of Egypt. I stood on top of one of the 142-foot-high towers of the entrance pylon and looked out over a bewildering assemblage of grandiose temples, pylons, courts, columns, and statues—a fantastic open-air museum of architecture built over a period of 2,000 years by numerous pharaohs. Martha Roy had suggested watching the sunrise over Karnak; so following her direction, I had arisen before dawn, taken a carriage to the pylon, and with the help of a guard had found my way to the roof.

Karnak once occupied the heart of Egypt's ancient capital and most splendid city, called Thebes by the Greeks and Wase or Wo'se by the Egyptians. The 62-acre spread of religious buildings here was once the Vatican City of Egypt's golden age, the New Kingdom or Age of Empire, which endured from 1567 to 1085 B.C.

From my vantage point I could see the Avenue of Sphinxes that once extended for almost two miles from Karnak to the Temple of Luxor. There were only a few of the stately stone figures still in place, but originally there had been about 500 of these ten-foot ram-headed sphinxes, built to honor Amon, the king of the gods. I could also count five temples and ten pylons within the central grounds, along with the tallest obelisk of Egypt, one of a pair of ninety-six-footers erected for Hatshepsut, the lady Pharaoh, which reared above a mass of stone near the large green sacred lake.[70]

---

69. A staff of 2,600 servants once maintained the 850-foot long temple. It formerly dominated the southern part of Thebes, the most magnificent and wealthiest city of the ancient world, and the imperial capital of the Pharaohs during the centuries when Egypt's political power and culture were at their height. King Amenhotep III commissioned the beautiful temple around 1,400 B.C., dedicating it to Amon-Re, his consort Mut, and their son Khons. Ramses II added a pylon and a great court surrounded by a double row of graceful lotus columns, each fifty-two feet tall.

70. At one time there were dozens of obelisks scattered over Egypt, but only five have survived. The others were destroyed either by earthquakes or settling, or were shipped off to other lands. Originally each obelisk was sheathed in copper, gold, or electrum (a natural alloy of gold and silver) to reflect the rays of the divine sun. The largest ancient obelisk is a 3,400-year-old 105-foot shaft built during the 18th dynasty for Thutmose III, now standing in front of the Church of San Giovanni in Rome.

Egyptian Obelisks

An obelisk is a square monolithic shaft tapering to a
pyramidal top. These tall stone pillars were placed in
the courtyards of ancient Egyptian temples to
symbolize either the presence of the sun-god or to
commemorate some important event. At the temple
of Amon at Karnak stands an 80-foot obelisk
weighing 149 tons that celebrates the thirtieth
anniversary of the rule of Thutmose I (1525–1512
B.C.). His daughter, Queen Hatshepsut (reigning
1503–1482 B.C.) added two more great obelisks, each
ninety-six feet tall and fifteen feet square at the base,
weighing 325 tons. The two most famous Egyptian
obelisks were known as "Cleopatra's Needles." One of
them stands in New York City's Central Park; the
other overlooks the Thames River in London. The
most prominent landmark of Washington, D.C., is
the 555-foot Washington Monument, an obelisk
memorial to the first president of the United States,
weighing more than 90,000 tons.

All the large Egyptian obelisks were cut from the
Aswan granite quarries and transported down the
Nile to the Pharoahs' most prominent cities aboard
200-foot barges, the largest boats in history at the
time. Hundreds of workers dragged them from the
river bank on sledges to the end of a sloping ramp.
They eased them base-down into a sand-filled brick-
lined hole in the ramp, then erected them on a
pedestal at their final resting place by gradually
removing the sand.

I lingered on the pylon roof for an hour, savoring the silky morning air, the eye-filling panorama of the antiquities below, and the placid Nile beyond; then I climbed down for a thorough ground tour and headed directly for "the greatest wonder of Thebes" and the most spectacular religious complex of the ancient world—the gargantuan Temple of Amon. It had begun as a small shrine to Amon in about 2000 B.C.; but during the succeeding thousand years, with ten pharaohs contributing to its splendor, it developed into an architectural wonder that for sheer magnitude surpasses all other Egyptian constructions, with the exception of the pyramids. The dominating and most important section of the Temple is the Hypostyle Hall, built by Seti I and his son, Ramses II, in the form of a colossal rectangle 400 by 1,200 feet, the largest columnar building ever constructed. I entered the vast hall and felt overwhelmed by a forest of 134 mammoth stone columns soaring around me to a height of sixty-nine feet. Each pillar is thirty-three feet in circumference and is covered with colored relief sculptures. The Hall constitutes only one-fifth of the temple yet has an area of 5,800 square yards—large enough to contain the entire Notre Dame Cathedral of Paris—with room to spare.

I didn't finish my tour of Karnak until late afternoon, spending the day wandering among the mammoth ruins, but I returned to Luxor in time to watch a big parade of local Moslems celebrating the eve of Ramadan, the Moslem holy month of fasting. The parade included mounted soldiers, gaily bedecked camels, scores of donkey carts pulling children of all ages, and hundreds of Egyptians shouting religious slogans and singing hymns from the Koran, and, most bizarre, a cart containing one young farmer displaying a goat he had just killed—while his companion wound the entrails around his head as a gruesome turban. Many of the younger boys had blackened their faces with charcoal and stood up in the carts with arms linked together, singing at the top of their voices.

I tried to film the colorful procession but gave it up after being threatened several times by some of the more fanatical marchers.

June 5: *Thebes*

Across the river on the west bank lies the Necropolis of Thebes, the famous City of the Dead, an ancient cemetery stretching along the tan cliffs of the Western Desert for two and a half miles. An Egyptian architect, Hassan Famy, refused to hear of our plans to take donkeys the several miles to the cliffs; instead he provided both a lorry and a driver.

We paused on the way to take pictures of the Colossi of Memnon, two immense portrait statues of Amenhotep III, each sixty-four feet high and weighing a thousand tons.[71] Then we headed for the fabled Valley of the Kings, rattling down a gravel road into the narrow valley deep into the cliffs where for 450 years the pharaohs of three dynasties were entombed, beginning with Thutmose I. The gorge was like a huge oven, so searingly hot that the lenses of Andre's still camera came unglued, making it impossible for him to take any more photographs during the trip.

There are sixty known tombs, some excavated as deep as 300 feet into the solid limestone walls and floors of several canyons. With a local guide bearing a lantern, we visited several of the most fascinating, descending long inclined passageways leading to the burial chambers. It seemed incredible that some of the vivid wall paintings we saw had been painted 3,000 years ago, but the airtight environment and the hot, dry atmosphere accounted for their remarkable preservation.

It was in this valley that the tomb of Tutankhamen was discovered in 1922 after six long years of searching by English archaeologist Howard Carter. The pharaohs had hoped to protect their rich burials from pillaging by concealing them in this remote area, but by 1,000 B.C. grave robbers had looted all but one, that of the boy-king Tutankhamen. This one survived only because the workmen excavating for the tomb of Ramses VI completely buried the entrance under the rubble they dug from the cliff. I experienced a thrill when I entered the legendary burial chamber of "King Tut" and stood next to the ponderous stone sarcophagus containing the young pharaoh's mummy. It was encased in a stunning gold coffin shaped to represent his face and figure. Serene eyes stared upward with a lifelike quality. The beautiful gold funerary mask that originally covered the bandaged face—a faithful likeness of his appearance—revealed the features of a young man who would be considered attractive by modern standards. Historians estimate that Tutankhamen was only ten years old when he became king and was eighteen at his death at about 1,325 B.C. Although he was the reputed son of the brilliant Amenhotep III and the son-in-law of Queen Nefertiti, he was supposedly a ruler of minor importance; yet many authorities consider the discovery of his tomb, with its fabulous treasure of 5,000 priceless objects, the greatest archaeological find of all

---

71. The northern colossus was damaged by an earthquake in 27 B.C., creating a freakish condition in which the statue would utter a melodious moaning sound each morning as the sun's rays warmed the sandstone head. This "Singing Memnon" was one of the biggest tourist attractions of the Roman Empire, but the mysterious sound disappeared when the damage was repaired 200 years after the quake.

time.[72] As we left the sepulcher, I thought of the "mummy's curse," a legendary inscription in the tomb: "Death shall come on swift wings to him who touches the tomb of Pharaoh." The mysterious deaths of the two Egyptian workers who had first opened the tomb were attributed to their breathing the foul air laden with the dust of centuries, and Howard Carter had lived until 1939—seventeen years after his momentous discovery. But Lord Carnarvon, his patron, had died in Cairo six months after entering the tomb. At the moment of his death, reputedly, all the lights in Cairo went out at the same time, and Carnarvon's pet dog on his estate in England uttered a loud howl and fell over dead. These events made sensational copy for the tabloids of the day and gave credence to the myth of the curse.

But much more memorable to me than any curse was the blessing inscribed on one wall, a prayer for the teenage king: "God be between you and harm in all the lonely places you must walk."

During the afternoon we visited the Valley of the Queens, where royal wives of the pharaohs and a few favored princes were entombed. There are seventy known burials in the Valley, and of the several we visited the most interesting was that of Nefertari, the favorite wife of Ramses II. Later, we explored the Ramesseum, the funerary temple of Nefertari's vain but spectacular husband, and clambered around on the shattered colossus of Ramses, once Egypt's largest statue, standing fifty-seven feet and weighing 1,000 tons. The sun had set behind the historic hills before we finished our touring. Our kind benefactor, Hassan, drove me to the river that night so I could return to the mission to have supper with Martha and write up my notes on the day's activities. André and Jean returned to Hassan's home for the night as his guests.

June 6: *Thebes*

We enjoyed another fascinating day exploring "the eternal abode of the dead"—Western Thebes. The golden Theban hills rising steeply above the green plain are honeycombed with hundreds of rock-hewn burial chambers and tomb-chapels of the nobles and officials who helped the pharaohs run their kingdom. In one funerary chapel after another we found walls and ceilings pul-

---

72. Howard Carter spent eight seasons (October to April) removing, cataloguing, and restoring the exquisite jewels, furnishings, and statuary in the four chambers of the tomb. The innermost coffin, one of three enveloping the king, is of solid gold and weighs more than a ton. Since this was considered a minor burial, the splendor of the tomb of a really great pharaoh, such as Ramses II or Amenhotep III must have been overwhelming.

In 1976 fifty-five of the fabulous treasures of Tutankhamen's tomb were brought to the United States for a three-year tour of six American cities.

sating with the vibrant colors of paintings that had remained unfaded after thirty centuries. The guides showed us the method the artists may have used for lighting the interior of the tombs thousands of years ago. One guide would hold a mirror at the entrance of each crypt, angling it to direct reflected sunlight inside, while another man holding a second mirror reflected the light around to the various walls, like the beam of a big flashlight.

The tombs were much more modest than those of their overlords but also contained charming vignettes of what daily life must have been like in ancient Egypt. There were animated paintings depicting the whole cycle of farming, detailed scenes of pottery and brick making, weaving, making bread, and other domestic activities. It was startling to look at these ancient paintings and recognize the same activities we had been observing along the Nile each day, the fellahin using the same tools and methods employed by their ancestors of three millennia ago.[73]

We also visited the magnificent mortuary temple of one of history's earliest ardent feminists, Queen Hatshepsut, who ruled Egypt jointly with her husband and half-brother Thutmose III.[74] This is an architectural melange of colonnades, chapels, and statues, fronted by three graceful terraces and spanned by a long ramp leading to a sanctuary cut deep into the rock. The whole elegant structure harmonizes with its dramatic setting at the base of a majestic 1,000-foot cliff.

At dusk after another unforgettable day of communing with the ancient world, we returned to Luxor and went to bed early to be rested for our departure the next morning, but the noise of local revelers kept us awake until midnight.

June 7: *Qift*

The Libyan hills retreated, and the cultivated banks spread wider as we moved downstream from Luxor. We stopped to film two fellahs working shadoofs in tandem side by side, scooping water up in large goatskin bags, with steady, rhythmic movements. They laughed when I took a turn and spilled

---

73. The paintings and inscriptions on the antiquities have provided scholars with their main source of knowledge about the history of ancient Egypt.

74. Hatshepsut was Egypt's first "woman's libber" and first full-fledged lady-king. (She wore the Double Crown indicating her authority over both the lands of Upper and Lower Egypt.) She proved 3,400 years ago that women could rule as well as men. During her successful twenty-one-year reign (1503–1482 B.C.) she forsook the traditional campaigns of conquest in preference to the development of peaceful trade abroad and the erecting of mighty monuments. (See photo, page 292.)

Goddard assists a fellah at a double shadoof.

water all over me. Both men seemed sickly and frail, and I realized they probably were suffering from "snail disease" or schistosomiasis, the curse of the fellahin since ancient times.

We bought a melon at Qus at about 4 p.m. Melons are one of our main sources of food and refreshment since we arrived in Egypt. It seemed as if half the village gathered around as I dickered with a merchant for one—and the whole assemblage followed me back to the river as if they had never seen a foreigner.

We have learned to savor the essences of life on this journey. The simplest pleasures seem delightful—a sudden cool breeze blowing over our overheated bodies, the soothing taste of Nile water, the refreshing thrill that runs through us when we dive into the river, the glint of sunlight on the wings of a gliding raven, the mouth-watering fragrance of cooking food subtly wafting out to us from a riverside village, the wonder shining in the eyes of children as we shake their hands. Such are the small joys that bring up happiness and make our days complete.

After a meal of pitta, the flat, round unleavened bread that is the fellahin's staff of life, and some buffalo's milk, we slept on a wooden bench at the home of the omdah of the small village of Qift.[75] But curious villagers kept dropping in every few minutes until about 3 a.m., preventing us from going to sleep. We felt no serious resentment, however; during the ordeal of Ramadan, each of the thirty interminable days of abstinence from food and drink is a torment, but once night comes on people are in a festive mood from the relief of being able to break the fast. Everyone stays up until all hours eating, drinking, and socializing.

June 8: *Qena (Only sixty miles from the Red Sea).*

A windless morning enabled us to reach Qena by eleven o'clock, where we watched naggars, or cargo feluccas, being loaded with ten-foot stacks of big white water pitchers called *ballas*—bulbous clay pots exactly like the ones we had seen in the 3,000-year-old tomb paintings at Thebes.[76] Qena is famous for

---

75. Qift was known as Coptos in ancient times, when it was an important center for caravans leaving the Nile to cross the Eastern Desert to ports on the Red Sea.

76. Qena's potters annually produce several million of these hand-crafted clay jugs in different sizes. Mixing ashes with the clay gives the jugs a porosity that enables them to "sweat," which keeps water surprisingly cool. The large pitchers are used as water containers all over Egypt and other Arab nations. Smaller pots called "gullas" are designed for sakieh irrigation, as many as thirty to one large water-wheel.

Schistosomiasis

Schistosomiasis or *bilharzia* is a group of
diseases caused by three species of
microscopic parasitic blood worms or
flukes that occupy the blood vessels of
humans and other mammals.* These
flatworms invade vital organs, where
they feed on red blood cells and release
hundreds of thousands of eggs that do
widespread damage to all parts of the
body, particularly the liver, intestine,
bladder, and lungs. The cluster of eggs
produces the major symptoms of
fatigue, fever, cough, pain in the
abdomen, and, in many cases, death. In
the majority of victims the resistance
and general health is lowered, and
susceptibility to other afflictions is
increased. In Egypt the flukes thrive in
the sluggish waters of the Nile and
irrigation canals. Their larval stage is
spent in the body of a snail, but man is

---

*Editor's note: During the expedition John Goddard
was afflicted with malaria, dysentery, a staphyloccus
infection, and tapeworm; but his most serious health
problem came from schistosomiasis, contracted while
he traveled through Egypt. Upon his return to Los
Angeles, he was cured, but only through the drastic
treatment of sixteen injections of a powerful and
dangerous drug, potassium antimony tartrate.

their true host. The Aswan High Dam has caused an alarming increase in the disease by stopping the Nile's annual flooding, which served to limit it by flushing out the snail-infested areas and by ending the inhibiting period of dryness before the flood. In 1977 authorities estimated that 70 percent of the fellahin had schistosomiasis, and one in every eight deaths in Egypt was caused by it. But the farmers are constantly and unavoidably exposed to infected water in their daily farming. It is not only the number one health problem of Egypt but of the entire world. With more than 400,000,000 people suffering from the infection, schistosomiasis has supplanted malaria as mankind's most widespread sickness. That it has been one of Egypt's plagues for thousands of years is evidenced by the presence of schistosoma eggs in the kidneys of mummies and by the frequent prescriptions against hematuria, or bloody urine, one of the common symptoms of the disease, in the medical papyri discovered in ancient tombs.

the pots, and we have been seeing village women filling and head-balancing them all along the Nile from Aswan.

The postmaster of Qena consented to open the post office to give me the mail from my friends and family, even though it was Friday, the Moslem sabbath. We passed a pleasant hour with this charming Egyptian discussing everything from politics to Shakespeare.

After lunch, André was picked up by a khaffir and was being taken to a local prison for having no passport—he had left it in his kayak—when the captain of police happened by, recognized him, and rescued him.

Across the river we visited the Ptolemaic temple of Dendera.

Since we came to Egypt, the word *ancient* has taken on a new meaning to us. So many relics in Egypt are four and five thousand years old that Ptolemaic and Roman ruins "only" 2,000 years old seem almost modern by comparison. Dendera's great hypostyle hall is supported by eighteen ponderous, man-dwarfing columns, whose tops have been carved to represent the head of the temple's chief diety, Hathor, goddess of love and fertility. On the back of the

Naggers and camels being loaded with Qena water pitchers.

274

temple we saw a relief portrait of Cleopatra in profile, wearing an elaborate headdress, and with one breast exposed. Next to her was her son Caesarion, whose father was Julius Caesar.

We paddled on until after sunset without finding a place to stop. It would have been foolish to pitch our tent on the banks—there were too many bandits around. We had been warned by boatmen and officials that on the way to Cairo we would be passing through areas notorious for armed robbery, where well-organized gangs of holdup men waylaid travelers on the river or the land.

Jean found a felucca crew willing to give him hospitality, while André and I, thinking he was still following behind us, kept going until eight o'clock, when we finally found a village where we could stay the night—Dishna, a town large enough to have two omdahs. We stayed with the one in the northern part of town, but before we retired, we had a chance to listen to a celebrated faky, or Moslem cantor, sing psalms from the Koran in our host's living room. The town's most prominent citizens had gathered to hear him present a concert; he was a virtuoso singer with a truly remarkable range, a resonant voice with perfect pitch, and a gift for making incredibly difficult arpeggios, extending three octaves, sound effortless. The concert lasted until midnight, and I enjoyed it immensely; afterward I complimented him and expressed my appreciation, and he invited me to sit with him and chat over a drink—apricot juice served hot, which he said was great for the throat.

June 9: *Nag Hammadi*

We left before our host was out of bed. The wind was particularly strong, causing the usual rough water and painfully slow progress all day. We completed the Nile's last extreme loop, which begins just above Luxor and is a miniature of the river's great curve in the Sudan.

Jean caught up with us by hitching a ride on a felucca, which made speedy progress downstream by tacking back and forth across the river. Today we stopped drinking directly from the Nile—now we fill our green canvas supply bags with filtered and boiled water. We try to take precautions about what we eat and drink and about our health in general, but there are times when we have no alternatives, and we are forced to take risks. The sun was in our eyes all afternoon, and each of us was sunburned raw again. Jean's poor nose never tans, but remains fire-engine red.

By evening we were at Nag Hammadi, thirty miles west of Qena, and we stopped to visit Egypt's largest sugar refinery; the Frenchman in charge of the plant was very hospitable and immediately had two rooms prepared for us at the large company rest house.

The colony is a miniature city, providing all the spiritual and temporal necessities for the more than 150 European employees—French, Italian, Greek, Belgian, and others. Beautifully landscaped grounds and gardens, a swimming pool, a club, an outdoor cinema, a church, and attractive apartment houses make a charming setting, and after supper we joined a large group to watch a hammy, B movie in Arabic at the outdoor theater.

An intelligent young Greek who calls himself Tim, a distillery expert in the factory, has been corresponding with an American girl in Georgia for the past two years and is an ardent rooter for anything Yankee—we talked until late, and then he left, promising to show us through the factory in the morning.

June 10: *Nag Hammadi*

True to his promise, Tim gave us a tour of the factory, which produces 8,000 pounds of sugar every twenty-four hours. The manager of the factory, hearing of our desire to visit the Temple of Seti I at Abydos, generously announced, "By all means you should see it. Take my car and go!" This pleased us, since it would have been too far from the river for us to visit otherwise.

I suspected the Egyptian chauffer of driving under the influence of hashish: he raced us along at breakneck speed, forcing villagers, donkeys, buffalos, and geese to scamper out of our way. It was a wild ride but an exhilarating contrast to traveling in our three-mile-an-hour kayaks.

At the mortuary Temple of Seti, once one of the most magnificent buildings along the Nile, we inspected its most unique feature—*seven* shrines in the interior rather than the usual one, six of them dedicated to the major gods of old Egypt, the seventh for the worship of the divine pharaoh, Seti. Etched on the fine-grained limestone walls of the temple were the most delicately colored reliefs we had seen. The most famous of the wall carvings is the scene of Seti and his son, Ramses II, making offerings to the seventy-six deceased kings who preceded them, beginning with Menes, the first ruler of the first dynasty (3,100 B.C.), who was born near Abydos. This list of kings has been invaluable to scholars in helping them reconstruct the succession of ancient Egyptian rulers. Seti was among the three or four most brilliant rulers of Egyptian history, yet Ramses II, his less gifted son, is the most famous of all the pharaohs.

June 11: *Sohag*

On this windless day I really stroked off the miles, despite the concentrated blast of heat radiating off the high, craggy hills on the east bank. When I ran out of boiled water, I risked drinking the river water again; otherwise I'm sure the sun would have shriveled me like Ramses' mummy. It is easy now to understand how Egyptians came to worship the sun. It is the most pervasive, dominating force throughout the lives of every creature of Egypt. We are at its mercy, without shade or shelter, from the time it appears above the hills of the Eastern Desert until it sets. But the supreme influence in our lives still is the Nile—the broad, glistening river flowing majestically on, seemingly to infinity, ever luring us northward to another adventure.

No food during the day, but we had a good supper in Sohag; the town streets, tea pubs, eating houses, and shops were flooded with revelers celebrating getting through another day of Ramadan. We slept on the river bank to guard our kayaks.

June 12: *Asyut*

After a breakfast of dates, I had my second longest day of continuous paddling—17½ hours, two days' travel in one, from Sohag to Asyut. André, however, preferring to enjoy a well-earned respite, hitched a ride to Asyut on a barge.

I passed an albino boy about ten years old playing in the water with several normally pigmented playmates. He was halibut-white from his hair to his toes, but he didn't seem to be suffering from any discrimination by his companions and appeared to be a happy child.

After my long paddle, I was happy to see the tall lighted minarets of Asyut, the largest city of Upper Egypt, at about 10 p.m.[77] After landing, I was directed to the local fire station, where I telephoned the American Presbyterian Mission Hospital, as Martha Roy had suggested I do. Orval Hamm, a young doctor from a small town in Kansas, and Everett McCleery, a lab technician who has spent twenty-five years in Egypt, came for me and drove me to the hospital.[78] I was introduced to the rest of the staff—all Americans. During the past eight months I hadn't seen more than a dozen Americans. Now, suddenly transplanted from my narrow cramped kayak on a moonlit, lonely river to a bright room full of personable fellow Americans, I was overcome. And adding to my pleasure, they sat me down to a midnight snack of cold meat, cheese, apple-

---

77. In Ptolemaic times Asyut was called Lycopolis because the wolf (now extinct) was there held in as special a reverence as was the crocodile at Ombos.

78. The American Presbyterian Mission Hospital and Leper Clinic was first established in 1891 as a small day clinic by a Kansas medical missionary, Dr. L. M. Henry. Despite initial distrust of Christians by the local fellahin and their belief that sickness is caused by evil spirits, the hospital steadily expanded from one doctor practicing in a one-room donkey stable to a modern well-equipped institution staffed by twenty skilled American and Egyptian doctors and nurses, who ministered to more than 8,000 patients a year.

Ramadan

Ramadan is the ninth
month of the Moslem year
and the annual holy thirty-
day fast observed
throughout the world of
Islam as a religious
discipline and as one of the
five "pillars" or absolute
requirements of the faith.
Its observance begins at
the new moon and finishes
when the moon disappears,
extending each day from
the time when a white
thread can be
distinguished from a black
one until the two threads
are indistinguishable at
sundown. No food, drink,
smoking, or sexual
intercourse is indulged in
during this time.
Ramadan is the
outstanding month of the
year for Moslems—a time
of atonement and renewal,
of debt-paying,
reconciliation, forgiving,
reunions, and happy
socializings.

sauce, tomatoes, cucumbers, ice cream, and milk. Dr. Hamm and I hit it off so well that despite my weariness we talked until late at night.

June 13: *Asyut*

Jean and André had spent the night on a felucca, having stopped at sundown.

All morning I watched Dr. Kraft, a Pennsylvanian transplant to Egypt, perform operations in the hospital. He removed a tumor the size of an orange from the uterus of one village woman, then adhesions from the large intestines of another, followed by another bit of gynecological surgery, and finally an appendectomy. I wore a cap, a mask, and a gown and felt like a medical student again.

I noticed that Mohammed's injunction, "Circumcision is honorable in women," had been followed in the case of the female patients, with the clitoris and labia minora missing from each woman. Orval told me that female circumcision is a widespread custom among the fellahin from the belief that a wife was more likely to remain faithful because of the accompanying reduction in sexual desire and pleasure. He said that the operation was performed with a razor and with no anesthetic on a girl at the age of seven by an old midwife-type woman, and that the incidence of infection was high since no antiseptic, except a locally made brandy, was used—and no stitches were made.[79]

Between operations I visited the Leper Clinic and watched several pitifully deformed patients gratefully receive their medicine. There were 135 outpatients with Hansen's disease who received treatment at the clinic twice a week.

Orval drove me around Asyut all afternoon, while Jean wrote letters and André visited the local French Catholic school nearby. From a hilltop we looked over Asyut's huge cemetery, where thousands of tombs of every description sprawl along the edge of the desert. This modern necropolis is actually larger and more attractive than the town of the living. It looked like a pleasant Mediterranean community of whitewashed villas instead of a city of the dead. Orval told me that there is an annual festival held here for three days and nights with the citizens of Asyut camping out in tents and visiting the tombs of deceased relatives and friends.

But the highlight of the visit was meeting the Nile Mother: sixty-three-year-old Lillian Trasher from Jacksonville, Florida, who for forty years has been

---

79. Female circumcision was customary in ancient Egypt. Some historians believe it may have preceded the practice of male circumcision.

a mother to thousands of Egypt's deserted and orphaned waifs. Her orphanage presently has 630 children of all ages, and she loves and cares for each one as if it were her own. She is helped by the older girls and boys, who look after their younger brothers and sisters, and by ten widows whom she has adopted, too.

As a young, inexperienced girl of twenty-three, she had come to Egypt to do missionary work for the Church of God. By chance she had come to found the orphanage with one little baby when its mother, whom Lillian had been nursing, suddenly died. The idea grew, but at first everyone who heard her idea of expanding the orphanage considered her a fanatic. Gradually, however, through persistence and hard work, she made the orphanage a growing concern and won the confidence of everyone from the neighboring fellahin to the Egyptian government.

Mama Trasher is a dynamic and powerful personality. Everything about her is prodigious: her body (she weighs about 250 pounds), her energy, her love for God and humanity, and her executive and administrative abilities. As we saw her with the children during the day we were impressed with the love she showered on every child she had contact with. Frequently children are brought to her near death from disease and malnutrition, but she feeds and loves and nurses them back to health and a good life. My last glimpse of her as we left was of her bending over the beds of two adorable twin girls, lavishing attention on the babies, a look of love and pride warming her work-worn face. She is a mother in every way but one; for Lillian Trasher, who has a heart as big as a cabbage and a leaf for each one of her numerous children, is a spinster.

June 14: *North of Asyut*

Again it was hard to say good-bye to new and good friends, knowing that I'll probably never see them again. But they gave me a big box lunch for the three of us; then I met Jean and André near the Catholic school where they had spent the night. We headed out into the river and passed through the locks of the half-mile long Asyut Barrage, a forty-one-foot-high barrier with more than a hundred sluices The four workers who helped us thought it a huge joke to have to go through all the effort of cranking open the giant steel doors of the locks for three *Kawareb Shawaya* (little boats). One of them suggested we throw the toys over the dam, but we told him to get back to work, that we had paid twelve good piasters for each boat. This was only thirty six cents American, since the transit charge is based on *tonnage,* but it is half a

280

day's wage for each worker. They gleefully increased their pace when I gave them some baksheesh for their labors.

I passed Manfalut around 3:30 p.m. and waited for my companions, but apparently they had fallen far behind, so I decided to continue to the next village and stop for the night. It was so squalid and the people so rough-looking that I decided to try another.

A lone fellah's hut a mile or two farther on looked promising, so I stopped to see if I could spend the night there. I was walking up the sand bank toward the dwelling when out streaked two mongrel dogs, who savagely attacked me. I had been warned that the vicious, half-wild village dogs of Egypt were notorious for killing and eating people traveling alone in the country; but I had no stick or weapon with which to defend myself. I whipped out my red bandana handkerchief and, by kicking and flicking the cloth at the crucial moment, I managed to hold them off until the fellah came to my rescue—and even he had to beat the crazed animals with his staff to get them away from me.

I had received several lacerations where the dogs grazed my legs with their fangs, and my bandana had been ripped to shreds and torn out of my hands by the beasts, but the fellah was very distressed and tried to apologize for the attack. However, the dogs had another idea, and when they started lunging at me even while I sat talking to their master, I thought it best to get out of there, fast! The animals followed me all the way back to my kayak, snapping and snarling and were held at bay only by the stout staff of my flustered host. This is one of the few times in my life I wasn't able to calm down a dog and make friends.

The wind was still blowing strongly as I paddled on downstream; I couldn't see any sign of a village downriver; so I beached the kayak on the west bank and applied penicillin ointment to the dog bites, fervently hoping neither animal was rabid. Then I wrapped up as best I could in my extra clothing and went to sleep in the bottom of my boat—which was much like sleeping on a woodpile.

I hadn't been asleep more than an hour when the silence of the night was fractured by the blast of a rifle shot. The explosion brought me upright and wide awake. I couldn't see anyone anywhere, though the gun had been fired not more than fifty yards away, and it was a moonlit night. I'm quite sure that my kayak, so starkly white in the moonlight, had been the target of the bullet. So I made haste to depart from so hostile a region, stopping only after I had paddled three or four miles downstream, where I slept until dawn.

June 15: *North of Dairut*

I had no idea when I awakened on the deserted beach that I was about to experience a life-or-death ordeal. I set off downstream to find a village and to wait for Jean and André. High palisades paralleled the river on the east bank, and stark, flat desert lay on the west. At about 9 a.m., as I fought to make headway against the stiff wind, I was hailed by two men on the right bank, who called out to me to stop and visit with them. They were a sinister looking pair, so I merely returned their greeting and continued on my way.

They persisted, however, running along the bank and shouting after me to come over to them. I began speeding up, edging toward the middle of the river, even though it was rougher there, whereupon the two men ran ahead of me downstream to a rowboat felucca, where four other hoodlums joined them. The six then began to row frantically, three on an oar, to reach me. It was only by paddling as fast as I could that I managed to keep ahead of them.

While the chase was on, I noticed men gathering on both banks, several carrying rifles and clubs and all bearing long staffs. A short time later other feluccas loaded with men began a campaign to bottle me up and intercept me.

Altogether five boats—two feluccas under sail and three rowboats—took part in the pursuit, and I was hard put to elude them. Just as it seemed that I was escaping them, a man on the left bank waded knee-deep into the river, leveled his rifle, and fired. The bullet struck the water a few feet in front of the kayak.

Immediately I became the target of all the outlaws with rifles, and they banged away. Two of the bullets nearly parted my hair; their eerie whine as they streaked over chilled me. I scrooched down in the boat as best I could to offer as small a target as possible, then paddled as if Satan himself were after me.

For once I found myself blessing the incessant wind instead of cursing it. The waves it created kept me bobbing and heaving like a cork and made me a difficult target.

The gunfire sounded exceptionally loud, although most of the snipers were one or two hundred yards away. One blast, apparently aimed at my head, sounded full in my ear, causing it to ring and throb. My pulse rate must have set a new high when the bullets began kicking up a spray around the kayak. It seemed a paradox that I found myself in mortal danger, fleeing for my life, when our expedition was nearing completion and, we thought, all the worst danger was behind us. But there I was, flailing the wind-tossed water with the last of my strength—bullets zinging all around and the blasts of the guns and the shouts and curses of the bandits resounding in my ears.

Most of them gave up the chase after I had paddled out of range of their guns, but a few, six or seven, continued to run along the left bank. It took me a few minutes to realize what they were trying to do. The Nile is so low at this time of the year that many sandbars and small islands that normally are submerged under several feet of water during the flood season are now exposed. The bandits were running downstream a couple of miles to a point where the river channel was narrowed by a big sandbar. Obviously they hoped to catch me as I passed through this narrow gap, which they could easily wade across.

My back and arms were aching, numb with fatigue from the terrific exertion I had already undergone; but when I saw this new danger, I forgot my exhaustion and paddled as never before to beat them to the slender passage. Once through, I knew I would be safe because the river beyond ballooned out more than 300 yards wide.

It was a nip-and-tuck race, the wind holding me back. As the river narrowed, I was forced nearer and nearer to my assailants, who took advantage of their good luck by hurling large rocks at me. Fortunately, none of them had a rifle, but some of the rocks struck my boat, not doing any real damage because the range was still too far.

Struggling against the wind with my attackers close behind, I heard them whooping like Apaches on the warpath as I shot through the narrow channel just before they reached it. They splashed and shouted in rage at losing me. I experienced a thrilling sense of victory as I turned around in my kayak and elaborately thumbed my nose at them.

At the next bend in the river I was grateful to see a small village on the left bank and hurried over to see if there was a khaffir to whom I could report the attack and secure protection for Jean and André, who had yet to pass that section of the river. The first person I met upon landing was a rifle-carrying Egyptian with two bandoleers of bullets crisscrossing his chest! But he was peaceful and led me to the home of the village omdah without saying a word.

I had a long wait before the mayor, dopey and heavy-eyed from slumbering, made an appearance. I explained the details of my holdup and asked what could be done to protect my comrades. He was sympathetic but philosophical about my harrowing experience. His first comment was "Malish," meaning roughly, "It is fate," or "Don't worry, it could've been worse." ("Malish" is one of the favorite expressions of the fellahin and exemplifies their fatalistic belief that all the problems of life, major and minor, are due to the indisputable will of Allah. For a long time he hemmed and hawed before finally dispatching some of his armed men upstream to help Jean and André get through safely. Then there was nothing I could do but sit and sweat out the wait for my friends.

They reached the village two hours later, seething with rage and excitement, and told me they had experienced a repetition of what had happened to me. Feluccas intercepted them, they were chased on foot and by boat, they were shot at, rocks were thrown at them, and they barely eluded their attackers. The guards sent by the omdah never showed up—no doubt unwilling to risk a showdown with the pirates.

As if to show his regret at our disconcerting experience, the pudgy little mayor had a lunch of mutton and macaroni prepared for us, with milk and a pastry for dessert, even though it was Ramadan.

We went on cautiously from there, but no further attacks came today. It was more like being at sea on a stormy day than on a river as we fought against the heavy swells stirred up by the wind. We would often plunge out of sight from one another in the troughs between the high waves. But we finally reached the town of Mallawi at dusk. Jean had dropped out of view behind us, which often happened. We left our boats in the care of a fellah who had a hut on the river's edge, then walked to a school building where an American woman, Regina Pearson, lived and taught two hundred Egyptian high school girls. Her name had been given us by the Americans at Asyut. We found her at home, and an Egyptian friend who was visiting with her, Nadie Bishay, had her driver take us to spend the night at her father's home next to the ginnery, which he owns and operates.

June 16: *El Minya*

The wind was fair today, and we reached El Minya at 4 p.m., where we met Jean and spent the evening in a fashionable sporting club with many prominent Egyptians. During the evening we learned that the new queen of Egypt was from Minya. [Only a year after our visit, her dissolute husband, King Farouk, was overthrown by a group of army officers, led by Gamal Abdul Nasser, who became president of Egypt in 1956.]

We spent the night at a French Catholic mission operated by Jesuit priests.

June 17: *North of El Minya*

Jean woke up with an infected nose and had to go to a doctor to have it attended to. As he was returning to the mission, his face swathed in bandages, a crowd of shouting villagers suddenly attacked him. They somehow had mistaken him for an Israeli para-commando and had shoved and tripped him and thrown stones at him. He escaped only by running as fast as he could back to

André Davy washes with the assistance of an Egyptian Omdah at a village near El Minya.

the safety of the mission. To avoid further clashes he would have to travel to and from the doctor's office in covered horsedrawn carriages.

The doctor told him he would have to stay at least two days in El Minya to have shots of penicillin for the infection, which was not yet critical but could develop into something serious.

After a discussion, André and I decided to paddle downstream thirty-five miles to a sugar factory, where we knew we could stay for two days as we had at Nag Hammadi. Jean would meet us there as soon as he could leave.

We spent the night at the home of a tough little omdah who had a crowd of youngsters carry our boats and baggage into his house for safekeeping. At 7 p.m. someone blew a whistle officially ending the day of fasting, and he sat down with us to a supper of fish and molakhia. As we tried to sleep on goatskins on the floor, we were kept awake half the night by the omdah's arguing with several elders of the village in the next room, who were all shouting.

June 18–19: *North of El Minya*

When we arrived at the sugar factory after fighting wind and waves for several hours, we found the factory completely shut down and most of the machinery moved out. We learned that it was closed for political reasons, to keep it safe, as a new agricultural project replaced sugar cane in the nearby fields.

The next day I spent writing letters and catching up on my journal.

June 20: *North of El Minya*

Jean arrived from Minya, having caught a ride on a barge. His nose is healing. And after a head cold simultaneously with a boil, so is mine!

We spent part of the day with a wealthy land baron, Taher Abaza, who lives like a feudal lord in a huge mansion in the heart of the worker village, surrounded by his farmers and their families, who work his extensive land holdings of cotton, wheat, and durra. Only thirty-five, slight in build, with black hair, brown eyes, and light olive skin, he is the omdah, boss, and overseer of more than 2,000 people. He is planning to visit the United States next year to study American methods of agriculture and irrigation.

June 21: *Biba*

Today we made good time—a strong current and no wind—but we were kept alert dodging naggars sailing upstream. The big cargo boats would change course and head directly for us, seemingly intent on running us down. Probably their pilots were curious about us or feeling mischievous. As I approached an anchored felucca, the river water next to it suddenly turned red. A crewman had just cut the throat of a large goat and was holding it over the side to drain. He almost dropped the carcass in surprise as I greeted him.

It seems strange that in Egypt we have not seen one stalk of wild papyrus, when in ancient times it was the most important plant in the country.[80]

We had some kisra and an egg for lunch with a fellah, and learned from him that a band of "Nile pirates"—outlaws who had been attacking river craft in the area and hijacking their cargoes, had been captured and imprisoned. He told us there were several areas along the Nile, including the one near Dairut where we were attacked, in which feluccas never ventured singly but always traveled in convoys, and never at night. We passed through another bandit region today, however, and met with no pirates, though when we spent the night with the omdah of Biba, he assigned one of his men to watch over the kayaks through the night.

To reach Biba, André and I had cut sharply to the left around a large island. Jean passed the island on the other side, missing Biba and ending up sleeping alone on a felucca moored downstream at a small village.

Word quickly spread through town of our arrival, and a mob soon formed outside the alarmed omdah's door. He sent for a khaffir to come and stand guard. The khaffir barred my way when I tried to step outside to stretch my legs, and I realized we were virtual prisoners for the night. Our nervous host told us the people had never seen strangers like us—and we wouldn't be safe.

We listened to another faky concert tonight, but this time the cantor had a voice that grated painfully on our ears—shrill and interminable. After an hour of polite listening we could bear it no longer and asked if we could take a stroll around town. The omdah insisted on sending an escort of four armed khaffirs with us, and we also had a growing crowd of curious villagers marching along behind. The chief of police stopped us along the way and made an ostentatious display of his authority by making a minute inspection of our passports and a tiresome interrogation that finally ended with a smart salute and a cheerful invitation for us to continue our walk.

---

80. Beginning 5,000 years ago, papyrus contributed importantly to the development of Egypt. In addition to providing the writing material so essential for recording their knowledge, papyrus enabled the Egyptians to construct large boats, giving them the ability to travel on the seas and thus to extend their empire. The great papyrus swamps of Egypt gradually dried up or were converted to farmland. By 1872 the valuable plant had disappeared from the country. A few specimens had to be imported from Italy to reestablish it in Egyptian botanical gardens.

June 22: *Beni Suef*

Around 5 a.m., after we had spent a night battling bedbugs that oozed out of the mattress, the omdah came in and brusquely demanded that we share breakfast with him. We had no interest in eating the boiled meat and watermelon set out for us, but as guests it was impossible to refuse the curt invitation.

A calm morning, but river traffic was heavy. Dozens of big feluccas, some with heavy loads of golden chopped hay, kept us busy staying out of their way. We passed a remarkable village on top of a high bluff with two Coptic Christian churches prominently rising from the midst of the dwellings—a strange sight in this Moslem country where a mosque is invariably the dominant building of each community.[81]

We stopped at Beni Suef in the hope of finding Jean, but no one had seen him.

June 23: *South of Cairo*

We had a hard paddle to Kormat, where we arrived just after sunset and spent the night with a sullen omdah. There was still no sign of Jean. We hoped that since we had been warned about bandits on this stretch of the river he had hitched a ride on a barge to pass this section safely. But we were genuinely worried.

June 24: *South of Cairo*

We found Jean in good condition at the big Hawamdieh sugar refinery fifteen miles from Cairo. As I had guessed, he had caught a ride on a barge.

Signor Maurice Falqui-cao, the Italian manager of the distillery plant, invited us to stay at his guest apartment and after visiting with us and feeding us, he took us to a French movie in the company's open-air cinema.

June 25–26: *Memphis Saqqara*

Our host provided us with a car for a two-day tour of Memphis, the capital of Egypt through most of its ancient history, and of Saqqara, its main ceme-

---

81. In 1977 there were more than 7,000,000 Christian Egyptians or Copts, and their Coptic religion is the oldest form of Christianity now practiced. Its teachings and rituals have remained unchanged since the sixth century. The Copts are the direct descendants of the ancient Egyptians and possess the purest blood lines of any modern Egyptians because of the prohibition they have always observed against intermarriage outside their faith.

tery.[82] At its height, Memphis extended for twenty miles and was regarded as one of the world's most important and opulent cities. But after its decline in Roman times, it deteriorated until it was little better than a convenient quarry of precut stones for the construction of new buildings—it was so thoroughly looted over the centuries that about the only worthwhile relics of its existence were a splendid alabaster sphinx and a reclining colossus of (of course) Ramses II in a palm grove.

We spent most of our time at Saqqara, the necropolis for Memphis, dominated by the famous Step Pyramid of Djoser, second king of the third dynasty. Built around 2650 B.C., this is Egypt's oldest known monument and the most ancient freestanding stone building in the world. This massive structure, forerunner to the true pyramid, rises steeply to a height of 204 feet in a series of six *steps* or terraces.

I was eager to climb to the top but changed my mind when I saw and touched the crumbly limestone surface. I was sure the pyramid was climbable, but it was obvious that the effort would have produced unavoidable damage to its badly eroded surface. So many of the priceless monuments of Egypt have been seriously marred or even destroyed by callous acts of vandalism—and tourism—that we were determined not to cause any more.

June 27: *Cairo (El Qahira)*

The fifteen-mile paddle to Cairo was marked by the heaviest river traffic we had yet seen on the Nile. We felt as nervous as student drivers venturing onto a highway for the first time as a continuous procession of broad-beamed, low-riding naggars, motorized barges, swift launches, and sluggish lighters swept past us traveling up and down the stream. We weren't used to having to share the river, and we had a hectic time scooting out of their way.

We were met near Cairo by a large, sleek cabin cruiser bearing a group of waving officials and journalists, who escorted us to the pier of the swank Maadi Yacht Club where a crowd of well-dressed men and women awaited us. We were embarrassed, but we were moved by a sudden burst of applause and shouts of "Bravo!" and "Well done!" as we docked and stepped out of our kayaks. We were fed, then grilled by reporters and interviewers from five of Cairo's most prominent newspapers and by feature writers from Egypt's two most popular magazines. Then we proceeded to the Royal Rowing Barge, anchored nine miles farther downriver, where we spent the rest of the evening in

---

82. Memphis was reputedly founded by King Menes around 3,100 B.C., when it became the first capital of a united Egypt.

the company of other officials and gentlemen of the press, who were keenly interested in our account of the bandit attack.[83]

And at last we were driven to the French College (just behind the American University) where we were provided with suites; and we drifted off to sleep with a glowing sense of happiness at having arrived in Africa's largest city.[84]

June 28 to July 9: *Cairo*

Our visit to this 1,000-year-old city (founded in A.D. 969) has been jammed with activity, but we have been having a marvelous time sightseeing, filming, and attending luncheons and parties held in our honor.

We have seen, I'm sure, every major attraction of Cairo, including the Citadel, built by Saladin, the grand opponent of the Crusaders; the mosque of Mohammed Ali, the dynamic nineteenth-century ruler of Egypt who once gave a banquet for 480 Mameluke grandees, after which he had them ambushed and slaughtered by his troops; Egypt's most beautiful mosque, a fourteenth-century masterpiece built by Sultan Hassan, with the tallest (265 feet) minaret in Cairo; 900-year-old Ben Ezra Synagogue; Al Azhar, the university that since its founding in A.D. 971 has been the intellectual center of the Arab world; and the University of Cairo, which produced the majority of Egypt's college graduates and specialized professionals.

We also ate a sumptuous lunch at Shepheard's—for almost a century Africa's most famous hotel.[85] And we spent hours shopping around Muski Street, the mile-long artery of the commercial quarter where separate bazaars branch off along narrow lanes, each specializing in specific merchandise such as rugs, copperware, gold jewelry, and leather goods. We had a fine time haggling for souvenirs with merchants in the crowded and noisy markets, with an unceasing stream of humanity flowing past us. There were turbanned Arab sheiks in splendid white robes, men in tailored business suits with red fezzes or tarbooshes on their heads, and veiled women wearing voluminous black gowns. There were also water carriers weighted down with large goatskins or pottery

---

83. The news reports of our bandit attack aroused prompt action from the authorities. A posse of 200 Egyptian soldiers was dispatched to hunt down the outlaws, who quickly surrendered after only a brief skirmish.

84. Cairo's population in the Fall of 1978 was approximately 9,000,000.

85. Six months later Shepheard's was burned to the ground when Cairo was devastated by a torch-carrying mob of anti-British rioters. During this catastrophe sixty-seven people were killed and $300,000,000 worth of buildings and other property were destroyed.

jars, camels and donkeys laden with various types of cargo, numerous horse-drawn carts and carriages, and rattletrap taxis.

Jean and I also drove in a government car six miles southwest of Cairo to visit the most famous of all antiquities, the three pyramids of Giza. With Jean at my side, I fulfilled another childhood goal by climbing to the top of the largest stone building ever built and the only survivor of the Seven Wonders of the Ancient World—the stupendous 4,500-year-old Great Pyramid of

Reclining colossus of Ramses II.

The mortuary temple of Queen Hatshepsut at Deir el Bahri. (See footnote, page 269.)

Cheops (*Khufu*). It is built of an incredible 2,300,000 limestone blocks, each weighing 2½ tons, stacked up in 210 layers to a height equivalent to a forty-story building. Its base covers thirteen acres, equivalent to nine football fields, yet the foundation sets only one-half inch off perfect level, and originally the four sides came within eight inches of a perfect match in length. From the thirty-six-foot square summit of the Great Pyramid, in one sweeping glance we could see everything characteristic of Egypt—the shimmering desert, the green

Goddard climbs the Great Pyramid of Cheops.

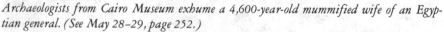
Archaeologists from Cairo Museum exhume a 4,600-year-old mummified wife of an Egyptian general. (See May 28–29, page 252.)

valley of the Nile, the antiquities, including the Sphinx below us, and, in the distance to the south, the Step Pyramid of King Djoser that I had refrained from climbing a few days before.[86]

July 11: *North of Cairo*

This clear, hot July day found us heading downstream again after two wonderful weeks in Cairo. We had an escort of six boats from the Royal and University Rowing clubs to send us off. I was amazed at how clear the Nile be-

---

86. On the seventy-two various sized royal pyramids of stone and brick erected during the Old and Middle kingdoms along a sixty-mile stretch of the Nile, only eleven remain intact. The three at Giza are the largest and most well preserved and were built by three kings of the 4th dynasty, Khufu, Khafre, and Menkure (or *Cheops, Chephren,* and *Mycerinus,* as the Greeks called them), to insure preservation of their mummified bodies and to glorify their names for eternity.

Fellahin women doing their laundry along the shores of the Beheira Canal in the Delta.

295

comes a few miles downstream from Cairo. Considering the enormous amount of garbage and waste the river receives from every city it passes, you would expect it to be murky and soupy.

Sixteen miles from Cairo we encountered the Mohammed Ali Barrage and found that we would have to take a detour of about thirty miles down the Beheira Canal because of the lack of water in the river beyond the dam. We made the short portage around the lock separating the Nile from the canal and were pleased to find a good current flowing in the Beheira, even though the stream is only eighty to a hundred feet wide. Beyond the barrage the Nile divides into two main channels, one flowing 146 miles northwest to Rosetta and the other flowing northeast for 151 miles to Damietta. In ancient times the Nile broke up into seven separate branches that flowed through the Delta to the sea, but five of them gradually silted up and disappeared.

Traveling down the Beheira en route to Rosetta gave us a splendid chance to observe and study the life and customs of the Delta villagers. We could paddle silently along within just a few yards of their dwellings and cultivations, often passing by fellahin without their being aware of our presence. But whenever I approached too near the women working along the banks, they would scatter like a covey of frightened quail.

The Egyptian Delta is one of the most densely populated and fertile regions in the world, where barely a square yard of land goes undeveloped. Everywhere we looked were fields of cotton, durra, corn, beans, melons, rice, okra, and marrow. Small villages fringed the canal and dotted the landscape, adorned with luxuriant banana groves, conifers, willows, and flowering vines—a dramatic contrast to the dry and treeless settlements in the Sudan and Upper Egypt.

At the farm estate where we spent the night, the overseer presented us with a supper of hard-boiled eggs, pitta bread, and three bottles of Coca-Cola! Then he kept us awake half the night by bounding into our room to open or close the window or start another conversation. I had to restrain myself from clouting him when he came in for the last time at about one a.m. and woke me up, nudging me with his rifle butt to ask me what time it was!

After that, except for fleas, we slept undisturbed.

July 12: *Minouf*

We were awakened at dawn by the obnoxious overseer; so we got an early start. We had a few moments of concern when, after I had filmed our passage through a lock, several policemen challenged me for photographing "an installation of strategic importance." Before I could produce my government pass and document of permission to photograph in Egypt, a mob of people gathered and began muttering curses and threats against me. I should have realized our troubles were not over even after I had identified myself.

About an hour later I began filming a fleet of high-masted, dutch-shoe shaped feluccas that were sailing toward me upstream. When some peasants saw me, a bearded foreigner in a strange boat, pointing a camera in the direction of a bridge (quite by accident), they must have concluded that I was a particularly reckless Israeli spy on a mission of espionage. Since Egypt is officially at war with Israel, the rabble quickly worked themselves into a state of hysterical agitation and began chasing after me along the bank in an ever-growing, loudly jabbering mob. I didn't quite understand what the ruckus was about, but I knew we'd better paddle out of the area as fast as possible. I shouted to Jean and André behind me to speed up and look out for trouble.

We hadn't paddled far when the mob began bombarding us with big, hard chunks of clay. Men who only a few moments before had greeted me in the most friendly manner were now lusting for my blood—earnestly doing their best to bean me with grapefruit-sized clods. Judging from the size of the clods and the violent force with which they were thrown, there was little doubt in my mind what my chances would have been of surviving a direct hit on the head.

Several other men, seeing their countrymen attacking a stranger, immediately joined in and began pelting me from the other bank with anything they could lay their hands on. If any of them had had firearms, it would have been the end of me.

I chanced a quick glance behind me to see how Jean and André were making out and was dismayed to see that they had landed and were in the custody of a crowd of excited fellahin. I was rapidly being overcome by the fusilade of stones, so I had no alternative but to surrender and take a chance on the consequences.

Even after I had capitulated, the crowd was in such a frenzy that they continued pitching sticks and clods at me. Miraculously I came through the intense bombardment with only two or three bruises on my arms and shoulder, but the kayak was struck several times.

About this time I started feeling somewhat belligerent myself. I furiously paddled to shore, jumped out of my boat onto the bank, grabbed the two attackers nearest me by their necks, and began to shake some sense into them. Everyone began to calm down, but I had a few tense moments when one of the peasants climbed onto my kayak and ordered me to paddle upstream with him perched on the prow. I knew he couldn't stay there a minute before the

The filming of these feluccas precipitated a stoning attack by the fellahin mob.

boat turned turtle. His attention, fortunately, diverted, and he instead requisitioned my two cameras and strutted back upstream toward the little village of Kaaf Shubra where Jean and André had been taken into custody, the mob following at his heels. I followed in my kayak, ready to burst with rage and indignation.

I tied up my boat, then joined my comrades, who were trying to show their passports to several khaffirs but were being so jostled by the mob that they could hardly stand. There must have been well over 300 people in the village, all of them crowding around us, shoving and cursing, and every one of them hostile to us. Somehow the rumor had swept through the mob that we were not Israelis but Englishmen, whom they hated almost as much as Jews.

The situation was getting out of hand. It seemed we might be murdered on the spot. I demanded that we be taken to the omdah immediately, whereupon we were herded down a winding narrow alley in a cloud of dust to the dwelling of the village chief. The crowd bustled along all around us, shouting, reviling, and even spitting at us. We felt like prisoners of a horde of savage warriors who were leading us to an altar of sacrifice.

The omdah, who met us in front of his ramshackle adobe, proved to be a doddering old man, completely confused by our appearance. We presented the two documents from government officials in Cairo identifying us and authorizing us to photograph. The papers written in flowing Arabic and affixed with important-looking stamps, seals, and signatures were supposed to protect us from precisely this kind of embroilment. All he had to do was check these papers, see that they were satisfactory, order our release, and allow us to continue on our way.

But from the way the ancient omdah and others in the mob turned the documents in all directions it was obvious that no one there could read them. He decided we should be taken to a police post two miles away. No amount of reasoning with him altered his decision, and since we were outnumbered a hundred to one, we had to fight down our anger and start marching to the post.

As we started to leave, we were startled to see three or four khaffirs brutally lash out with their long staves at the masses of villagers crowding around us to clear a path. When one young fellah protested at the whippings, he received a vicious slap across the face, which made him cry. Another man, incensed when a khaffir struck his boy across the back, raising a long red welt, grabbed the guard's arm to restrain him. He received a hard kick in the pants and a punch to his head from the arrogant guard.

I thought for a minute that a fight would start between the villagers and the khaffirs, but the latter beat or kicked everyone who got in their way and in that manner cleared a path for us to leave.

It was a long, hot walk to the little police station, but we finally arrived, with the cocky hero who had captured me leading the way astride a white donkey. I tried several times to rescue my cameras from the grubby roughneck to protect them from the clouds of dust and sand kicked up by our feet—but each time I made the attempt, he jerked them so savagely from my grasp that rather than jeopardize the precious equipment, I let him have his way.

We were held prisoners for over four hours in the squalor of the vermin-infested jail until a police lieutenant arrived from a neighboring town. He was about the twentieth person to examine our passports and other official papers, and like all the others he was completely perplexed as to what to do. So he loaded us in his pickup truck and drove to the commandant of police at the large town of Minouf to decide our case.

Fortunately, the commandant, Medhat el Morrass, could speak English, and as he put it, had "followed the expedition with envy from the beginning." He apologized profusely for the attack and tried to make amends by extending an invitation to have supper and spend the night at his home. Since it was too late to continue our journey, we accepted. But first we had him drive us back to our kayaks at the small village to make certain a khaffir was stationed to guard them during our absence.

When we returned to Minouf, Medhat drove us on a tour of the city, introduced us at the club, and provided us with an excellent supper and comfortable beds. His kind hospitality soon soothed our anger at our harsh treatment from the mob, and I began to realize we were lucky to have escaped with our lives and without serious injury. Besides, the incident had afforded us the opportunity to see something of one of Egypt's most densely populated regions, the five districts around Minouf. In each of our worst experiences on the Nile—as in the calamities of life—we have found *something* to be grateful for.

July 13–16: *South of Rosetta*

Just before we left, our host informed us, "I'm arranging for your protection along the way to Rosetta so that you may finish your travels in peace"—a masterpiece of understatement, as we were soon to discover.

We found the kayaks undisturbed, with two guards watching over them and a remarkably subdued crowd lining the banks. They humbly stepped aside as we threaded our way past them to our kayaks; then they respectfully waved us on our way as we shoved off. "They seem genuinely sorry that they tried to kill us," I said to André.

As we set off, a green police pickup with two lieutenants in the cab and six policemen crowded together in back appeared along the dirt road paralleling the canal. All day long they stuck close to us, sometimes racing ahead to alert villages of our arrival and in general keeping things under control by their presence. The villagers we passed were so awed by our police escort and strange boats that they stood transfixed, allowing themselves to be approached and photographed with no reaction other than smiles of bewilderment.

When the road veered away from the canal the next day, as we returned to the main channel of the Nile, the truck was replaced by three khaki-clad policemen wearing red tarbooshes, carrying rifles in their saddle holsters, and mounted on three magnificent Arabian stallions. Every few miles a fresh team

Three of the mounted policemen who served as a protective escort through the Delta.

301

would take over the job of escorting us, so that in all twenty-four men and their beautiful horses guarded us the remaining hundred miles to Rosetta. We had traveled more than 7,000 miles through remote regions of six countries of Africa virtually unarmed and completely on our own. Now, in the heart of civilization, we found it laughable that we had to have an armed guard watch over us as we completed our expedition.

In addition to providing the protective escort, Medhat had thoughtfully arranged our itinerary for the days ahead. We found ourselves scheduled to stay overnight with the omdah of one village, to lunch with another, to take tea with an official here and to meet and pose for pictures with another one there. This was all very pleasant and convenient, but how we longed for the freedom of our former days.

Late in the afternoon on July 16 we arrived at the last dam on the Nile, the Idfina Barrage.[87] A French construction company was just completing the project, which they had built of Aswan granite, the favorite stone of the ancient Egyptians. We were welcomed and invited to stay the night by a delegation of French engineers and their families, who seemed almost as excited as we were that we were so near the end of our journey.

July 17: *Rosetta (Rashid)*

At ten o'clock a.m., with our alert guards and a crowd of French and Egyptian bystanders watching, we portaged our kayaks around the dam, taking them out of the fresh water of the Nile for the last time and launching them into the salt water of the Mediterranean lapping at the front of the dam.

As we paddled the twenty-mile stretch from Idfina to Rosetta, the green cultivations gradually fell away and were replaced by low, flat sand dunes deposited through the ages by the flooding Nile and molded into what looked like petrified waves by the sculpturing sea winds.

My heart began thudding with fear when I spotted several mysterious dark forms swimming rapidly on the surface toward us. My first impression was that we were about to be attacked by a school of sharks, but I laughed with relief as they drew near and I recognized them for what they were: those most

---

87. This final barrier was constructed to conserve the precious waters of the Nile throughout the low-water season to supply the Delta's growing demands. With the arrival of the annual flood, the sluices were formerly opened to permit the excess water to flow through and into the Mediterranean. These nutrient-laden waters nourished large schools of fish, which were harvested by Egyptian fishermen. Now that the Aswan High Dam blocks the flood and prevents it from reaching the sea, the fish have largely disappeared from around the Nile outlets.

The three Nileteers near the mouth of the Nile, with the Idfina Barrage in the background.

lovable creatures of the sea, dolphins—like a happy delegation from Neptune's court sent to welcome us to the Mediterranean. They spread out, and, for a few moments, cavorted around us like acrobatic clowns, at times even bumping impishly into our kayaks as if trying to nudge us into joining them in their play. And then suddenly they were gone.

As we approached Rosetta, a small port town near the sea, three hand-rowed feluccas loaded with men began closing in around us, but edged away at a shouted command from one of our mounted guards watching from shore.

We stepped out of our battered and patched kayaks for the last time. And as we stood on the dock, Jean, André, and I, overcome with emotion, gave each other spontaneous hugs of congratulation for this triumphal moment we had waited so long and worked so hard to achieve. Nine arduous and action-filled months after beginning our "impossible" expedition, we had arrived at the

The three Nileteers on the Mediterranean shore near the mouth of the Nile, with the flag of the Los Angeles Adventurers' Club.

Mayor of Rosetta, government officials, and journalists welcome the Nileteers to the Mediterranean.

The Rosetta Stone

In 1799 near Rosetta a
French engineer of
Napoleon's army found
the now famous Rosetta
stone, a carved tablet of
black basalt inscribed in
two languages—
Egyptian and Greek—
and three alphabets—
hieroglyphic (sacred),
demotic (common),
and Greek.
The slab records a
decree written by the
priests of Memphis in
196 B.C. mostly in
praise of Ptolemy V, the
ruler at the time. The
inscriptions provided
scholars, beginning
with Thomas Young,
an English physicist,
and the French scholar,
Jean-François
Champollion, with the
key for translating the
written language of
ancient Egypt.

end of the Nile. Each of us had dipped at least a million paddle strokes since our start on the Kagera River, and we had become, through the grace of God, the first men in history to have explored the Nile from its remote headsprings to its mouth—4,145 miles of the longest and most historic of all rivers.

Our devoted police guards dismounted and stood at attention next to us as the debonair mayor of Rosetta, wearing a white silk coat, black pants, and red tarboosh and leading an entourage of dignitaries and journalists from Cairo and Alexandria, extended an exuberant official welcome.

Afterward came the press interviews, picture-taking, and celebrating, and then we slept on the sandy shores of the Mediterranean at a nearby fort and lighthouse where two antique cannons pointed seaward.

The next day a caravan of cars from the European colony at Alexandria picked us up and drove us to their lovely seaside city, where we were lavishly hosted by the French consul-general and others before boarding ship to return to France and then home.

I felt a deep sadness at leaving the Nile. It had so totally dominated our lives and had been the supreme subject of our thoughts, plans, dreams, and energies for so many months that it didn't seem possible we were leaving it for good. For so long we had awakened each morning to behold its gleaming expanse leading endlessly to the next horizon. It had borne us thousands of miles through many of the earth's wildest regions. Its waters had cleansed, cooled, and provided sustenance for our bodies. We had been enthralled by its beauty, enraged by its perversity, awed by its magnitude, and frightened by its power.

In short, we had just finished the greatest experience of our lives, and I was sorry to see it come to an end.

I had had a personal motto about exploring the Nile: "It should be done. It can be done. It shall be done." Now, at last, I could add, "It has been done!"

Postscript

There is an ancient Egyptian saying: Whoever once drinks the water of the Nile, though he may travel to the ends of the earth, yet will he return to drink again." This promise has been fulfilled for my French companions and me.

In 1956 Jean returned to the Victoria Nile in Uganda with Jacques Blein to paddle by kayak on a stretch of river below Lake Victoria. It was at this time that Blein met his death.

André returned to Egypt and Khartoum on a journalistic assignment in 1957.

I returned to the Nile basin and revisited various areas along the river in Uganda, the Sudan, and Egypt in 1956, 1958, 1968, and 1973. But the lure of the Nile continues to be a powerful force in my life—and there will be additional visits in the future.

Index

282, 284, 287, 288, 298
Fezara tribe, 166
Fifth Cataract, 200
Fires, 59, 95, 114, 115, 157
First Cataract, xii, 35, 189, 251
Fish, 124, 161, 170, 194, 201, 302
Fish eagle, 52
Fishermen, 35, 37, 44, 55, 135, 157, 161, 163, 164, 166, 216, 255, 261, 302
Fishing, 35, 37, 135, 161, 261
Fola Rapids, 100
Foods, 20, 25, 31, 40, 41, 44, 45, 51, 84, 85, 90, 103, 107, 108, 113, 114, 115, 121, 124, 131, 141, 146, 155, 156, 159, 161, 164, 165, 168, 170, 171, 173–75, 187, 190, 191, 199, 201, 203, 206, 211, 213–17, 224, 235, 237, 239, 240, 271, 227, 279, 284, 288, 296
Foot safari, 100–15
Fortresses, Arab, 201, 204, 205, 217, 221, 235; Egyptian, 227
Fourth Cataract, 204, 207, 213
Francolin birds, 103
France, 148
French College, 290
French Explorers' Society, 2, 121
Funeral, 98
"Fuzzy Wuzzies," 199

Gaaliin tribe, 190
Gadawag, Sudan, 197–99
Ganetti, Sudan, 213
Garf Hussein, Egypt, 247
Gazelle, Dorcas, 227
Gebel el Silsila (quarries), 257
Geddi, Sudan, 219
Geese, 162, 164, 190, 218, 276
Gelot, Monsieur, 12, 13
Gemai, Sudan, 228
Gessi, Romolo, 127, 130
Gezira Irrigation Project, 168
Ghart Benna, Sudan, 217
Gilbert, W. S., 212
Gimma tribe, 166
Giraffe, 154
Giza, Egypt, 291
Goats, 174, 191, 206, 235, 243

Gold mine, 223, 224
Goose, Egyptian, 155, 156
Gordon, General Charles George, 177, 180, 194
Gotch, J. D., 84
Graffiti, ancient, 219
Grant, James A., 26
Great Britain, 27, 118, 148, 149
Great Pyramid of Cheops, 292, 293
Greeks, 95, 118, 121, 185; ancient, 210, 237, 246, 251, 259, 276
Guinea fowl, 103, 105, 106
Gule tribe, 165, 167
Gum Arabic, 166

Haboobs, 172, 194–97
Hadendowa tribe, 199
Hadj, 244
Halfa Province, Sudan, 219
Hamitic race, 28, 116; language, 131, 199
Hamm, Dr. Orval, 277, 279
Hamza, Ahmed, 172–74
Hansen's disease, 279
Harkhuf, Prince, 252, 254
Hassan, Sultan, 290
Hathor, 237, 273
Hatshepsut, Queen, 264, 265, 269, 292
Hawamdieh sugar refinery, 288
Hawks, 52; Horus, 259
Heat, 225, 226, 228, 232, 240, 276
Hebrews, 235
Helmy Ahmed, 173
Herodotus, xiii, 65, 254
Herons, 69, 164
Heston, Charlton, 177
Hippos, 6, 8, 9–11, 16, 18–20, 24, 33, 54, 55, 57, 58, 68, 70, 71, 73, 81, 85, 87, 90, 102, 122, 124, 151, 154, 157, 159, 162, 194
Hittites, 237
Hog, giant forest, 24, 25
Hoima, Uganda, 67
Honeycomb, 155
Hoopoe bird, 206
Hornbill bird, 6
Horus (god), 259, 260
Howe, Sir Robert, 184

Ramses VI, King, 267
Rapids, 10–17, 37, 70, 100, 111, 188, 200, 201, 204, 205, 206, 207, 209, 218–21, 227–29
Rashid, Charles, 232; Joseph, 217
Rats, 227
Ravens, 218
Red Sea, 92, 156, 271
Rejaf, 112
Rhino Camp, Uganda, 81, 83, 85
Rhinoceros, black, 100, 101, 102; white, 30, 100, 101
Rift Valley, 59, 60
Ripon Falls, Uganda, 35
Robichon, Dr., 262
Roman fortress, 239
Romans, 208, 237, 238
Rosetta (Rashid), Egypt, xiv, 35, 296, 300, 302, 304, 305, 306
Rosetta Stone, 306
Roy, Martha, 262, 264, 268
Ruffs (birds), 164
Ruins, 191–93, 201, 202, 204, 205, 209–11, 224, 225, 227, 235, 239, 251
Ruvuvu River, Burundi, 1
Russian engineers, 250
Rutana, Burundi, 1
Ruwenzori Mountains, xi

Sablukah Gorge, Sudan, 187, 188
Sahara Desert, 219, 226
Sakieh (water wheel), 166, 185, 186, 213, 217, 254
Saladin, 290
Salt industry, 63, 64
Sand dunes, 170, 190, 197, 204, 207, 209, 225, 226, 233, 302
Sandpipers, 164
Sandstorms, 172, 194–97
Saqqara, 288, 289
Scarring, tribal, 104, 105, 154
Schistosomiasis, 271–73
Scoones, Major-General, 183, 207
Scorpions, 171, 244
Second Cataract, 35, 218, 227, 229, 231, 232
Semna, Sudan, 227

Seti I, 266; Temple of, 275
Shabasha, Sudan, 170
Shadoof, 254, 269
Shambe, Sudan, 133
Sheep, 211, 235, 261
Shellal, Egypt, 249
Shendi, Sudan, 190–92
Shepherd's Hotel, 290
Shilluk, 79, 104, 116, 135–40, 150, 151, 152, 154, 156
Shrike (bird), 168
Sixth Cataract, 188, 189, 217
Skimmers, African, 164
Skulls, ancient, 257, 259
Sleeping sickness, 34, 88
Snake, 232
Sobat River, 128, 140, 141, 173
Sohag, Egypt, 277
Somerset Nile, 57
Southern Cross, 205
Sparrows, 54
Speke, John Hanning, xii, 26, 35
Sphinxes, 240, 264, 289, 294
Stanley, Henry Morton, 1, 26, 27
Steamboats, 37, 56, 63, 74, 127, 131, 133–35, 163, 194, 209, 233
Storks, 143; Marabou, 69; Whale-headed, 135–36
Storkmen, 118, 119
Suchos (crocodile god), 255
Sudan, 75, 90, 91, 92, 93, 118, 128, 129, 157, 166, 178, 191, 206, 209, 210, 232, 233, 275
Sudan Defense Force, 183
Sudanese, 166, 170, 171, 173, 178, 184, 187, 190, 191, 211, 213, 225
Sudan Railroad, 232
Sudan War Memorial Ceremony, 183, 184
Sudd, 46, 126, 127, 130
Sudd Swamp, 46, 126–30, 133–35, 161, 164, 237
Sugar cane, 255, 257
Sulb (ancient temple), 224, 225
Sun, 277
Swahili, 37, 40, 56, 74, 78, 81, 118
Swallows, 14, 173
Synagogue, Ben Ezra, 290

*About the
Author*

"To dare is to do . . . to fear is to fail." This philosophy has guided John Goddard since he was fifteen, when he set 127 lifetime goals for himself—including
exploring the length of the Nile River (goal number one), climbing Mount
Ararat to search for Noah's ark, reading the Encyclopaedia Britannica, and
becoming a professional explorer. Number 97 on the list was writing a
book, and with the completion of this Nile manuscript he has now accomplished 106 of these ambitions.

A graduate of the University of Southern California, where he majored in
anthropology and psychology, Goddard has conducted anthropological stud-
ics of numerous isolated tribal cultures on every continent. During his adventurous life he has visited 117 countries and logged in excess of one million
land, sea, and air miles. He has climbed many of the world's highest mountains, including Kilimanjaro, Popocatepetl, and the Matterhorn; he has explored 15 remote rivers and has filmed underwater from the Red Sea to Truk
Lagoon. He is a member of the Explorers' Club of New York, the Royal
Geographical Society of England, and the Adventurers' Clubs of Chicago
and Los Angeles.

Goddard has flown forty-six different types of aircraft, including the F-111
on a record-setting 1500 miles-per-hour flight. But of all his experiences he still
considers the Nile Expedition his most memorable and outstanding achieve-
ment.

In 1978 John Goddard was chosen by its board of editors as Encyclopaedia Britannica's Gold Medal Winner in Exploration.